A HARD DAY'S WRITE

A HARD DAY'S
WRITE

The Stories Behind Every Beatles Song

Steve Turner

HarperCollins*Publishers*

This book is dedicated to the memory of
T-Bone Burnett and Larry Norman in memory
of many hours of Beatle-talk over the years.

THIS IS A CARLTON BOOK

First published in the UK in 1994
This new edition published by Carlton Books Limited
1999
Text copyright © Steve Turner 1999
Design copyright © Carlton Books Limited 1999

Design: Stephen Kirk
Art editor: Zoë Maggs
Executive editors: Lorraine Dickey and Tessa Rose
Editor: Nicola Hodge
Picture research: Juliet Duff
Production: Sarah Schuman

HarperCollins books may be purchased for educational,
business, or sales promotional use. For information,
please write: Special Markets Department, HarperCollins
Publishers, Inc., 10 East 53rd Street, New York, NY
10022

LIBRARY OF CONGRESS CATALOGING-IN-PUBLICATION DATA
Turner, Steve
    A hard day's write: the stories behind every Beatles
song/ by Steve Turner. — 1st ed.
    p. cm.
    ISBN 0-06-273698-1
    1. Beatles.   2. Rock music—England—History and
criticism.
    I. Title.
    ML421.B4T87   1994
    782.42166'092'2—dc20   94-9687
                                                    MN

First US edition 1999

00 01 02 03 10 9 8 7 6 5 4 3 2

COPYRIGHT CREDITS

'Baby, Let's Play House', words and music by Arthur
Gunter © Williamson Music Inc./Carlin Music Inc.
'Daydream', words and music by John Sebastian © 1966
Hudson Bay Music Corporation. Reproduced by kind
permission of Robbins Music Corp. Ltd, London.
'I'm Wishing', words and music by Larry Morey and Frank
Churchill; and 'Please', words and music by Leo Robbin
and Ralph Rainger © Warner Chappell Music Ltd,
London. Reproduced by kind permission of International
Music Publications Ltd.
'Something in the Way She Moves', words and music by
James Taylor © 1968 EMI Blackwood Music Inc./Country
Road Music Inc., USA.
The songs of the Beatles, words and music by John
Lennon and Paul McCartney or George Harrison ©
Northern Songs. Reproduced by kind permission of
Music Sales Group Ltd.

PICTURE CREDITS

The publishers would like to thank the following sources
for their kind permission to reproduce the pictures in this
book:

Apple Corps Ltd; Barnaby's Picture Library: Tom
Charles; BFI; Bristol Old Vic; Camera Press; Richard A.
Cooke; Corbis-Bettman/Reuters; Lucy O'Donnell;
Edinburgh Photo Library; Royston Ellis; Mary Evans
Picture Library; Art Fein; Hulton Deutsch Collection:
Apple Corps Ltd; Colin Harrison; International Music
Publishers Ltd; Thelma McGough; London Features
International; Mail Newspapers Plc: Solo Syndication;
Mirror Syndication International; The Robert Opie
Collection; Pictorial Press; Popperfoto; Redferns; Astrid
Kirchherr, David Redfern; Rex Features: Archetti,
Blackbrow, Decaux, Lari, Magnus, Mondial, National
Trust/Dennis Gilbert, Parker Publishing, SIPA, Ward; The
Salvation Army; Theatre Museum; The Steve Turner
Collection.

Every effort has been made to acknowledge correctly
and contact the source and/or copyright holder of each
picture. Carlton Books Limited apologises for any unintentional errors or omissions, which will be corrected in
future editions of this book.

PREFACE

A *Hard Day's Write* tells the stories behind the Beatles' songs, which I've defined as songs written and recorded by the Beatles. This book doesn't include songs by other writers which the Beatles covered, Lennon-and-McCartney numbers recorded by other artists or songs which have surfaced only on bootleg. It looks at the how, why and where of the songwriting and traces the inspiration back to source. Alongside the stories there are over 200 illustrations, including pictures of the people and places that prompted the group members to write. In essence, *A Hard Day's Write* is a scrapbook for those seeking insight into the best-known popular songcatalogue of modern times.

Having said that, this is not a book about how the Beatles recorded the songs, nor about who played what on which sessions. Mark Lewisohn has done that job definitively in *The Complete Recording Sessions* and anyone who writes about the Beatles now cannot fail to refer to Mark's book. I have only mentioned production details where they have had a significant bearing on the actual construction of a song, such as when George Martin suggested beginning a song with the chorus, or when lyrics were written or altered in the studio. Neither is *A Hard Day's Write* a book of in-depth musical analysis. I haven't attempted to describe to the reader what he/she has been listening to for all these years in the language of pentatonic melismas and syncopated stresses. For a musicological take on the Beatles, see *Twilight Of The Gods* by Professor Wilfrid Mellers (Schirmer Books, 1973) or *Revolution in the Head* by Ian McDonald (Fourth Estate, 1994).

This is also not a book that explains what the Beatles 'were really trying to say'. Although I've given outlines of many songs for those who may not be familiar with the lyrics and have referred to psychological factors that I believe influenced the standpoint of the writing, I've left the task of interpretation to others. If you do want to know what Paul was saying, read a book like *Paul McCartney: From Liverpool To Let It Be* by Howard DeWitt (Horizon Books, 1992) or, if you want to catch the drift of John's intellectual development, read *The Art and Music of John Lennon* by John Robertson (Omnibus, 1990) or *John Lennon's Secret* by David Stuart Ryan (Kozmik Press, 1982).

What I have tried to do is simply to tell the story of how each song came into being. It could have been a musical inspiration, such as wanting to emulate a Little Richard single, or trying to write in the style of Smokey Robinson. It could have been a phrase that just wouldn't go away, like the 'waves of sorrow, pools of joy' line that forced John to write 'Across The Universe'. Or it could have been an incident like the death of socialite Tara Browne which led to the writing of part of 'A Day In The Life'.

Not every song has a great story behind it. Some of the earlier material, particularly the soundtrack for the films *A Hard Day's Night* and *Help!*, was written to deadline and owed more to the vernacular of other songs than the Beatles' own experience. Four numbers from *A Hard Day's Night* were apparently churned out in one intense session. There are also songs from this period which neither John nor Paul had any clear memory of once the Beatles had split up. Paul has referred to them as "work songs" and John commented that many of them were written "with no thought to them", dismissing them as "garbage". Later songs, like 'Dig It' and 'Dig A Pony', were 'knocked off' in a different way. By this time, the pair were each in their own way disenchanted with the Beatles and were only in the studio to fulfil contractual obligations, so they began to make up nonsense lyrics while jamming. For the purposes of this book, the most fruitful period was between 1965 and 1969 when the group recorded *Rubber Soul*, *Revolver*, *Sgt Pepper's Lonely Hearts Club Band*, the *Yellow Submarine* soundtrack, *Magical Mystery Tour*, *The Beatles* (The White Album) and *Abbey Road*. During this time, the Beatles challenged the conventions of pop songwriting, drawing on everything around them for inspiration instead of adhering to the narrow range of subjects usually considered appropriate for pop.

My primary source is the words of the Beatles themselves. I was fortunate enough to meet John, interviewing him and Yoko at the Apple office in Savile Row in the summer of 1971, shortly before *Imagine* was released. I remember complimenting him on the personal nature of his new songs which had come after an intense period of therapy. "My songs have always been personal," he responded. "'Help!' was personal. 'You've Got To Hide Your Love Away' was personal. 'I'm A Loser' was personal. I've always been on that kick."

Now that John is dead, I had to refer questions arising from this book to Elliot Mintz, a close friend of his who represents the John Lennon Estate. He was helpful throughout, sharing memories of discussions he'd had with John about his writing and keeping Yoko informed of my research. I didn't meet Paul until 1992 when I was asked to help Linda in the writing of the text for her photographic book *Sixties: Portrait Of An Era*. I had hoped that Paul would contribute his own memories to *A Hard Day's Write* but after reading through an early draft of the manuscript, he decided that he couldn't just dip into a project like this and yet didn't have the time to give a full account of every song. He did, however, point out some discrepancies in the stories I had collected which I was then able to change.

If the most reliable comments on the songs are those made by the Beatles themselves, I've also drawn on the published interviews I have personally collected since beginning my first Beatles' scrapbook in 1963. Those that I had missed, I searched out at the National Newspaper Library and the National Sound Archives in London. There were six invaluable written accounts which I found myself coming back to repeatedly and without which I wouldn't have known where to start. In order of publication these were: Alan Aldridge's interview with Paul McCartney published as *A Good Guru's Guide To The Beatles' Sinister Songbook* in the *Observer* magazine, London, on November 26, 1967; *The Beatles* by Hunter Davies, 1968; *Lennon: The Greatest Natural Songwriter of our Time* by Mike Hennessey in *Record Mirror*, October 2, 1971 (reprinted in *Hit Parade*, April 1972); *Lennon Remembers* by Jann Wenner, 1971; *I Me Mine* by George Harrison, 1980; *The Playboy Interviews* with John Lennon and Yoko Ono, 1981 and *Paul McCartney: Many Years From Now* by Barry

Miles. There were also two radio series which shed light on the songwriting: Mike Read's *McCartney On McCartney*, broadcast on BBC Radio 1 during 1989, and *The Lost Lennon Tapes*, an American production co-ordinated by Elliot Mintz, featuring demo tapes from John's private collection which Yoko had allowed to be broadcast for the first time.

As informative as all these were, they didn't tell me the whole story. Many of the anecdotes are already well known. William J Dowlding's book *Beatlesongs* (Fireside, 1989) does a very good job of listing the session information from Mark Lewisohn's book alongside Beatle quotes from newspapers and magazines. I wanted to go a step further than this by interviewing the people who were around when the songs were written, or who had even been the subject of songs. I also wanted to track down the newspaper stories which had provided ideas, the books from which they'd taken lines and the places which had inspired them. I wanted to surprise even the Beatles themselves because I knew that they didn't know who Mr Kite was or what happened to the girl whose story inspired 'She's Leaving Home'. I knew they would have also long since forgotten the letters' column which supplied them with the title 'From Me To You' and the face of the girl who became Polythene Pam.

The definitive book on this subject won't be written until John's journals, letters and work books are made public and Paul, George and Ringo sit down in front of a microphone and share everything they remember about the 208 songs which the Beatles recorded. The chances are though that John's material will remain locked in vaults for the foreseeable future because much of it refers to people still living and Yoko believes that it is too sensitive to release. The six-part television series *The Beatles Anthology* was disappointing to anyone expecting the remaining members of the Beatles to tell hitherto unheard stories which would reveal the sources of their inspiration.

That's why it was worth compiling *A Hard Day's Write*. It may be the closest we'll ever get to understanding how the Beatles conjured up their songwriting magic.

STEVE TURNER • LONDON, MARCH 1999

▲ **George, John, Ringo and Paul seen here in 1964 with Maureen Cleave, feature writer and pop columnist with the *Evening Standard*. One of the first London journalists to cover the group, she wrote the interview in which John claimed that the Beatles were now "bigger than Jesus".**

ACKNOWLEDGEMENTS

For interviews carried out specifically for this book I thank: Al Aronowitz, Diane Ashley, Margo Bird, Tony Bramwell, Prudence Bruns, Iris Caldwell, Maureen Cleave, Melanie Coe, Richard A Cooke, Nancy Cooke de Herrera, Meta Davis, Rod Davis, Pat Dawson, Richard DiLello, Royston Ellis, Peter Fonda, Johnny Guitar, Paul Horn, Kevin Howlett, Michael Hurll, Stephen James, Rod Jones, Tony King, Timothy Leary, Donovan Leitch, Julian Lennon, Dick Lester, John Lowe, Angie McCartney, Roger McGough, Thelma McGough, Elliot Mintz, Rod Murray, Delbert McClinton, Denis O'Dell, Lucy O'Donnell, Alun Owen, Little Richard, Jimmy Savile, John Sebastian, Helen Shapiro, Don Short, Joel Schumacher, Derek Taylor, James Taylor, Doug Trendle, Dr John Turner, Jan Vaughan and Gordon Waller.

I drew on past interviews conducted with Lionel Bart, Hunter Davies, John Dunbar, Cynthia Lennon, George Martin, Barry Miles, Spike Milligan, Roy Orbison, Ravi Shankar, Bruce Welch and Muriel Young.

For supplying information or setting up interviews I thank: Tony Barrow, Penny Bell, Gloria Boyce, Eleanor Bron, Murray Chalmers, Lynne DeBernardis, Liz Edwards, Mike Evans, Peggy Ferguson, Roberta Freymann, Sarah Jane Freymann, Lynda Gilbert, Matt Godwin, Adrian Henri, Corinna Honan, Shelagh Jones, Andrew King, Martha Knight, Carol Lawrence, Mark Lewisohn, Brian Patten, Mrs Juan Mascaró, Robbie Montgomery, Iona Opie, Peter Rhone, Bettina Rose, Juliet Rowe, Phil Spangenberger, Alvin Stardust, Jean Stein, Sue Turner, Lisa Ullmann and Linda Watts.

I used facilities supplied by these organizations: American Federation of Musicians, ASCAP, BMI, Beatles Shop (Liverpool), Bristol Library, Bristol Old Vic, British Library, Chiswick Library, Highland Bookshop and Wildlife Art Gallery (Traverse City, Michigan), National Newspaper Library, National Sound Archives, Nigerian High Commission, Performing Rights Society, Rochdale Library, Theatre Museum, UCLA Library and Westminster Library.

Finally, I would like to thank my agent Lisa Eveleigh who never gave up on the project and Piers Murray-Hill and Jonathan Goodman at Carlton Books.

INTRODUCTION

Researching a feature for the 20th anniversary of the Beatles' *Sgt Pepper's Lonely Hearts Club Band* album, I was delighted to be able to track down Lucy, the girl who as a four-year-old had unwittingly starred in John Lennon's song 'Lucy In The Sky With Diamonds'. I soon discovered that she hadn't given much thought to her immortalization. After all, the Beatles had broken up by the time she was seven and she was well into her teens before she learned that John's inspiration had come from a nursery school painting his son Julian had made of her floating in the sky surrounded by diamonds. Yet here she was, a girl who had been resident in my consciousness for 20 years and who therefore appeared to me to be a celebrity. She was of course an ordinary person, made extraordinary by the touch of a Beatle's pen.

Anyone who, like me, had grown up with the Beatles' music would have been similarly impressed to meet Lucy, with or without diamonds, because our memories are thronged by a cast of characters created by John Lennon, Paul McCartney and, to a lesser degree, George Harrison. The fireman with an hourglass and the banker without a mac have become as familiar to us as any incidental character in Dickens and, from Peking to Peru, there must be people who can sing about Dr Robert or who can hum 'Strawberry Fields Forever' and 'Penny Lane'. It is precisely because these people and these places are now part of us, that it becomes fascinating to discover where they came from: the true identity of Dr Robert, what Penny Lane really looked like, or the emotional truth behind the writing of songs like 'And I Love Her', 'Yesterday' or 'We Can Work It Out'.

Of course, knowing the inspiration behind the songs doesn't make them any better or worse. The songs exist as creations in their own right, enhanced by the memories surrounding the time when we first heard them. If you loved 'A Hard Day's Night' in 1964, you're not going to love it any better for knowing that Ringo supplied the quip which became the title, or that John wrote it on the back of a birthday card in a small flat behind London's Cromwell Road. It is just that these songs are so much a part of us and we are so much a part of what the songs have become, that it is almost an act of self-discovery to learn the stories behind them. Looking closely at the songs also gives us an insight into the Sixties and the lives of the Beatles, who have been examined frequently as celebrities, performers and businessmen but rarely as composers.

▲ George, John and Paul outside the back door of the McCartney home at 20 Forthlin Road, Allerton, Liverpool. John and Paul wrote over 100 songs in the front room here, before 'Love Me Do' became their first British hit in 1962.

Most of the early interviewers completely ignored the Beatles as songwriters. Even after turning out the splendidly-crafted *A Hard Day's Night*, the first album to consist of nothing but Lennon and McCartney songs, no-one seemed interested in how they did it or where the ideas came from or how much of themselves they were revealing in the lyrics. Instead, to their increasing frustration, they had to put up with questions on the level of "Do you prefer filming to making records?" or "When is Paul getting married?". No wonder they turned their backs on touring midway through their recording career and restricted the access of journalists.

It was only with the arrival of the more serious albums (*Revolver, Sgt Pepper*) and the interest of the more serious press (*The Sunday Times, Rolling Stone*) that the Beatles began to be interviewed as artists capable of discussing the creative process. Although they often volunteered invaluable information, no-one, as far as I know, has properly followed up the clues to discover the full story. We may know, for example, that 'She's Leaving Home' was based on a newspaper story of a teenage runaway but do we know who she was? Did she ever come back home? Did she ever know that she was the subject of a Beatles' song? What about 'Ob-La-Di Ob La-Da'? Paul has, at various times, said it was the phrase of a London night club habitué called 'Jimmy', or perhaps 'Scott', which he appropriated for his reggae-inspired number. But how did this character react to having a song written around one of his catch phrases?

By the time the Beatles released their first single in 1962, there was already a considerable Lennon and McCartney catalogue because they'd been writing together for five years, meeting mostly at Paul's family home in Allerton, Liverpool, to polish off songs that they'd begun on their own. Starting a song may have meant having an idea for a melody, or arriving with an almost complete song which just needed the essential middle eight 'hook'. It may also have meant coming up with a great title and a first line and needing help with direction, or having heard a great new rock'n'roll song and wanting to make a version that was all their own.

From fairly early on, each song bore the distinctive signature of either John or Paul because although they were united in their love of primitive American rock'n'roll, they were markedly different in their approaches to songwriting. Crudely put, Paul's songs were melodic and optimistic while not giving a lot away about his passions and anxieties. John's songs tended to be more rhythmic, his outlook was pessimistic and, even before he'd heard of Bob Dylan, he was letting his feelings show.

These different styles of writing owed everything to their different backgrounds. Paul grew up in an old-fashioned working-class home where music brought people together. If you wanted to get a party going, you would persuade someone to bang out a tune on the piano and everyone would stand around and sing along. Although Paul's mother died when he was 14, his father was always encouraging and praised the values of hard work and ambition. His own tastes in music - he'd been a band leader in the Twenties - were passed on to his son and songs like 'When I'm 64', 'Your Mother Should Know' and 'Honey Pie' were Paul's affectionate tributes to the pre-war music he knew his dad loved. It was Jim, his dad, who advised Paul to learn to play the piano because, he said, it was people who played the piano who got invited to the best parties.

In a way, that's how Paul got on. He mastered several instruments and songs and became the life and soul of the party. After all, it was the fact that he could play guitar chords rather than banjo chords and knew the words to 'Be Bop A Lula' and 'Twenty Flight Rock' that so impressed John Lennon when he first met him at a church fete in the summer of 1957 and got him the job with John's group the Quarry Men.

Although John is often seen as the working-class Liverpudlian, a perception encouraged by his song 'Working-Class Hero', he really came from a middle-class background where the deprivations were emotional rather than material. He grew up in a semi-detached private home on one of Liverpool's grandest avenues and was an only child whose father ran out on him as a child and whose mother abandoned him to the care of her sister. By contrast, Paul's father had to work hard to bring up his motherless sons in a council house, but there was always a lot of affection in the McCartney home. Perhaps this is what made Paul and John such a perfect match. Each

of them seemed to have what the other lacked. Where Paul was bright and uncomplicated, John was serious and brooding. Where Paul looked on the bright side, John always suspected the worst. Where Paul wanted show business with flashing lights, John wanted to be taken seriously as an artist.

It worked well for a decade. When Paul wanted 'beauty queen' to rhyme with 'just seventeen' in 'I Saw Her Standing There', John told him it was 'crap' and thus saved a beat music classic. When they were writing 'Getting Better', John offered the line 'couldn't get much worse' and, for the similarly optimistic 'We Can Work It Out', it was he who added the contrasting middle eight that started: 'Life is very hard...'

In restraining each other's excesses, they were pulled back to the central cause, which was always the Beatles. At the same time, Paul and John became each other's main rival. It's impossible to underestimate the creative power that was unleashed by the desire to top the other's achievements. There was always an unspoken contest to write the A side of the next Beatle single and this pressure drove standards ever higher. The Beatles didn't really have to fear the competition of the Rolling Stones or the Byrds or even of the Beach Boys, but John had to fear the competition of Paul and vice versa. If John wrote a cracker of a song, Paul would have to go away and come back with something twice as good. This often resulted in them trying to write in the other's style just to show that they could do it. One such example, the gritty, dirty, minimalist piece 'Why Don't We Do It In The Road?' was composed by Paul and recorded without John's help. At around the same time, John was working on 'Julia', a song as tender as anything Paul had written.

Now that Beatle songs saturate the airwaves and can safely be regarded as a soundtrack for an era that started with Kennedy's assassination and ended with Neil Armstrong's moon walk, it's not easy to pinpoint the changes they ushered in. It's particularly difficult

▲ John's main childhood home at 251 Menlove Avenue, where he lived with his Aunt Mimi. The Quarry Men and then the Beatles used to rehearse inside the front porch; John wrote 'Please Please Me' in the bedroom above.

While Paul and John wrote the songs that provided a soundtrack for a generation, it was the older and more conservative George Martin who helped translate their ideas into recordings. His experience and maturity were an important ingredient in the final Beatles' mix.

for those born and raised in the post-Beatle era to see what all the fuss was about. After all, the average rap or ambient record uses more sophisticated technology than *Sgt Pepper* required and songwriters such as David Byrne, Morrissey and Elvis Costello all write lyrics which transcend the old Tin Pan Alleyisms of moon and June, love and above. As T S Eliot responded when told that contemporary writers knew so much more than their forebears: "Precisely, and *they* are that which we know." In other words, what were breakthroughs for the Beatles have become commonly accepted work practices for those who have followed.

It was the Beatles, under the guidance of producer George Martin, who pioneered multi-tracking in the studio and the idea of recording songs that were too complex to be duplicated live in concert. Before the Beatles it was rare in rock'n'roll for songwriters to perform, or for performers to write. Indeed in Britain it was rare that performers had anything to say at all, except perhaps to confess a love of milk shakes and steak and kidney pies, or a desire to buy a cottage for mum and dad. Nearly all the rock'n'roll songs at this time were about love, fashion and adolescence. One of the great legacies of the Beatles was to extend the subject matter of pop. Fewer than half the songs on *Revolver* were about love. The rest of the songs on this album ranged from taxation, through submarines, to altered states of consciousness, drugs and Tibetan Buddhism.

John Lennon and Paul McCartney were the first major pop stars to have benefited from an extended education. Before the Beatles, the assumption was that a typical pop star would be an academic failure who had turned to music for a quick ride to fame and fortune. Elvis Presley was a truck driver, Cliff Richard had worked as an office clerk, but John Lennon had been to art school in Liverpool and Paul McCartney had studied for his A level exams at the best grammar school in the city. This was significant because it meant that for the first time rock'n'roll had reasonably well-educated performers who were able to produce work informed by art and literature. It also meant that the Beatles would later rank alongside painters, poets and novelists in the popular culture of the Sixties. Expecting more of their chosen medium than Gene Vincent or Billy Fury had ever envisioned allowed the Beatles to outgrow the teen market. Before them, no-one had managed the transition from heart throb to 'serious' artist but, between 1966 and 1970, the Beatles had extended their appeal to college and university students. The John Lennon look of centre-parted hair and granny glasses became a familiar campus stereotype.

The early songs were hardly profound because they were written within the limitations of the pop singles market, as well as for an increasingly adoring female audience. "We were just writing songs à la Everly Brothers, à la Buddy Holly," John once admitted. "They were pop songs with no more thought to them than...to create a sound. And the words were almost irrelevant." John would later say that he deliberately kept himself out of the early songs, channelling his personal observations and feelings into poems and short stories, some of which would eventually make up the books *In His Own Write* and *A Spaniard In The Works*. "I was already a stylized songwriter on the first album," he said. "To express myself I would write... personal stories which expressed my personal emotions. I'd have a separate songwriting John Lennon who wrote songs for the sort of meat market, and I didn't consider the lyrics to have any depth at all. They were just a joke."

Some of the songs from these days lived on to become Beatle songs. 'Love Me Do' became their first single. 'I Call Her Name', 'I'll Follow The Sun' and 'The One After 909' became album tracks. Other songs such as 'Thinking Of Linking' and 'Just Fun'

didn't make it on to record. Iris Caldwell, an early girlfriend of Paul's from Liverpool, remembered him singing a song he'd written called 'I Fancy Me Chances With You' which had a chorus of: 'I fancy me chances with you, I fancy me chances with you, When I'm at the dances, I fancy me chances, I fancy me chances with you'.

The Quarry Men became the Silver Beetles, then the Beetles, before metamorphosing into the Beatles with George Harrison joining on lead guitar and Pete Best on drums. For a while Stuart Sutcliffe, an art school friend of John's, also played bass guitar. Their repertoire was dominated by covers of songs associated with Elvis, Little Richard, Jerry Lee Lewis and other American rock'n'rollers but gradually they became confident enough to insert Lennon and McCartney originals into the set.

In 1961, Stuart Sutcliffe left and the following year Ringo Starr, drummer with Rory Storm and the Hurricanes, replaced Pete Best. Managed by Brian Epstein and produced by George Martin, the Beatles became a national phenomenon and their musical interests expanded to include black American girl groups like the Shirelles and the Chiffons and the new Motown sound of the Miracles and Barrett Strong. They admired Gerry Goffin and Carole King who were then at their peak as a songwriting team writing pop hits such as 'Will You Still Love Me Tomorrow?', 'Chains', 'One Fine Day', 'Take Good Care Of My Baby' and 'Please Don't Ever Change' for a variety of American artists.

"First of all, Paul and I wanted to be the Goffin and King of England," said John, and you can see the hallmarks of that Brill Building style of songwriting, where hits were written to order within office hours, in many of their early compositions. As with Goffin and King, they too began to write for other artists,

▲ **Stuart Sutcliffe was a poor musician, but his devotion to painting and rock'n'roll was an inspiration to his friend John, who invited him to play bass guitar with the Beatles. Sutcliffe's death in 1962 was indirectly referred to in John's moving song 'In My Life'. In 1994, Sutcliffe was the focus of *Backbeat*, a feature film about the early Beatle years.**

▲ Manager Brian Epstein, pictured here with Paul and George, encouraged other artists to cover Beatles' songs and persuaded John and Paul to write for Cilla Black, Billy J Kramer, Tommy Quickly and the Fourmost, who he also managed.

major pop star to write songs which dealt with defeat and insecurity; songs that, for example, made statements like 'I'm a loser' or 'I need help' or 'I don't want to spoil the party and so I'll go'. The only thing that cushioned the impact was the Beatles' jaunty image, sustained particularly by films like *Help!*. As the film was a rollicking romp, the title song was generally assumed to be a joke. It wasn't though because, as John himself admitted years later, he was desperately unhappy at the time and literally crying out for help.

Paul was affected in different ways. Through Jane Asher, his girlfriend, herself an accomplished film, television and stage actress, her brother Peter, and their mother, a professor of music, Paul was introduced to students of psychology, classical musicians, actors, theatre directors, film makers and members of London's fledgling 'underground' scene. He developed a fascination for the avant-garde and hung out in art galleries. The effect could be heard in ambitious new songs in which he developed characters and told stories like 'Eleanor Rigby', songs which used orchestral settings like 'Yesterday' and songs like 'For No One' which looked at the world through a film maker's eye. This was the period during which the Beatles began to impress those who had once dismissed them as just another noisy pop group. They weren't to be just an overnight sensation. They had made the transition from Liverpool stars to British stars to international stars and were clearly writing songs destined to become standards.

Until 1965, the Beatles simply refined and synthesized accepted notions of 'rock'n'roll. From that year on, they stretched and dislocated it, challenging all the conventions. In the mid-Sixties they were taking inspiration not from Buddy Holly but from Karlheinz Stockhausen, the German electronic composer, and Ravi Shankar, the classical sitar player. They experimented with rhythms and recording techniques, reinvented the concept of the pop album and, in deserting the stage for the recording studio, changed forever the public perception of pop stars. Through their unbridled imaginations the Beatles transformed pop music. From the outset they were determined to avoid clichés, whether that was cliché of lyric, cliché of rhyme or cliché of chord change. They imagined new sorts of songs and believed if they had the

finding themselves so prolific in 1963 and 1964 that they had material to spare. Thus, they gave 'World Without Love', 'Nobody I Know' and 'I Don't Want To See You Again' to Peter and Gordon (Peter Asher was the brother of Paul's girlfriend, Jane) and 'Bad To Me' and 'Do You Want To Know A Secret?' to Billy J Kramer (who Brian Epstein also managed).

These songs became hits and the rush was on to record Lennon and McCartney songs. Stephen James, son of the Beatles' original music publisher Dick James, remembers that the first task they had when the Beatles sent in a demo was to find the right act to cover the songs. By the mid-Sixties, almost every song on a Beatles album would crop up as a single by another artist, some of them like 'Michelle' by the Overlanders, 'Ob-La-Di Ob-La-Da' by Marmalade and 'Got To Get You Into My Life' by Cliff Bennett and the Rebel Rousers becoming major UK hits.

The second stage of songwriting came in 1964 when Paul and John's horizons were broadened in other ways, by other influences. Although it was Paul who first got hold of a Bob Dylan album it was John who was the most obviously affected. With songs like 'I'm A Loser', 'You've Got To Hide Your Love Away' and 'Help!', there came a new intensity and honesty which signalled that John had discovered that he could be as revealing in song as he had been in his poems and jottings. It was startling at the time for a capacity to imagine something, then producer George Martin would be able to get it down on tape.

Their great burst of creativity in the mid- to late Sixties came about because they accepted no limits. Accidents such as studio feedback or twisted tapes were seized upon and incorporated into their art. Random lyrics, which made no literal sense, were kept because they sounded better. Songs were plucked from newspaper headlines, snatches of conversation, posters, television commercials, religious tracts, dreams and letters. In the studio they demanded the impossible and usually got it. '"Make me sound like a thousand chanting Buddhist monks, George', 'Get me a piccolo sound like I heard last night on the Brandenburg Concerto, George', 'Stick these two half-written songs together and make a new song.'" John and Paul had started by scrawling lyrics in old school notebooks and imagining themselves as Leiber and Stoller (the songsmiths behind Elvis' 'Hound Dog'), or even Rodgers and Hammerstein. Now they were every bit as well-known as their idols.

The third stage of Beatle songwriting was heavily influenced by drugs and eastern meditation. The phrase 'turns me on' had appeared in 'She's A Woman' but the first real fruit of the new altered states was John's song 'The Word' with its message that love can solve all our problems. Songs such as 'Tomorrow Never Knows',

'She Said She Said' and 'Strawberry Fields Forever' would never have been written without marijuana and LSD. Equally, George Harrison's 'Within You Without You' and 'The Inner Light' wouldn't have been possible without the experience of India. John's ability to write was first enhanced and then hampered by his experimentation with drugs. He later confessed that LSD had virtually destroyed his ego and that in turn cost him the unacknowledged leadership of the Beatles. In 1964 and 1965, most of the hit singles were songs where John was the major contributor. After Sgt Pepper, the hits were almost all written by Paul - 'Hello Goodbye', 'Magical Mystery

Tour', 'Lady Madonna', 'Hey Jude', 'Get Back', 'Let It Be'. By 1967, the world was wondering not so much whether the Beatles could push the form of the popular song any further but where they would take it to next. The general feeling was that their recordings would be even more complex and full of tricks.

The fourth and final era of the Beatles' songwriting began in 1968. Against all expectations, it marked a return to simplicity. They released 'Lady Madonna', as basic a rock'n'roll song as they had ever written, and then went off to India where they composed a set of acoustic songs. The album cover this time was plain white. By now the Lennon and McCartney partnership was falling apart. Although most of the songs were still credited to them as a pair, it was clear that The Beatles (The White Album as it is popularly known) relied on solo contributions. In private life too, they were pulling in different directions. John had a new partner in Yoko. Paul had a new partner in Linda. There weren't the same reasons for being together anymore.

In 1969, the Beatles decided they had done everything they could ever do together and parted company. Abbey Road, with its tales of financial woes, arguments and discord was the last album the group recorded, although Let It Be was the final album to be released. In seven years they had gone from young Liverpudlians happy to sing about the delights of chatting up a girl in a ballroom to worldly-wise men waxing philosophical about the power of love and groaning under the weight of their business empire.

Somehow they had managed to take us along with them, particularly those of us who were 13 when they sang 'I Saw Her Standing There' and 20 when they sang 'Come Together'. They seemed to have documented the whole struggle of adolescence, from the desire to simply touch a loved one ('I Wanna Hold Your Hand'), through the feelings of loneliness ('Help!'), moving on to inquisitive experimentation with drugs and religion ('Within You Without You'),

The wooded grounds of the Salvation Army children's home in Liverpool lying beyond this gate post came to represent the idyllic world of John's lost childhood. Today, the old building has gone but the posts remain and are a significant tourist attraction.

to facing up to the burdens of earning a living ('Carry That Weight') and marriage ('The Ballad Of John and Yoko').

The Beatles' songs were never as dense as Bob Dylan's or as raunchy and direct as the Rolling Stones'. At the time, however, they were taken no less seriously, as Beatles' songs were always believed to 'mean' something. Thirty years after the band stopped playing, those songs still mean something to us. They are like old friends who we met when we were young and who made life a little more exciting and easier to cope with. Because of what they did for us, we have great affection for them. It is because we hold such affection for them that it makes sense to find out where they came from.

▲ **Several of the Beatles'**
songs were inspired by
items in newspapers
and magazines,
including 'A Day In The
Life', 'She's Leaving
Home' and 'Lady
Madonna'.

PLEASE PLEASE ME

One of the great strengths of the Beatles was that by 1962, the year they cut their first record, they were already seasoned performers, well-versed in American soul, gospel, rhythm and blues and rock'n'roll. Most of what they knew had been learned the hard way. They knew how songs were constructed because, unable to afford sheet music, they had to decipher lyrics and work out chord changes by listening to records over and over again. Having played rock'n'roll to adoring teenagers at the lunchtime Cavern Club sessions in Liverpool, as well as to inebriated German businessmen in Hamburg, they also knew how to excite, calm and seduce an audience.

John and Paul had been together for five years; George had been with them for almost as long. Ringo was a recent member, having replaced Pete Best on drums, but they'd known him since 1959 and his previous position with Rory Storm and the Hurricanes meant that they had all played the same venues.

At this time, the Beatles' material was standard beat group fare – the best-known songs by the best-known rock'n'roll artists. Top of their list was Elvis Presley. They covered almost 30 of the songs he'd recorded, as well as numbers by Chuck Berry, Buddy Holly, Carl Perkins, Gene Vincent, Fats Domino, Jerry Lee Lewis, Larry Williams, Ray Charles, the Coasters, Athhur Alexander, Little Richard and the Everly Brothers. Studying the music of these artists taught John and Paul the basics of songwriting. When they came together at Paul's house to write their own material, it was a case of reassembling the familiar chords and words to make something distinctively theirs. This is how a bass riff from a Chuck Berry number came to be incorporated into 'I Saw Her Standing There', a song about seeing a girl at the Tower Ballroom in New Brighton, and explains how the sound of Roy Orbison's voice came to be the inspiration behind 'Please Please Me', the Beatles' first Number 1 single.

Sometimes their songs were 'about' incidents from their lives but often the words, like the chords, were borrowed from what had gone before. At this stage, the words were important to create sounds and impressions, rather than to convey a message.

Most of their debut album was recorded in a single session on February 11, 1963. It was released on March 22, 1963 and reached the top spot in the British charts. In America it was titled *Introducing The Beatles*, and released on the little-known Vee Jay label. The US version didn't include 'Please Please Me' or 'Ask Me Why', and failed to make the charts.

I SAW HER STANDING THERE

Producer George Martin's initial idea had been to tape a Beatles' show at the Cavern Club in Liverpool but it was eventually decided to get the group to play their live show in the studio and cut the album in a day. This was done on February 11, 1963, when in a 15-hour session the Beatles recorded ten new tracks which were then added to both sides of their first two singles and released as the album *Please Please Me*.

'I Saw Her Standing There' was the perfect song with which to open the Beatles' first album because it set the group firmly in its context of sweaty ballrooms, full of adoring teenage girls and dancing. They decided to keep the 1-2-3-4 'intro' as this added to the feeling of a raw Liverpool beat group captured in live performance.

Originally titled 'Seventeen', the song tells the simple story of a boy who sees a girl dancing at the local ballroom and, after deciding that her looks are 'way beyond compare', determines to dance with no other from that day on.

There's a wonderful mixture of youthful arrogance and insecurity as the story unfolds, for there is no hint that the boy has considered the possibility of rejection and yet, in that unforgettable beat group rhyme, we're told that as he 'crossed the room' his heart 'went boom'.

Paul started composing this song one night in 1962 driving back to his home in Allerton, Liverpool. He liked the idea of writing about a 17-year-old girl because he was conscious of the need to have songs which the group's largely female audience could easily relate to. "I didn't think a lot about it as I sang it to myself," he said four years later. "Originally the first two lines were 'She was just seventeen, Never been a beauty queen'. It sounded like a good rhyme to me at the time. But when I played it through to John the next day, I realized that it was a useless line and so did John. So we both sat down and tried to come up with another line which rhymed with 17 but which meant something." After a while, John came up with 'you know what I mean', which as Paul recognized, could either be dismissed as a filler or be seen as sexual innuendo. It was also a very Liverpudlian phrase avoiding the borrowed Americanisms which littered most rock'n'roll of the time.

The two boys completed the melody on their acoustic guitars and wrote the lyrics in a Liverpool Institute exercise book. Paul later explained in an interview with *Beat Instrumental* that the bass riff was stolen from Chuck Berry's 1961 song 'I'm Talking About You'. "I played exactly the same notes as he did and it fitted our number perfectly," he confessed. "Even now, when I tell people about it, I find few of them believe me. Therefore, I maintain that a bass riff doesn't have to be original."

In December 1961, Paul started dating Iris Caldwell, sister of local beat singer Rory Storm, whose group the Hurricanes featured Ringo Starr as drummer (he joined the Beatles in August 1962). Just like the girl in 'I Saw Her Standing There', Iris was only 17 at the time when Paul saw her dancing the twist at the Tower Ballroom in New Brighton (situated 25 minutes out of Liverpool). She was a trained dancer and Paul was apparently impressed by her legs, which were displayed in fishnet stockings, and the fact that she was already working professionally in show business.

Paul became a frequent guest at the Caldwell family home at 54 Broad Green Road, Liverpool 15, which was known to the local beat groups as Hurricaneville. He became close to Iris' mother, Violet, and would often drop in with John to sit around and write songs. "Paul and I dated for a couple of years," says Iris. "It was never that serious. We never pretended to be true to each other. I went out with lots of people. I was working away in different

Mrs Violet Caldwell pours tea for her son Rory Storm who was one of Liverpool's top performers in the years before Beatlemania. Rory's sister Iris (in the photo on the wall) met Paul when she was demonstrating the twist at the Tower Ballroom. She was 17.

theatres at the time but if I was back home then we would go out. There were never any promises made or love declared." According to Iris, Paul intended giving 'I Saw Her Standing There' to her brother Rory to record. "He thought it would be a good song for him but it wasn't dealt out that way. Brian Epstein didn't want Rory to have it."

Certainly, by 1962, 'I Saw Her Standing There' was part of the Beatles' stage act, one of the earliest Lennon and McCartney songs slipped between those of Buddy Holly and Little Richard. The first cover version of the song was by English rock'n'roll singer Duffy Power in 1963. In America, it became the flip side of 'I Want To Hold Your Hand', the single released in January 1964 that was the Beatles' first US Number 1. It was one of five songs which the Beatles performed on the celebrated *Ed Sullivan Show* of February 9, 1964, which was watched by 70 million people, then the largest US TV audience ever recorded. In November 1974, John performed the song with Elton John at Madison Square Garden.

MISERY

By January 1963, with 'Love Me Do' a British Top 20 hit under their belt, the songwriting confidence of the McCartney-Lennon team (as they were initially credited) had grown, but when plans were made to record their first LP, they were suddenly under pressure to come up with some new songs .

Although not all the songs were going to be their own compositions - they had chosen material by American songwriters to fill almost half the album - they were determined to stamp their own mark on the recording and not become yet another British act making a living out of cover versions. In the climate of the times, this was a bold move. Traditionally British rock'n'roll acts didn't record their own songs but,

In February 1963, it was Helen Shapiro, pictured here with her hand on Ringo's shoulder, who was the big British star and the Beatles were invited to be one of her seven support acts. Shapiro became the first performer to have a song specifically written for her by Lennon and McCartney, although her recording manager eventually turned it down. Also shown here are *Ready Steady Go* television presenter Keith Fordyce and British singers Dusty Springfield and Eden Kane.

aping the US sound, covered promising American singles before they were released in the UK. Cliff Richard, Britain's top pop star when the Beatles began recording, had broken the mould slightly by recording songs written by Ian Samwell, a former member of his backing group, but no-one in the UK had succeeded in producing genuinely British-sounding rock'n'roll.

It was against this background that Paul and John began to pull together the five new unreleased songs for their debut album *Please Please Me*. Backstage at the King's Hall, Glebe Street, Stoke-on-Trent, where they were playing a concert on January 26, 1963, they huddled together and wrote 'Misery', with John as the major contributor. Just as Paul had been irrepressibly optimistic that he would get to dance with the girl in 'I Saw Her Standing There', John kicked off his career as an album artist by complaining about a girl who has left him and made him lonely. 'The world is treating me bad' was the song's portentous first line. "Allan Clarke and Graham Nash of the Hollies helped on that song," remembers Tony Bramwell, then an employee of Brian Epstein. "John and Paul were desperate to get it finished and got stuck on one of the lines and Allan and Graham began throwing in suggestions. The boys wanted to get it ready for Helen Shapiro."

Within days they had made a tape and sent it to

Helen Shapiro said that John was like a big brother to her. The last time she saw him was at a literary luncheon in 1964 where his book *In His Own Write* was celebrated. "I remember that he signed a copy for me ... nutty as he was with me he was always really lovely."

Norrie Paramor of EMI's Columbia label for him to consider for Shapiro, who they knew would shortly be recording in Nashville. Indeed, Paul told Alan Smith, the editor of *New Musical Express*, that it was a song to be covered: "We've called it 'Misery' but it isn't quite as slow as it sounds. It moves along at quite

a steady pace and we think Helen Shapiro will make quite a good job of it."

Just 16 at the time, Helen had been having Top 10 hits in Britain since early 1961 and the Beatles were due to debut on the cinema circuit as one of seven support acts on her 14-date February tour. It would only be in the final shows, with 'Please Please Me' a Top 10 sensation, that the Beatles were upgraded, although even then they only got to close the first half. Package tours still formed part of the British entertainment scene at the time, despite being a hangover from the days of variety shows where singers followed jugglers and magicians on to the stage. For this tour, the Beatles had time to deliver four songs and were sandwiched between performances by comedians.

"I got on great with them," remembers Helen, "and John was like a brother to me. Very protective. He and Paul certainly offered 'Misery' to me first, through Norrie, but I didn't know anything about it until I met them on the first day of the tour (February 2, Bradford, Yorks). Apparently he'd turned it down even though I hadn't heard it." The offer was taken up by another artist on the same tour, Kenny Lynch, a black singer from Britain, whose biggest success to date had been a Top 10 hit with a cover of the Drifters' 'Up On The Roof'. 'Misery' wasn't a hit for him but it gave him the distinction of being the first non-Beatle to record a Lennon and McCartney song.

ASK ME WHY

Written in the spring of 1962, with John as the major contributor, 'Ask Me Why' was a lightweight love song from the Beatles' set at the Cavern Club that year, and was premiered on the BBC radio programme *Teenagers' Turn* on June 11, 1962. It was one of four songs which they took to their first recording session on June 6, 1962 at EMI Studios in Abbey Road, north London, but George Martin didn't think it was strong enough to be their debut single. Re-recorded in February 1963, it was released in Britain as the B side of 'Please Please Me'.

PLEASE PLEASE ME

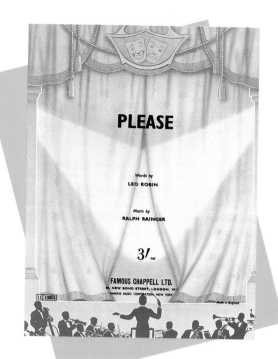

▲ The lyric of 'Please Please Me' had an unlikely origin in a 1932 song recorded by Bing Crosby.

It was American star Roy Orbison's voice that John conjured up as he wrote the original slow version of 'Please Please Me' in his Liverpool bedroom. Months after the song became a hit, the Beatles found themselves supporting Orbison on a British tour.

Please Please Me' was one of those innocent-sounding pop songs with a subversive subtext. Some critics have seen it as a plea for equality in sexual pleasure. Robert Christgau, music editor of New York's *Village Voice*, has more explicitly claimed that it's about oral sex.

Iris Caldwell remembers Paul coming over to her house one night and reading her the words to the just-completed song. "He used to pick up my brother's guitar and play it but that night he didn't bother" she says. "He just read out the lyrics. They didn't seem to make any sense to me at the time and I thought they were absolutely awful." The song's origins were certainly innocuous, as the chorus was suggested by the 1932 Bing Crosby song 'Please', written by Leo Robin and Ralph Rainger, which starts off by playing with the homophones 'pleas' and 'please': 'Oh please, lend your little ear to my pleas, Lend a ray of cheer to my pleas, Tell me that you love me too'. Later, John recalled his mother, Julia, singing this to him as a child, adding that he'd always been fascinated by the dual use of the 'please' sound.

When John came to write this song, in his front bedroom at 251 Menlove Avenue in Liverpool ("I remember the day and the pink eyelet on the bed"), he imagined Roy Orbison singing it because he'd just been listening to the hit single 'Only The Lonely'. It's easy to imagine Orbison singing the original, slow version of 'Please Please Me'. With his pallid, dough-like complexion and permanent shades, Orbison might have looked an unlikely pop star, but he was a brilliantly soulful singer and wrote his own songs. He was someone whom John in particular could relate to because his lyrics explored dark moods of loss and loneliness.

Within months of 'Please Please Me' being released as a single and reaching the Number 2 spot in the British charts, the Beatles were picked to support Orbison on a three-week tour of Britain. "We never talked to each other about songwriting on that tour," remembered Orbison years later. "The basic thing they wanted to know at that time was how I thought they would get on in America. I told them to let people know they were British and to get on something like the *Ed Sullivan Show*. If they did that, I said they could be just as big in America as they were in Britain. I said that in an article for *New Musical Express* which came out during the tour. I thought it was important that they let people know they were British because we hadn't heard much from Britain except for the Blue Streak missile and the Profumo scandal."

His exact words, recorded in May 1963, were: "The Beatles could well be tops in America. These boys have enough originality to storm our charts with the same effect as they have done here, but it will need careful handling. They have something that is entirely new even to us Americans and although we have an influx of hit groups at home I really do believe they could top the charts...It's a change to see new stars who are not just watered-down versions of Elvis Presley. This seems to be a sound they have made famous all on their own and I really think it is the greatest. Though you know it as Merseyside music, I am sure this will be hailed as the new British sound in America."

Orbison didn't discover that John had written 'Please Please Me' in emulation of his style until pro-

ducer George Martin mentioned it to him in June 1987 at an Abbey Road celebration for the 20th anniversary of *Sgt Pepper's Lonely Hearts Club Band*. "He told me that it sounded so much like me that they had to change it a little bit," Orbison commented. "That's a nice thing to find out."

In March 1963 John had revealed that they had intended 'Please Please Me' as a B side for their first single until Martin complained about this similarity. "He thought that the arrangement was fussy, so we tried to make it simpler," said John. "In the weeks following (the 'Love Me Do' session), we went over it again and again. We changed the tempo a little. We altered the words slightly and we went over the idea of featuring the harmonica, just as we'd done in 'Love Me Do'. By the time we came to record it, we were so happy with it that we couldn't wait to get it down."

The Beatles' fondness for Orbison was to survive the Sixties. John described his last single, 'Starting Over', as 'Elvis Orbison' and in 1988 George Harrison joined Orbison, Bob Dylan, Tom Petty and Jeff Lynne in recording the critically-acclaimed *Traveling Wilburys* album.

When George Martin first heard the Beatles play 'Please Please Me' in 1962 he told them it was too mournful and needed some speeding up. "It was Paul singing a very kind of winsome, Roy Orbison slow ballad," said Martin. "It was very dreary."

LOVE ME DO

In Britain, 'Love Me Do' was the Beatles' first hit and, like the group's image, it was all pretty strange to a generation which had spent the last two or three years listening to fairly insipid pop performed by men with short haircuts and big grins.

An early song written by Paul, the lyrics of 'Love Me Do' were as basic as could be, with most words consisting of only one syllable and 'love' being repeated 21 times.' I love you for-ever so please love me'. That was the entire message. What set it apart from the teen love songs of the time was a gospel-blues tinge to the singing – a feeling which was heightened by John's harmonica and the slightly mournful close harmonizing. (John's fondness for gospel was confirmed when he listed R&B and gospel as his 'tastes in music' in the *New Musical Express* of February 15, 1963).

During 1962, American star Bruce Channel had enjoyed a British hit with 'Hey Baby' which featured a harmonica solo by Nashville session musician Delbert McClinton. John was impressed by this and when he met McClinton in June 1962 at the Tower Ballroom, New Brighton, where the Beatles were playing sup-port for Channel, he asked him how he played it. "John was very interested in harmonica and, when we went on to play another couple of dates with the Beatles, he and I hung out a lot together," says McClinton. "He wanted me to show him whatever I could. He wanted to know how to play. Before our time together was over he had his own harmonica ready in his pocket." It was only three months later that the Beatles recorded 'Love Me Do', in which John was able to include a distinctive harmonica break.

John went on to play harmonica on the next two singles, 'Please Please Me' and 'With Love From Me To You', as well as on six other tracks including 'Little Child' (*With The Beatles*) and 'I Should Have Known Better' (*A Hard Day's Night*). The last time he used it on record was on 'I'm A Loser'(*Beatles For Sale*) recorded in August 1964. By that time he reckoned it had turned into a Beatles' gimmick.

'Love Me Do' was included on the group's first

four-track extend-ed play record which had sleeve notes written by Tony Barrow, a Lancashire journalist who was then working as the Beatles' press officer. Barrow's com-ments on the four tracks ('From Me To You', 'Thank You Girl', 'Please Please Me' and 'Love Me Do') were remarkably prescient. "The four numbers on this EP have been selected from The Lennon and McCartney Songbook," he wrote. "If that description sounds a trifle pompous perhaps I may suggest you preserve this sleeve for ten years, exhume it from your collec-tion somewhere around the middle of 1973 and write me a very nasty letter if the pop people of the Seventies aren't talking about at least two of these titles as 'early examples of modern beat standards taken from The Lennon and McCartney Songbook'. "

In 1967, when every Beatle song was believed to be drenched in meaning and they had been elevated into 'spokesmen for a generation', Paul commented to Alan Aldridge in an interview for the *Observer* "'Love Me Do' was our greatest philosophical song...for it to be simple, and true, means that it's incredibly simple."

▲ **Although 'Love Me Do' was a fairly restrained Beatles' number, the quirkiness of the group was brought out in John's harmonica solo. This was inspired by Delbert McClinton's harmonica playing, featured on Bruce Channel's hit 'Hey Baby'.**

PS I LOVE YOU

Written in 1961, 'PS I Love You' was another early song by Paul which the Beatles considered recording as their first single. In Britain, it became the B side of 'Love Me Do'. In America, almost two years later, it became a single in its own right and made the Top 10.

It had become fairly routine for British beat groups of the time to play stints in German night clubs where there was a great demand for the new American-style music but few musicians around who could actually play it. In April 1961, the Beatles – John, Paul, George, Pete Best (drums) and Stuart Sutcliffe (bass) – started a gruelling 13-week residency at the Top Ten Club in Hamburg, Germany, playing for over five hours each night, seven days a week. It was the best

apprenticeship they could have had. The continuous playing of other artists' songs taught them how songs were constructed and the pressure to entertain taught them what worked and what didn't.

Paul's girlfriend at the time was Dorothy 'Dot' Rhone, an elfin Liverpool teenager who worked for a chemist and lived at home with her parents. She was a shy but sweet girl whom Paul had been dating for a while and who had become a regular guest at his family home in Liverpool. "She was very much in love with Paul," remembered her friend Sandra Hedges. "He in turn would jealously guard her by placing her amid the group while they were playing." Dot became close to Cynthia Powell, John's girlfriend from art school, and during the Easter holidays the two girls decided to visit their boyfriends in Germany, Cynthia staying with Astrid Kirchner, Stuart Sutcliffe's girlfriend, and Dot staying with Paul on a houseboat.

After Dot had returned to Liverpool, Paul wrote this song which she assumed was for her although, years later, Paul denied that he had anyone specific in

mind. Written letter form, 'PS I Love You' was the precursor of Paul's other letter songs, 'Paperback Writer' and 'When I'm 64'. Paul's relationship with Dot was picked up after returning from Hamburg but ended in the summer of 1962 just as the Beatles began recording. At the time, she was sharing a flat with John's art school girlfriend Cynthia Powell at 93 Garmoyle Road, Liverpool, close to Penny Lane.

Paul came round late one night and broke the news to Dot. Cynthia remembered her collapsing in tears. "Poor little defenceless Dot," she wrote in her book *A Twist Of Lennon*. "She wouldn't hurt a fly but had been hurt so much that she couldn't even tell me without renewed convulsions and outbursts of uncontrollable crying. As it happens, she didn't need to tell me anything. Only one thing would have done that to Dot and that was Paul giving her the push...he was too young to settle down. He wanted desperately to be footloose and fancy free and I suppose I let Dot down very gently under the circumstances."

▲ **Billy J Kramer, seen here sitting above Ringo and George, was also managed by Brian Epstein.**

DO YOU WANT TO KNOW A SECRET?

Around the same time that Paul finished with Dot Rhone, Cynthia discovered that she was pregnant. On August 23, 1962, she and John did the conventional thing by getting married at a registry office in Mount Pleasant, Liverpool. The best man at this small affair attended by Paul, George, and a handful of relations, was manager Brian Epstein, who offered the newlyweds the privacy of a ground floor flat he rented at 36 Faulkner Street to start their married life. This wasn't Epstein's main home but a place in the city centre which he kept for his own discreet homosexual liaisons.

Cynthia remembered being ecstatic at the unexpected wedding gift as they hadn't given much thought to where they would live and there was no time in the busy Beatles' schedule for a honeymoon. "It was the first apartment I'd ever had that wasn't shared by 14 other art students," John later admitted.

It was while living here that John wrote 'Do You Want To Know A Secret?', the secret in question being that he had just realized that he was really in love. As with 'Please Please Me', it had its genesis in a song his mother used to sing to him, which she in turn had picked up from Walt Disney's 1937 film *Snow White And The Seven Dwarfs*. In one of the opening scenes in the film, Snow White is working as a kitchen maid and, as she stands by the castle well, she begins to sing to the doves: 'Wanna know a secret?, Promise not to tell?, We are standing by a wishing well' ('I'm Wishing', words and music by Larry Morey and Frank Churchill).

In an interview with *Musician* magazine, George Harrison was later to reveal that the musical inspiration for the song came from 'I Really Love You', a 1961 hit for the Stereos.

John made a demo of 'Do You Want To Know A Secret' on an acoustic guitar while sitting in a bathroom (a fact that became obvious because of the flush of a toilet at the end of the song). This was offered to another Epstein artist, Billy J Kramer, who

▲ **Brian Epstein's early successes as Beatles' manager were really to do with presentation – smartening their image and ensuring that they handled themselves well in interviews and on tour. He had virtually nothing to do with the songwriting.**

took it with him to Germany as part of his stage act. Kramer's real name was Billy Ashton, and he was Epstein's third signing following on closely from Gerry and the Pacemakers. Epstein then acquired the Big Three, the Fourmost, Tommy Quickly and Cilla Black, all of them Liverpool acts.

Kramer came back from Germany convinced that 'Do You Want To Know A Secret?' wasn't a crowd pleaser but EMI liked it enough to offer him a recording contract after hearing a test tape of it. It went on to become a Number 2 hit for him in Britain during the summer of 1963; the first time a Lennon and McCartney song by another artist had made the Hit Parade.

Although John had written it with his own voice in mind, when the Beatles recorded it, the song was offered to George. "I thought it would be a good vehicle for him," John said, "because it only had three notes and he wasn't the best singer in the world."

THERE'S A PLACE

Just as 'Misery' indicated the feelings of isolation and rejection which would become a major preoccupation in John's songs, so 'There's A Place' introduced what was to become a recurring theme of finding comfort in his thoughts, dreams and memories. In 'There's A Place', John deals with his life's sorrow by retreating into the safety of his inner thoughts and, in a more sophisticated way, this is what would characterize later songs such as 'Strawberry Fields Forever', 'Girl', 'In My Life', 'Rain', 'I'm Only Sleeping', 'Tomorrow Never Knows' and so many others. "The usual Lennon thing," he would comment with reference to 'There's A Place'. "It's all in your mind."

"He was a combination of introversion and extroversion," says Thelma McGough who as Thelma Pickles dated John while they were both at Liverpool School of Art. "He appeared very extrovert and yet it was all front. He was actually very deep but he'd keep that pretty well hidden until you were on your own with him."

Although John spoke as though the song was entirely his, Paul has since claimed that the original idea for it came from him, the title derived from the *West Side Story* song 'There's A Place For Us' (1957) which he had in his Forthlin Road record collection

Musically John admitted that 'There's A Place' was his attempt at "a sort of Motown, black thing", referring to the hot new sound emerging from Detroit on Berry Gordy's fledgling independent label. Motown hits were mostly written by production line writers and performed by groups trained in the label's own school — it was dance music driven by inventive bass lines, gospel-style splashes of tambourine and vocal harmonies.

The Beatles were to play a crucial role in popularizing the label, initially by recording Motown songs such as 'Please Mr Postman', 'You've Really Got A Hold On Me' and 'Money' and later by dropping the names of new Motown artists and records in interviews. In 1964 Berry Gordy said: "It helped when we had several songs of ours recorded by the Beatles. I met them and found out that they were great fans of Motown and had been studying Motown music, and they went on to become some of the greatest songwriters in history. We were absolutely delighted."

John was both an introvert and an extrovert. The bookish, introspective side revealed itself in songs like 'There's A Place', where he confessed to wanting to avoid the harshness of life by retreating into his imagination.

The other side of John was abrasive and outspoken. Performing rock'n'roll brought out his more assertive tendencies but close friends have said this loudness was largely a protective shield.

▲ After six years honing
their stage act, the
Beatles were keen to
explore the studio.

WITH THE BEATLES

The Beatles had five years to prepare for their first album and five months to prepare for their second. After years of meeting up at Paul's house, with hours of spare time on their hands, they were now forced to write in hotel bedrooms, on tour buses and in dressing rooms – anywhere they could snatch a quiet moment.

Such pressures cause some songwriters to freeze up, but it proved to be a positive stimulus to John and Paul who, as time went on, developed the ability to write Number 1 hits to order.

John and Paul seemed to have an innate sense of what their public wanted to hear. Believing that it was important for each girl in the audience to feel that they were singing personally to her, many of their songs had the word 'you' in the title – for example, 'From Me To You', 'Thank You Girl', and 'I'll Get You'.

However, if in the early days they'd been able to write for an audience they could see and for people they knew on first name terms, everything changed once they became successful. Suddenly, the police had to devise ingenious ways of smuggling them in and out of venues, and they were even becoming popular in countries they hadn't visited.

Nonetheless at the height of Beatlemania, often pursued by scores of screaming fans, they still managed to write a steady stream of successful singles. 'I Want To Hold Your Hand', for example, was written with the American market in mind, and propelled them to the top of the *Billboard* charts, making them the first British recording artists to truly conquer America. Indeed, constant international travel and the move to London were beneficial for their songwriting as it exposed them to a greater variety of influences. Everybody they met seemed to want to turn them on to something new. Through his relationship with the actress Jane Asher, Paul was becoming more familiar with stage musicals, theatre and classical music. Meanwhile, John was holed up in his Kensington flat listening to imported albums by black American groups like the Miracles, the Shirelles and the Marvelettes.

With The Beatles, their second album, was a much more considered recording than their first, with sessions spread over a three-month period. It went to Number 1 in Britain shortly after its release in November 1963 and became the first pop album to sell over a million copies. A version of *With The Beatles*, titled *Meet The Beatles*, was released in America in January 1964 and also went to Number 1.

FROM ME TO YOU

From Me To You', the Beatles' third single was written on February 28, 1963, while travelling by coach from York to Shrewsbury on the Helen Shapiro tour. Helen can't remember them actually writing it, but can recall it being played to her when they arrived at Shrewsbury in the afternoon ready for their evening concert at the Granada Cinema. "They asked me if I would come and listen to two songs that they had," she says. "Paul sat at the piano and John stood next to me and they sang 'From 'Me To You' and 'Thank You Girl'. They said they sort of knew their favourite but hadn't finally decided, so they wanted me to tell them which one I thought would make the best A side. As it happened I liked 'From Me To You' and they said, 'Great. That's the one we like.'"

The Beatles played the Odeon Cinema in Southport, Lancashire, the next day, the closest the tour would go to Liverpool, and here they were able to play their new song to Paul's father to get his opinion. They knew the lyrics were simple enough but they were worried that the music was "a bit on the complicated side" and that "it wouldn't catch on with the fans." It was Paul's dad who convinced them that it was "a nice little tune".

The title was suggested by From You To Us, the letters' column in the weekly pop newspaper *New Musical Express*. Paul and John were reading the issue dated February 22, which had their tour dates advertized on the front page and stories about Cliff Richard, Billy Fury and Elvis Presley inside. They started to "talk about one of the letters in the column", as John revealed in May 1963, when asked about the origins of the song. There were only two letters and it's hard to see which could have provoked comment. One letter complained about 'maniacal laughter' on two recent limbo dance records and the other relished the fact that Cliff Richard appeared to be getting the better of Elvis Presley in the charts. Perhaps it was this last letter that fired the Beatles' own ambition.

THANK YOU GIRL

Apparently Paul and John started the song by trading lines, making it one of the few Beatle hits that they built from scratch together. The song's great gimmick was the use of the high-pitched 'ooooh' sound, inspired by the Isley Brothers' recording of 'Twist And Shout'. When Kenny Lynch heard them singing this on the coach, he said to them, "You can't do that. You sound like a bunch of fairies", and they replied, "It's okay. The kids will like it." In April 1963, John commented: "We were just fooling about on the guitar. This went on for a while. Then we began to get a good melody line and we really started to work at it. Before the journey was over we'd completed the lyric, everything. We were so pleased…"

A year later, again talking about how the song was written, John said: "Paul and I kicked some ideas around and came up with what we what we thought was a suitable melody line. The words weren't really all that difficult – especially as we had decided quite definitely not to do anything that was at all complicated. I suppose that is why we often had the words 'you' and 'me' in the titles of our songs. It's the sort of thing that helps the listeners to identify with the lyrics. We think this is very important. The fans like to feel that they are part of something that is being done by the performers."

From writing to recording took five days although, as John remembered, "We nearly didn't record it because we thought it was too bluesy at first, but when we'd finished it and George Martin had scored it with harmonica, it was alright."

In April 1963 'From Me To You' became the Beatles' second British Number 1 hit but, released on the Vee Jay label in America, it didn't even make the Top 40.

◄┈┈┈┈┈┈┈┈┈┈┈┈┈┈┈┈┈
'From Me To You' was written on the Helen Shapiro tour bus. Here John and Helen fool around for the cameras.

John and Paul claimed in the early days to have written over 100 songs together between the summer of 1957 and 1962, Paul now admits that the number was closer to 20. When they became stars, they could no longer afford to hang about, as almost everything they wrote from this point on would have to have hit potential. Between 1963 and 1965, they released at least three singles a year and two albums, an incredible output for a group who were touring, filming, meeting the press and writing most of their own material.

When the Beatles came into the industry, pop music was formulaic and rather stale. The B sides of singles tended to be throwaway, often written by the producer under a pseudonym to reap the benefits of mechanical royalties, and albums contained one or two recent hits plus filler material. The Beatles changed all this. Suddenly, every song counted. Each of their singles had a B side which was arguably as good as the A side and each album was full of potential singles. Only rarely did their singles appear on albums.

'Thank You Girl', originally 'Thank You Little Girl', was a follow-up to 'Please Please Me', with 'From Me To You' actually composed as its B side. In the end, 'From Me To You' sounded like the obvious single, and so they swapped the two around. At the time, John seemed proud of the song but, in 1971, he dismissed it as "just a silly song that we knocked off" and, in 1980, as "one of our efforts at writing a single that didn't work". Paul appears to agree. "A bit of a hack song," he has said, "but all good practice."

▲ **The Beatles altered the public's perception of B sides which had traditionally been filled with a throwaway track. Beatles B sides were of as high a standard as their A sides, because they were almost always written as potential singles themselves.**

SHE LOVES YOU

Although the Beatles had already taken Britain's Number 1 spot twice in 1963, it was 'She Loves You' which took them to the 'toppermost of the poppermost' as they mockingly used to call it. Its sales outstripped anything they'd done before and it went on to be the country's best-selling single of the decade, entering the Top 20 in August 1963 and staying put until February 1964.

It wasn't simply a commercial triumph. In just over two minutes of vinyl, the Beatles distilled the essence of everything that made them fresh and exciting. There was the driving beat, the fine harmonizing, the girlish 'wooo' sounds which had gone down so well on 'From Me To You', as well as the bursting enthusiasm of its pace. And on top of this, the distinctive 'Yeah, yeah, yeah' tag which became a gift to headline writers.

The rapid expansion of Beatlemania from regional to national phenomenon can be put down to the Beatles' appearance on *Sunday Night at The London Palladium*, a television show broadcast live from the heart of London on October 13, 1963. Witnessed by a national TV audience of 15 million, screaming fans mobbed the theatre and many of those who packed the streets outside found themselves on the front page of next day's Fleet Street newspapers. Not only had the Beatles transformed popular music but they had become a phenomenon of post-war Britain. Suddenly they found their photos plastered all over the national papers, not just *Melody Maker, New Musical Express* and *Boyfriend*. The single that just happened to be in the centre of this storm was 'She Loves You'.

The song was written by John and Paul in Newcastle after playing the Majestic Ballroom on June 26, 1963. They had a very rare day off before continuing the tour to Leeds on the 28, and Paul remembered being with John at the Turk's Hotel, sitting on separate beds, playing their acoustic guitars. Their first three singles had been declarations of love with the word 'me' in the title. This time, it was Paul's idea to switch the approach by removing themselves and writing about a love between two other people – 'she' and 'you'. The song he had in mind at the time was Bobby Rydell's then current British hit 'Forget Him'

At first sight, this is a song about reconciliation. The writer is offering to patch up a broken relationship by passing on messages ('she told me what to say') and offering counsel ('apologize to her'). However American rock critic Dave Marsh, detected 'darker nuances' in the text. In *The Heart Of Rock And Roll,* he wrote: "What Lennon sings boils down to a warning to his friend: You'd better appreciate this woman's friendship, because if you don't, I will." The song remains ambiguous because whether this is really being said as confidential advice to a friend, or through gritted teeth to a rival, largely depends on how you interpret the tone of voice.

The 'Yeah, yeah, yeah' chorus proved to be a perfect catch phrase for an optimistic era. If Paul's father had had his way though, things would have been different. On hearing the song for the first time, he suggested that they might revise it to 'Yes, yes, yes'; the Queen's English maybe, but not exactly rock'n'roll. The Beatles were not the first group to use 'yeah yeah'. It was frequently used as an aside in Fifties skiffle music, as well as by Elvis Presley in 'Good Luck Charm'(1962) and 'All Shook Up' (1957).

The sixth chord which ends the song was unusual in pop music, although the Glenn Miller Orchestra had used it often on their recordings in the Forties.

During 1963, the Beatles became a familiar sight in the BBC canteen, after appearing in programmes like *Saturday Club, Parade Of The Pops* and *Easy Beat.*

"George Martin laughed when we first played it to him like that," said Paul. "He thought we were joking. But it didn't work without it so we kept it in and eventually George was convinced."

I'LL GET YOU

▲ Recording *Pop Go The Beatles* for BBC Radio in August 1963, when 'She Loves You' was riding high in the British charts.

'll Get You' was written by John and Paul together at John's house as a follow-up to 'From Me To You', and then became the B side of 'She Loves You', a song they wrote days later but which they felt was better. For Paul, who still regards this as one of his favourite Beatles tracks, the use of the word 'imagine' evoked the beginning of a children's fairy tale and offered an invitation into a fictitious world.

One of the song's musical tricks, the shift from D to A minor to break the word 'pretend', was taken from Joan Baez's version of the traditional song 'All My Trials', which had been included on her debut album *Joan Baez*.

Released as a single in America during 1963 and again in 1964, it never made the pop charts.

Caught mid-air at a photo-call for their celebrated Royal Command Performance at the Prince of Wales Theatre on November 4, 1963. ▶

IT WON'T BE LONG

With *The Beatles* was released in November 1963 and Beatlemania swept Britain. Robert Freeman's black and white cover portraits, where half of each face was in shadow, provided a defining moment in Beatle iconography. Whereas the debut album had been recorded in a day, the sessions for *With The Beatles* were spread over three months, allowing the rawness of a live beat music session to give way to the beginnings of sophisticated pop. "That was when we discovered double-tracking," John later commented. "When I discovered it, I double-tracked everything. I wouldn't let him have anything single-tracked from then on. He (George Martin) would say, 'Please. Just this one,' and I would say, 'No'."

'It Won't Be Long' was the album's opening track, started by John as a potential follow-up single to 'She Loves You', but discarded because, as John said, "it never really made it." Composed as a love song, this could be the story of John's early life. Lonely and rejected, he sits at home waiting for the girl who has walked out on him to come back and make him happy. As in so many later songs, he contrasts the carefree life he imagines everyone else is having with his own anguish, believing that once he's reunited with his loved one all his problems will be solved.

Thelma McGough, who started dating John a month after his mother died in July 1958, believes that his songs of rejection weren't based on broken romances but on the fact that his father had left him as a child and then his mother had effectively left him again by handing him over to her sister to be brought up. "I lost my mother twice," he was to say. "Once as a child of five and then again at 17."

"Rejection and betrayal were his experience of life," says Thelma. "When I met him, the first proper conversation we ever had was all about this because my father had done exactly the same thing and so we felt we had something in common. It was that which helped to draw us close. Also, you have to remember that his mother was run down by a car and, although he appeared very controlled about it, you knew that he was hurting inside. We both felt very let down and abandoned. There was a big difference between Paul and John, although as teenagers they'd both lost their mothers. Paul had a very close-knit family with a network of cousins and aunties. His dad was absolutely wonderful. John's life was very isolated. He lived with Mimi (his mother's sister) who looked after him extremely well but there was no closeness. There was nothing tactile about the relationship."

One of the things that excited John and Paul at the time of writing was the word play that they had introduced around the word 'belong'. Although it was a small innovation for them it was to become a hallmark of their more sophisticated writing.

A rare photograph of the young John Lennon with fellow college student Cynthia Powell, who would later become his first wife.

ALL I'VE GOT TO DO

Half of the 14 songs on *With The Beatles* were written by John and Paul and most of these were written specifically for the album. 'All I've Got To Do', however, was written entirely by John in 1961. The track was, he said, an attempt "to do Smokey Robinson again". His earlier attempt had been with 'Ask Me Why', which was reminiscent of Robinson's 1961 song 'What's So God About Goodbye'. This time he appears to have used 'You Can Depend On Me' as his model. In 1980, while in the studio recording his vocal track for 'Woman', Yoko commented that John sounded like a Beatle. "Actually I'm supposed to be Smokey Robinson at the moment, my dear," John answered, "because the Beatles were always supposing that they were Smokey Robinson."

Bob Dylan, with perhaps only half of his tongue in his cheek, once referred to Robinson as his favourite living poet. The Beatles also covered his song 'You Really Got A Hold On Me' on this album, which had been a US Top 10 hit for the Miracles in February 1963. "When they recorded that, it was one of the most flattering things that ever happened to me," said Smokey. "I listened to it over and over again, not to criticize it but to enjoy it."

▲ Smokey Robinson, left, with his Miracles: Claudette Rogers, Ronnie White, Pete Moore and Bobby Rogers. This line-up lasted from 1955 until 1965, during which time John was influenced by Smokey's voice and style of songwriting.

ALL MY LOVING

The Beatles appeared twice on *Juke Box Jury*, a popular Sixties TV show in Britain, in which a panel of celebrities listened to the latest single releases before declaring whether they would be a hit or a miss.

.......................▶

On April 18, 1963, the actress Jane Asher was in the audience at London's Royal Albert Hall to see the Beatles and other acts in a show which was being recorded by BBC Radio. Although only 17, she was already a successful actress, besides being a regular guest on BBC TV's pop show *Juke Box Jury*. She was sent to the concert as Britain's 'best-known teenage girl' by the BBC magazine *Radio Times* which wanted to record her comments.

The resulting article, designed to show the effect that the Beatles were having on young people, was published in May 1963, with a photograph of Jane early on, looking mature and pensive, contrasted with a later photo of her feigning hysterics. Her comment on the Beatles was: "Now these I could scream for". Little did she know at the time that she would become the best-known of all Paul McCartney's girl-friends and would inspire some of his greatest love songs. She met up with the group after the show back at the Royal Court Hotel in Chelsea and it wasn't long before she and Paul became locked in conversation. Shortly afterwards they began dating and, before the end of 1963, Paul had moved into a room at the Ashers' Wimpole Street home.

It was a significant change for Paul because, within a year of leaving his council house in Allerton, he was in one of the most expensive areas of London's West End with a family which had important social connections. Jane's father was a medical consultant and her mother a professor at the Guildhall School of Music. They had a study filled with paintings and scattered with scientific journals, where talk could range from pop music and theatre to some new development in psychology. It all helped to broaden Paul's horizons, in turn affecting his songwriting.

'All My Loving' was conceived as a poem by Paul one day as he was shaving. It wasn't until he'd finished his day's work that he put music to it, initially imagining it as a country and western song as he worked on the tune backstage at a British theatre

.......................▶

Paul met Jane Asher, a popular young guest on *Juke Box Jury*, when she was sent to report on an appearance by the Beatles at London's Royal Albert Hall. During their five-year relationship, Jane was to inspire some of Paul's finest love songs, including 'All My Loving'.

while on tour. "It was the first song I ever wrote where I had the words before the music," he said. Like so many Beatle songs now that they were almost permanently on tour, it was about being separated, but whereas John would have been filled with apprehension, Paul is confident that things will work out. John, who was often grudging in his praise for Paul's songs, called it "a damn good piece of work".

LITTLE CHILD   DON'T BOTHER ME

As the lyrics to 'Little Child' are about a 'sad and lonely' boy wanting a girl to take a chance on him, the initial idea probably came from John. Asked about 'Little Child' in 1980, all John would say was that is was another effort to write a song for somebody, "probably Ringo". Paul later remembered that part of the song's melody was inspired by 'Whistle My Love', a 1950s song recorded by the British folk singer Elton Hayes.

The Beatles were now entering a period in which they were being asked to provide songs for other artists. In April 1963, John had gone on holiday to Spain with Brian Epstein who used the opportunity to try to persuade him to write original material for the other acts he managed. The Beatles duly complied, and the result was that they wrote 'I'll Be On My Way' and 'Bad To Me' for Billy J Kramer and the Dakotas, 'Tip Of My Tongue' for Tommy Quickly, 'Love Of The Loved' for Cilla Black, and 'Hello Little Girl' for the Fourmost.

Don't Bother Me' was the first song by George Harrison ever to be recorded by the Beatles and indeed the first lyrical composition that he had ever come up with. He wrote it in August 1963 while staying at the Palace Court Hotel in Bournemouth. The Beatles were playing six nights at the seaside town's Gaumont Cinema, and it was during this week that photographer Robert Freeman came down to take the celebrated album cover photographs.

"I wrote the song as an exercise to see if I could write a song," George said. "I was sick in bed. Maybe that's why it turned out to be 'Don't Bother Me'." Bill Harry, the founder of the Liverpool music paper *Merseybeat*, has suggested the title had another origin. Apparently Harry used to pester George whenever he saw him to find out if he'd written anything since his first instrumental composition 'Cry For A Shadow' which was included on an album by Tony Sheridan in 1962. "When George was about to go out one night, he thought he might bump into me," Harry wrote," so he started writing a number which he called 'Don't Bother Me'."

HOLD ME TIGHT

The Beatles covered two songs which had earlier been recorded by the Shirelles (pictured here) and cited the group as an influence on the writing of 'Hold Me Tight'.

A version of 'Hold Me Tight' was recorded for the Beatles' first album but not used and rather than go back to the old tape they re-cut it for *With The Beatles*. Written by Paul, who considered it a "work song", John's only comment was that he "was never really interested in it either way".

Musically it was influenced by the work of the Shirelles, the New Jersey vocal group who in 1961 had become the first all-girl group to make the Number 1 spot in the American charts. The Beatles were consistent champions of girl groups and girl singers, citing acts such as the Chiffons, Mary Wells, the Ronettes, the Donays and the Crystals as influences on their close harmony vocals. Even before they arrived in London, they were including Shirelles' songs in their act and on their debut album they included two of them – 'Baby It's You' and 'Boys'.

The Shirelles – Shirley Owens, Micki Harris, Doris Coley and Beverly Lee – had seven Top 20 hits in America and three in Britain but 1963 proved to be their last year of chart glory. Ironically, they found themselves pushed aside by the British beat group invasion spearheaded by the Beatles.

Although Ringo didn't have much of a singing voice he sang one number in each show that was within his limited vocal range and this tradition was carried on with the albums, with a doleful Ringo spot slotted in almost as light relief. It was with Ringo in mind that Paul started writing 'I Wanna Be Your Man', a basic four-chord number whose lyric didn't progress much beyond the five words in the title.

Shortly after, in September 1963, Paul spotted Andrew Oldham riding along Jermyn Street with John in a taxi after attending a Variety Club lunch. He asked the driver to stop and collect Oldham, so that they could talk.

The Beatles had known Oldham since they first arrived in London because Brian Epstein had briefly hired him as the group's publicist. In April 1963, Oldham had been tipped off about the Rolling Stones who were playing at the Station Hotel in Richmond. Soon afterwards he became their manager. Oldham was a born hustler who created the Stones' bad boy image by getting the group to look mean when photographed, playing up any signs of anti-social behaviour and suggesting controversial headlines to newspapers and magazines.

Five months after taking the Stones on, Oldham was anxious about finding them good material for singles. Mick Jagger and Keith Richard were not yet writing and their first single, which had sold 100,000 copies, had been a cover of the Chuck Berry song 'Come On'. He shared this concern with the two Beatles who had seen the Stones perform twice in London clubs and Paul immediately mentioned 'I Wanna Be Your Man'. The taxi was rapidly diverted to Studio 51 in Great Newport Street, a club run by jazz man Ken Colyer, where the Stones were rehearsing.

It was here that the song was played to the Rolling Stones and Brian Jones, then their acknowledged leader, said that he liked it and Decca was pressurizing them for a single. John and Paul talked it over for a moment and then John said, "Listen, if you guys really like the main part of the song, we'll finish it for you right now." They went off to a separate room and a few minutes later emerged with the completed song.

It was meant to emulate the feel of the Shirelles' song 'Boys' which Ringo sang in concert. It was the

I WANNA BE YOUR MAN

sound of the song rather than the lyrics that mattered to him. The dragged out 'maaaan' of the chorus was inspired by Benny Spellman's song 'Fortune Teller'.

'I Wanna Be Your Man' went to Number 12 in Britain and helped to turn the Rolling Stones into a major act. The press liked to portray the Beatles and the Stones as the deadliest of enemies but in fact they were always close friends, turning up at each other's sessions and socializing in clubs. John later commented that, as far as the Beatles were concerned 'I Wanna Be Your Man' was a 'throwaway' song, which they were happy to give it away before they had even recorded it themselves (which they did the next day with Ringo as vocalist). "We weren't going to give them anything *great*, right?", John said.

▲ **A Chuck Berry song had provided the Stones with their first single but it was John and Paul's song that propelled them into the Top 20 for the first time.**

NOT A SECOND TIME

P aul has said that the musical inspiration behind 'Not A Second Time' was Smokey Robinson and the Miracles, whereas the main writing honours were claimed by John. It was another example of John allowing his feelings, in this case of being wounded, to wash all over his work. After having been let down and made to cry the writer's response is to shut down his emotions because he can't face the possibility of being hurt all over again.

It was one of the first of the Beatles' songs to be subjected to critical analysis by a quality newspaper. William Mann, then music critic of *The Times* (London), compared part of it to Gustav Mahler's 'Song Of The Earth'. John would later say that this review was responsible for "starting the whole intellectual bit about the Beatles".

"Harmonic interest is typical of their quicker songs too," Mann wrote, "and one gets the impression that they think simultaneously of harmony and melody, so firmly are the major tonic sevenths and ninths built into their tunes, and the flat-submediant key-switches, so natural is the Aeolian cadence at the end of 'Not A Second Time'..." John's comment on this was, "I didn't know what the hell it was all about". Another time he said that he thought Aeolian cadences sounded like exotic birds.

....▶

Although the Beatles were largely regarded as a teenage fad in 1963, serious music critics like William Mann of *The Times* thought their compositions were worthy of closer scrutiny.

I WANT TO HOLD YOUR HAND

▲ **The Beatles stayed at the George V Hotel (above) when they played in Paris in 1964.**

There was a piano in the basement den of the Ashers' home in Wimpole Street where John and Paul would sometimes work. It was here that they came up with 'I Want To Hold Your Hand', the song that was to finally break them in America when it reached the Number 1 spot in January 1964.

It was a remarkable achievement because no British pop artists had ever really cracked America. In 1956 Lonnie Donegan, the 'king of skiffle', had reached the Top 10 with 'Rock Island Line' but only after four months of touring. Cliff Richard had toured, released movies and appeared on the *Ed Sullivan Show* but had only managed a minor hit with 'Living Doll'. The only British records ever to make the Number 1 position in the American charts had been Vera Lynn with 'Auf Wiedersehen' in 1952, Acker Bilk with 'Stranger On The Shore' in 1961 and the Tornadoes with 'Telstar' in 1962. After disappointing sales on the Vee Jay and Swan labels, the Beatles were now with Capitol in America and Brian Epstein had promised that the first single for them would be designed with an 'American sound' in mind.

According to John, 'I Want To Hold Your Hand' sprang into being when, having come up with an opening line, Paul hit a chord on the piano. "I turned to him and said,' That's *it*! Do that again!' In those days, we really used to absolutely write like that — both playing into each other's noses." Gordon Waller, schoolboy friend of Jane Asher's older brother Peter (with whom he had formed the singing duo Peter and Gordon), also remembered being in the house that day. "As far as I can remember John was on a pedal organ and Paul was on a piano," he said. "The basement was the place where we all went to make our 'noise' and they called us down to let us hear this song they'd just written. It wasn't totally complete but the structure and the chorus were there."

The Beatles were, of course, still playing to their market, the teenage girls for whom hand holding and kissing was the ultimate in physical expression. 'I Want To Hold Your Hand' certainly wasn't an indication of their own sexual reticence.

Robert Freeman, the photographer who took the

cover photo for *With The Beatles*, lived in a flat beneath John at 13 Emperor's Gate in Kensington, and tried to educate him in jazz and experimental music while John directed him towards rock'n'roll. "He (John) was intrigued by a contemporary French album of experimental music," Freeman recalled. "There was one track where a musical phrase repeated, as if the record had stuck. This effect was used in 'I Want To Hold Your Hand' – at my suggestion – 'that my love, I can't hide, I can't hide, I can't hide'."

The Beatles heard that 'I Want To Hold Your Hand' had made it to Number 1 in America when they were playing in Paris and it triggered plans for their first Stateside visit. It was because they knew that Cliff Richard had failed to set the charts alight there, despite having toured, that they determined only to make appearances when they could warrant top billing.

Gordon Waller (left) and Peter Asher (right) were around when John and Paul wrote 'I Want To Hold Your Hand' at the Ashers' Wimpole Street home.

To promote their Parisian concerts at the Olympia Theatre, the Beatles were dressed by photographers in 'typical' French outfits.

I CALL YOUR NAME

John, the Quarry Men material...

J ohn reckoned that he wrote 'I Call Your Name' back when "there was no Beatles and no group". As the Quarry Men, his first group, was formed very shortly after the acquisition of his first guitar in March 1957, he must have either written it as he was learning to play or even earlier when he could only play banjo, although Paul can remember working on it in John's bedroom at Menlove Avenue. The Quarry Men was initially a skiffle group made up of friends from Quarry Bank High School for Boys. Rod Davis, who played banjo with them, can't recall John writing songs in those days. "What we did was to listen to the latest singles when they were played on the radio and try to copy the words down," he says. "The trouble was, if you couldn't make them out, or couldn't write quickly enough, you were stuck. So what John used to do was to add his own words to these tunes. No-one ever seemed to notice because they didn't know the words either. There was a song called 'Streamline Train' which John rewrote as 'Long Black Train'. He also put new words to the Del Vikings' hit 'Come Go With Me' and I didn't realize what he'd done until I heard the original version many years later."

If the song was written as long ago as John thought, it's interesting that even in his schooldays he was writing about despair. The lines 'I never weep at night, I call your name' are close to his 1971 lines 'In the middle of the night, I call your name' in 'Oh Yoko' on the *Imagine* album.

John added the Jamaican blue beat instrumental break in 1964. Blue beat and ska, brought to Britain by immigrants from the West Indies, were becoming popular with British mods and the Blue Beat label, founded by Ziggy Jackson in 1961, had released 213 singles in the previous three years. Two weeks after the recording of 'I Call Your Name', the *New Musical Express* asked whether ska and blue beat were going to be the major new talking point in pop music. With the Beatles around, there was no chance of that.

THIS BOY

John, pictured above taking photographs of his fellow Beatles, began a creative surge in 1964 which didn't really end until drugs and lethargy set in during 1967.

T his Boy' was written by John and Paul in a hotel bedroom as an exercise in three-part harmony, which they had never attempted before, inspired, as so much else was at the time, by Smokey Robinson and the Miracles. "The middle eight", said George, "was John trying to do Smokey."

The lyrics, John said, amounted to nothing. All that was important was "sound and harmony". Harmony was integral to the early Beatles' work, and the influence of the Everly Brothers in particular is evident in this song. They'd become familiar with three-part harmonizing by singing Phil Spector's 'To Know Him Is To Love Him', a 1959 hit for the Teddy Bears.

Saying that the lyrics amounted to nothing, was not the same as saying that they were without meaning, for again John was portraying himself here as a loser waiting for his loved one to return.

A HARD DAY'S NIGHT

A *Hard Day's Night* marked a breakthrough as it was the first of their albums where every track was a Beatles' original. Personally, it was also a tour de force for John, who was the major contributor to 10 of the album's 13 tracks. Being the oldest in the group and the founder member of the Quarry Men, John was the unacknowledged leader in those days. Although Paul was more musically accomplished – he had mastered guitar and piano ahead of John – they still maintained the same junior to senior pupil relationship that started when they met in 1957.

John later recognized that this was the period of his greatest dominance in the Beatles and it was only when, in his own words, that he became "self-conscious and inhibited" that Paul began to take over. The majority of the group's singles up to this point, John claimed , had either been written by him, or featured him as lead vocalist. The only reason Paul sang on the track 'A Hard Day's Night' was because John couldn't reach the high notes.

Seven of the songs were written for the film *A Hard Day's Night* although one of these, 'I'll Cry Instead', was eventually dropped in favour of 'Can't Buy Me Love', a single which Paul had written under pressure. The Beatles were still writing pop songs to order but putting more of themselves into the lyrics. For example, 'If I Fell' was one of the most revealing songs about John's troubled psyche. Equally, 'And I Love Her' was one of Paul's most personal songs yet

A HARD DAY'S NIGHT

— a declaration of his love for Jane Asher. At the time, few people knew how or why the songs had been written. It wouldn't be until the Beatles broke up that the authorship of individual songs would be known and details, such as the marriage breakdown between John and Cynthia, would be revealed.

At first, the film of A Hard Day's Night was conceived purely to sell a soundtrack album but, as with everything the Beatles touched in 1964, the film turned into a great commercial success, recouping its production costs almost 30 times over. The idea was to re-create the delirium of Beatlemania, charting the group's astonishing rise to fame in the style of a black and white television documentary. Little more than a vehicle for their musical talent, the Beatles were provided with undemanding acting roles and a strong supporting cast of character actors to cover any weaknesses.

"I was with the Beatles in Paris when they played there in January 1964," says screenwriter Alun Owen. "I was also around them in an unofficial capacity on a lot of other occasions. The biggest nonsense that has been written about the film is that it was ad-libbed. It wasn't. They were at the time 22 or 23 years old. They had never acted before. If you go through the script, you'll see that no sentence is longer than six words, because they couldn't have handled any more. The only ad-libs were made by John."

The Beatles were pleased with the final result. Although they knew it only showed one side of their personalities and wasn't as realistic as it could have been, they recognized that A Hard Day's Night avoided the clichés of most pop movies.

The album was released in Britain in July 1964 and a month earlier in America, making the Number 1 spot in both countries. The American version was substantially different, featuring only the seven soundtrack songs and 'I'll Cry Instead'. It was made up to a 12-track album by including several of George Martin's orchestral versions of Lennon and McCartney's songs.

In the early Sixties, it was customary for pop stars to make a movie after a decent string of hits, just as Elvis Presley had done in the Fifties. The Young Ones (1961) and Summer Holiday (1962) were big box office hits in the UK for Cliff Richard, and even lesser British names such as Adam Faith, Tommy Steele, Billy Fury and Terry Dene had all made it on to the silver screen.

The Beatles wanted to do something from a different angle and were fortunate in being introduced to director Dick Lester, whose fast cuts and imaginative camerawork captured the excitement and freshness of pop. Negotiations over the film had begun in October 1963 and, in November, Liverpool-born writer Alun Owen, who had an ear for the Beatles' natural speech patterns, accompanied the group to Dublin and Belfast to observe them at work and catch the flavour of Beatlemania.

Without having seen the script, the Beatles had to write seven songs for the film. Two of these were written in Paris during January 1964, four were written the next month in Miami during one two hour burst and the title track was written in London. "All of the songs, except for 'A Hard Day's Night', were written independently of what I was writing," says Alun Owen. "Paul and John wrote them and they were woven into the script as things came up. None of them bear any relation to the story. They were just numbers."

The Beatles didn't have a title for the film, having already rejected 'On The Move', 'Let's Go' and 'Beatlemania'. 'A Hard Day's Night' was the last song written and it eventually became the title to both the album and the film. The phrase was attributed to Ringo Starr who said in 1964: "I came up with the phrase 'a hard day's night'. It just came out. We went to do a job and we worked all day and then we happened to work all night. I came out, still thinking it was day and said, 'It's been a hard day...looked around, saw that it was dark and added...'s night.'"

If Ringo did invent the phrase he must have done so in 1963, and not on the set of the film as has been reported, because John included it in his book *In His Own Write* which was written that year. Whichever way it came about, Dick Lester liked it as a title because it summed up the frenetic pace of the film as well as the humour of the Beatles and, as he was driving him home one night, he told John that he planned to use it. The next morning John brought in a song to go with it.

Evening Standard journalist Maureen Cleave, who had been one of the first London journalists to write about the Beatles, can recall John coming into the studio on April 16, 1964, with the lyrics written on the back of a card to his son Julian, who had just had his first birthday. Initially the song ran: 'But when I get home to you, I find my tiredness is through, And I feel alright'. Cleave told him that she thought 'my tiredness is through' was a weak line. John took out a pen, crossed through the line, and wrote; 'I find the things that you do, They make me feel alright'. Maureen has said that "The song seemed to materialize as if by magic. It consisted of John humming to the others, then they would all put their heads

together and hum and three hours later they had this record."

Although Paul hadn't written the lyric, when promoting the film in America, he was asked to explain how it was put together. "It seemed a bit ridiculous writing a song called 'A Hard Day's Night'," he said, "because it sounded a funny phrase at the time but the idea came of saying that it had been a hard day's night and we'd been working all day and you get back to a girl and everything's fine. So it was turned into one of those songs."

'A Hard Day's Night' was featured over the opening and closing credits of the film. It was the first cut on the soundtrack album and became a Number 1 single in Britain and America. The comic actor Peter Sellers, once a member of John's favourite radio comedy group the Goons, recorded 'A Hard Day's Night' by speaking the lyric as if he was Laurence Olivier delivering a Shakespearean monologue. It made the British Top 20 in December 1965.

A copy of the novelized version of *A Hard Day's Night* autographed by the Beatles and Brian Epstein, as well as by actors Wilfred Brambell and Victor Spinetti.

A Hard Day's Night was based on the group's frenetic lifestyle at the height of Beatlemania.

I SHOULD HAVE KNOWN BETTER

The songs in *A Hard Day's Night* were written before the Beatles saw the script – and then dropped in wherever needed by director Dick Lester. ▼

Released as the flip side of 'A Hard Day's Night' in America, 'I Should Have Known Better' was the first song in the film and was performed in a sequence where the Beatles and Paul's 'grandfather' (played by Wilfred Brambell) are on a train and banished to the mail van. They start playing cards and, several cuts later, appear with guitars, harmonica and drums. "It just seemed the natural place to have the first number," says Alun Owen.

Although much of the filming took place on trains travelling between London and the West Country, 'I Should Have Known Better' was actually filmed on a set at Twickenham Film Studios.

Surprisingly for a song by John it is very optimistic: he loves her, she loves him and everything is fine.

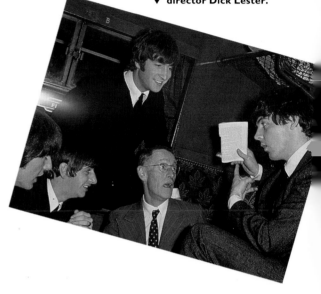

John and wife Cynthia on a flight between London and New York in February 1964. ▼

IF I FELL

The logistics of fitting it into an already-written script and the decision not to give any of the Beatles a love interest in the film, meant that John had to sing this love song to Ringo. "We're in the television studio and Ringo is supposed to be sulking a bit," Paul explained in 1964. "John starts joking with him and then sings the song as though we're singing it to him. We got fits of the giggles just doing it."

'If I Fell' is one of John's most beautiful songs and one of his most revealing. It's about an illicit relationship. He is asking the woman in question for an assurance that if he leaves his wife for her that she'll love him more than he's ever been loved before. It is the story of someone eager to avoid confrontation. He knows that if he walks out of his marriage he will cause pain and so he only wants to do it if he gets a guarantee of commitment from his lover.

John said that the song was 'semi-autobiographical'

and it is known that he was unfaithful to his wife Cynthia although, at the time, she was oblivious to what was going on. "Of course I'm a coward," he said in 1968 when discussing his first marriage. "I wasn't going to go off and leave Cynthia and be by myself."

John saw this as his first proper ballad and a precursor to 'In My Life', his song about growing up, which was to use the same chord sequence.

Paul's love of rock'n'roll was never a way of heaping scorn on the popular music that had preceded it. He loved the big band music of the Twenties and Thirties which his father played, the Victorian music hall songs which his relatives would sing around the piano and the show tunes of the Forties and Fifties.

Even in the days of Hamburg and the Cavern Club in Liverpool, Paul had sung 'Till There Was You', a song from the 1957 Broadway musical *The Music Man,* later popularized by Peggy Lee, and this was included on *With The Beatles*. From these early performances Paul must have realized that ballads enriched the Beatles' show, and wrote 'And I Love Her' as a first attempt to fill this space. John said it was Paul's first 'Yesterday'.

The initial idea was to write a song with a title that began mid-sentence. Paul said it was, "the first song I ever impressed myself with." It didn't escape his notice that almost a decade later Perry Como recorded a song titled 'And I Love You So'.

Recording on the song began in February 1964 and it was the first Beatle track to feature just acoustic instruments (Ringo played bongos). In the film *A Hard*

I'M HAPPY JUST TO DANCE WITH YOU

John and Paul wrote 'I'm Happy Just To Dance With You' for George to sing in the film "to give him a piece of the action" and it was filmed on stage at the Scala Theatre in Charlotte Street, London. As the youngest Beatle, George was living in the shadow of Paul and John. When he started writing his own songs, he became resentful that more weren't considered for the albums.

John was equally hurt in 1980 when George published his biography *I Me Mine* and made no mention of his influence on his songwriting. Paul has admitted that 'I'm Happy…' was a 'formula song'.

AND I LOVE HER

Day's Night, they are shown recording it for a television show.

Only the month before recording, Jane Asher commented to American writer Michael Braun: "The trouble (with Paul) is that he wants the fans' adulation and mine too. He's so selfish. That's his biggest fault. He can't see that my feelings for him are real and that the fans' (feelings for him) are fantasy." Paul has since said that it wasn't written with anyone in mind but it's hard to believe that in his first flush of love with Jane Asher he was writing such tender songs to an imaginary girl.

Jane Asher was the perfect Beatle girlfriend – attractive, discreet and professionally accomplished. She inspired jealousy amongst the fans as well as some of the best love songs of the Beatles.

TELL ME WHY

T ell Me Why' was written to provide an 'upbeat' number for the concert sequence in *A Hard Day's Night*. John thought of something the Chiffons or the Shirelles might do and "knocked it off".

It's a typical John scenario. He has been lied to and deserted. He's crying. He appeals to his girl to let him know what he's done wrong so that he can put it right. Children whose parents either leave them or die suddenly are often left with a feeling that they must in some way be responsible. 'If there's something I have said or done, Tell me what and I'll apologize', John sang.

It was only when he underwent primal therapy in 1970 that he came to terms with these subconscious fears. Therapist Arthur Janov set him the exercise of looking back through all his Beatles' songs to see what they revealed of his anxieties. On his first post-therapy album, *John Lennon/Plastic Ono Band*, he was able to sing about these traumas in their original context in songs such as 'Mother', 'Hold On', 'Isolation' and 'My Mummy's Dead'.

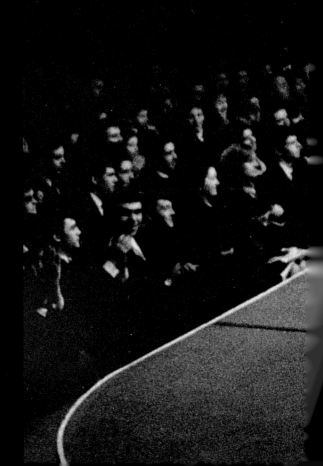

Every night for three weeks the Beatles played in Paris. During the day they were busy writing songs for *A Hard Day's Night*, recording their follow-up to 'I Want To Hold Your Hand' and planning their US debut.

...........................▶

CAN'T BUY ME LOVE

In January 1964, the Beatles went to Paris for 18 days of concerts at the Olympia Theatre. They stayed at the five star George V hotel, just off the Champs Élysées, and an upright piano was moved into one of their suites so that songwriting could continue. It was here that John and Paul wrote 'One And One Is Two' for fellow Liverpool group The Strangers and Paul came up with 'Can't Buy Me Love'.

With a new single due in March, and the news that 'I Want To Hold Your Hand' had rocketed to the top of the American charts, there was no time to waste. George Martin, who had come to the Pathé Marconi Studios in Paris to record the newly-written song, made the suggestion of starting it with the chorus. Although 'She Loves You', 'I Wanna Be Your Man', 'Don't Bother Me' and 'All My Loving' were all used in *A Hard Day's Night*, 'Can't Buy Me Love' was the only previously-released song to be included on the soundtrack album. This was because it was pulled into the film at a late stage to replace 'I'll Cry Instead', which director Dick Lester didn't think was right for the scene in question.

'Can't Buy Me Love' was used in the film as the group ran down a fire escape at the back of the

theatre (actually the Odeon in Hammersmith, London) and fooled around on some open ground (partly playing fields in Isleworth). It was the group's first experience of freedom in the film after having been locked for days in cars, trains, dressing rooms and hotels. Screenwriter Alun Owen remembers: "My stage direction at this point was very simple. It read: 'The boys come down the fire escape. It is the first time they have been free. They run about and play silly buggers'."

American journalists asked Paul in 1966 whether 'Can't Buy Me Love' was a song about prostitution. He replied that all the songs were open to interpretation but that suggestion was going too far.

John and George sorting through fan mail at the George V hotel in Paris.

◄ ·······················

The Beatles worked hard to promote their concerts in Paris – even when it involved wearing silly hats and posing as Frenchmen.

◄ ·······················

ANY TIME AT ALL

Having written the songs which would be used in the film, the race was on to come up with a number for what would be the second side of the soundtrack album.

John was obviously the more prolific songwriter at the time, having written five of the seven songs in the film and going on to write all but one of the tracks on the other side. This had not been achieved without some difficulty. 'Any Time At All', he later admitted, was a rewriting of his earlier song 'It Won't Be Long', using the same chord progression from C to A minor

and back and, when it came to recording, employing the same bawling vocal style.

In January 1964 he spoke about some of the changes in his songwriting techniques. "If I found a new chord (I used to) write a song around it," he said. "I thought that if there were a million chords I'd never run out. Sometimes the chords got to be an obsession and we started to put unnecessary ones in. We then decided to keep the songs simple and it's the best way. It might have sounded okay for us but the extra chords wouldn't make other people like them any better. That's the way we've kept it all along."

There were only three other occasions when he claimed Beatles' songs had been recycled. 'Yes It Is' he said was a rewrite of 'This Boy', 'Paperback Writer' was "Son of Day Tripper" and 'Get Back' was a "pot-boiler rewrite" of 'Lady Madonna'.

A Hard Day's Night was the only Beatles' album to be written entirely by John and Paul, seen here in New York during February 1964.

I'LL CRY INSTEAD

'Il Cry Instead' was originally the song which was going to be used over the fire escape sequence in A Hard Day's Night but which was then dropped in favour of the already-released 'Can't Buy Me Love'. However, when the film was re-mastered for video release in 1986, the song was put back in by running it over a collage sequence preceding the opening credits.

John had written about crying in many of his songs to date but 'I'll Cry Instead' marked a difference as he said that he'd cry now rather than get his own back, but once he'd finished crying he would return to seek

vengeance. He imagined coming back and breaking girls' hearts around the world, as if by causing people to fall for him and then spurning them, he would be able to punish everyone who had ever rejected him. He would later admit having been violent at times and in 'Getting Better' he was able to write about his cruelty to women as something he had overcome.

This was also the first song in which John admitted having a chip on his shoulder, an indication that he was entering a period of intense self-examination, that was to continue until his first solo albums, after the break-up of the Beatles.

THINGS WE SAID TODAY

In May 1964, having completed the filming of *A Hard Day's Night* and after fulfilling some performing commitments in England and Scotland, the Beatles and their partners took off for a holiday break. John and George made a round-the-world trip with stop-offs in Holland, Polynesia, Hawaii and Canada, while Paul and Ringo went to France and Portugal before taking off for the Virgin Islands.

While in the Carribean, Paul hired a yacht called *Happy Days* and it was while on board with Ringo, Maureen and Jane that he wrote 'Things We Said Today' on his acoustic guitar.

The song was a reflection of his relationship with Jane in light of the fact that he knew, by the nature of their work, that times together would be few. When they were separated, he said, he would take comfort from the memory of the things they'd said that day.

Paul and Jane pictured returning from their holiday together in the Virgin Islands. Beside Jane is Beatle press officer Derek Taylor and, over his left shoulder, Ringo Starr.

WHEN I GET HOME

When I Get Home' was described by John as a "four-in-the-bar cowbell song", influenced by his love of Motown and American soul music. Around the time it was recorded, he was asked what song he wished he had written and he said his first choice would be Marvin Gaye's 'Can I Get A Witness'. "Then there's other stuff on Tamla Motown that we like," he went on. "It's harder to write good 12-bar numbers because so much has been done before with them. I'd rather write a song with chords all over the place."

An unusually optimistic song for John, the lyric revealed his thoughts about what he was going to say and do to his 'girl', when he got home. Slightly close in subject matter to the single 'A Hard Day's Night' ('when I get home to you...') it shows that he still thought of home as the place where true love would be waiting. Despite his image as the 'lad' in the group, John was really a 'homebody' who liked nothing more than to curl up in front of a television with a supply of books and magazines. It's fitting that he spent much of his final decade as a 'house husband', happy to be confined to his rooms in the Dakota Buildings in New York.

George and Paul being directed by Dick Lester during the shooting of *A Hard Days's Night*, April 1964.

YOU CAN'T DO THAT

In both Britain and America 'You Can't Do That' became the B side of 'Can't Buy Me Love'. In this song, instead of weeping, John tries threatening. He tells his girl that if he catches her talking to another boy he's going to leave her immediately. He knows what it feels like to be spurned and he's determined that it won't happen again.

The musical influence, John later said, was Wilson Pickett, the former gospel singer from Alabama who at the time had only released three singles under his own name in America, only one of which had been a minor hit. However it wasn't until 1965, his contract then having been acquired by Atlantic Records, that Pickett became known as one of the great soul singers of the Sixties with hits such as 'Mustang Sally', '634-5789' and 'In The Midnight Hour'. It was at the suggestion of guitarist Duane Allman that Pickett recorded 'Hey Jude' in 1969 and managed to have a hit with it at the same time that the Beatles' version was in the charts.

On the recording of 'You Can't Do That', John played lead on his newly-acquired Rickenbacker while George played 12-string guitar for the first time on a Beatles' record. "I find it a drag to play rhythm guitar all the time," John told *Melody Maker*. "I like to work out something interesting to play. The best example is what I did on 'You Can't Do That'. There wasn't really a lead guitarist and a rhythm guitarist on that because...rhythm guitar is too thin for records."

▲ **Soul singer Wilson Pickett, who John later credited as the inspiration behind 'You Can't Do That'. Pickett went on to have a hit with the Beatles' song 'Hey Jude' in 1969.**

I'LL BE BACK

John found the chords for 'I'll Be Back' while playing a Del Shannon song. This was probably 'Runaway' which the Beatles had played in their early shows and which also starts in a minor chord and has a descending bass line.

Shannon had hits in 1961 and 1962 with 'Runaway', 'Hats Off To Larry', 'So Long Baby' and 'Hey Little Girl'. In 1963, after a hit with 'Little Town Flirt', he played London's Royal Albert Hall (April 18)

with the Beatles and suggested to them that he could help expose their work in America by covering one of their songs as a single.

The Beatles agreed and Shannon went back home and recorded a version of 'From Me To You' which, although it only reached Number 77, was the first Lennon and McCartney composition to feature in the American charts.

Del Shannon had hits in Britain just before the Beatles took off in a big way, and was the first person to take one of their songs into the US charts. John returned the compliment by reworking the chords of a Shannon hit into 'I'll Be Back'.

BEATLES
FOR
SALE

▲ The Beatles' fourth
album was put together
either side of their first
American tour in the
summer of 1964.

The *Beatles For Sale* sleeve revealed the flip side of Beatlemania – the exhaustion, dejection and loneliness of life at the top. John, Paul, George and Ringo look frazzled and world-weary in Robert Freeman's cover photographs and, with the sparkle temporarily missing from their songwriting, the group were only able to come up with eight of the 14 tracks themselves. Cover songs from their early rock'n'roll heroes made up the rest of the album.

The songs they did manage to write showed all the signs of being written under pressure. Although 'Eight Days a Week' was a love song, the title actually came from a comment Ringo had made about the superhuman demands of being a Beatle. John's songs were bleaker than anything he'd written before, with 'I'm A Loser' a foretaste of his confessional style of songwriting. For 'I'll Follow The Sun', Paul had gone searching back through his old school notebooks to find a song he'd last played in the Cavern days.

The album's most significant new influence was Bob Dylan, who Paul and John both heard and met for the first time during 1964. In the early days, the Beatles had concentrated mainly on mastering the musical side of the songs – chord construction, arrangement and delivery. Dylan was the first recording artist to affect them primarily as lyricists. Initially, Paul was the big Dylan fan, but John soon caught up with him. They were drawn to Dylan because his words were just as important as his tunes.

In writing what he felt rather than following any conventions, Dylan's intensely personal style of expression contrasted starkly with the anodyne pop lyrics of the day. His words were always made-to-measure rather than bought off the peg.

The shift towards a narrative style that Dylan initiated particularly excited John, because he had been writing poems and short stories for years, mostly for the amusement of friends. Some of these were published in a book *In His Own Write* in 1964, when he was hailed as 'the literary Beatle' and comparisons were made with Lewis Carroll, Edward Lear and the James Joyce of *Finnegan's Wake*. Dylan, and later the British journalist Kenneth Allsop, impressed upon him the fact that there need not be that great a gap between his 'literary' outpourings and lyric writing. John interpreted this to mean that, "Instead of projecting myself into a situation, I would try to express what I felt about myself (as I had done) in my book."

Beatles For Sale took two and a half months to record and was released in December 1964, reaching Number 1 in Britain. The American equivalent, *Beatles '65*, also hit the top spot and sold a million copies in the first week.

The Beatles' first US album Meet The Beatles! went to the top of the Billboard charts in February 1964, as did the single 'I Want To Hold Your Hand'. While in New York, the group was presented with gold discs for both these recordings.

...................................►

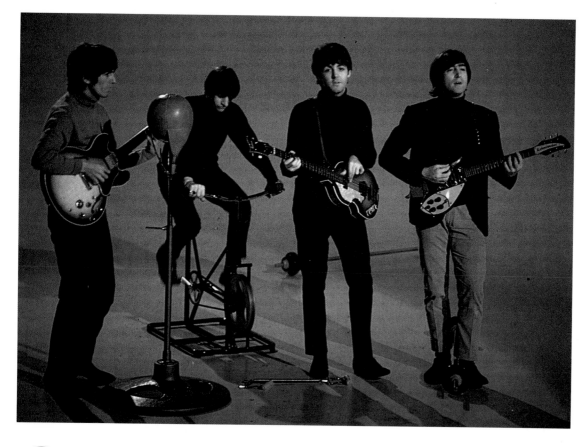

◄ In November 1965, the Beatles performed for their first video promotional clips at Twickenham Film Studios, a move which anticipated the pop video revolution by over a decade. Although it had been released a year earlier, their hit single 'I Feel Fine' was one of the five songs filmed.

I FEEL FINE

The Beatles completed the album *A Hard Day's Night* in June 1964 and by mid-August were back in the studio to start work on *Beatles For Sale*. On August 19, they left Britain to tour America and returned a month later to pick up where they had left off. *A Hard Day's Night* had been the first album to consist solely of Lennon and McCartney songs but, with so little time between projects, they found it impossible to come up with all their own songs for *Beatles For Sale*.

On October 6, while recording 'Eight Days A Week', John was working out the guitar riff that would become the basis of 'I Feel Fine', a song they recorded only 12 days later. "I actually wrote 'I Feel Fine' around the riff which is going on in the background," John said in December 1964. "I tried to get that effect into every song on the LP, but the others wouldn't have it.

"I told them that I'd write a song specially for this riff so they said, 'Yes. You go away and do that,' knowing that we'd almost finished the album. Anyway, going into the studio one morning I said to Ringo, 'I've written this song but it's lousy', but we tried it, complete with riff, and it sounded like an A side, so we decided to release it just like that."

Apart from the riff, the distinctive feature of 'I Feel Fine' is the sound of feedback which slides into the opening chords. It was one of those discoveries made in the studio. John's guitar was leaning against an amplifier after a take and set up an electronic whine. This marked a subtle shift in their approach to recording. Having mastered the studio basics, they started encouraging George Martin to take them further, finding fresh sources of inspiration in noises previously eliminated as mistakes (electronic goofs, twisted tapes, talkback). Feedback was to become a familiar part of recording – used by artists such as Jimi Hendrix and the Who – but John remained proud of the fact that the Beatles were the first group to actually put it on vinyl.

'I Feel Fine', John's most optimistic song to date, became a Number 1 single in Britain and America.

SHE'S A WOMAN

She's A Woman' was conceived by Paul on the streets of St John's Wood on October 8, 1964 and was finished that day in the sudio, Paul perfoming it in the high-pitched scream which he used to emulate little Richard. It was a conscious effort to bring a more bluesy sound to the Beatles. Some lines and a middle eight were added by John. "We needed a real screaming rocker for the live act," said Paul. "It was always good if you were stuck for something to close with or if there was a dull moment."

The song praised Paul's woman for being selflessly devoted to him. It was perhaps a little unfortunate that in order to find a rhyme for 'presents' he also had to commend her for being 'no peasant'!

'She's A Woman' was also the first Beatle's song to contain a veiled drug reference. John later confessed that they were quite proud to have inserted the line 'turns me on when I get lonely' and for it to have escaped the attention of the censors.

When they used the phrase 'turn you on' three years later (in 'A Day In The Life'), it led to a radio ban: by then, the authorities had become aware of the growing drug culture and its terminology.

Significantly, it was just five weeks before recording 'She's A Woman' that the Beatles had smoked marijuana for the first time. Until then, their only experience of drugs had been Drinamyl and Preludin tablets and the contents of Benzedrine inhalers. They were introduced to marijuana in the company of Bob Dylan, who met them for the first time in their suite at the Delmonico Hotel in New York City. The Beatles were happy to drink cheap wine into the small hours, but Dylan wanted to smoke a joint and assumed that they were all dope smokers because he mistakenly thought they had sung 'I get high', instead of 'I can't hide' in 'I Want To Hold Your Hand'.

The Beatles were apprehensive about joining in at first, but before long the lights were lowered, candles and incense were lit and towels were stuffed along the bottoms of the doors. For the next few hours, the musicians were "legless with laughing" as George Harrison put it later. Paul thought that he'd suddenly been blessed with amazing insights and asked road manager Mal Evans to take notes.

'She's A Woman' was released as the B side of 'I Feel Fine' in Britain and America. "At first, it wasn't so well received," said Paul in 1965. "A lot of people thought that I was just singing too high and that I'd picked the wrong key. It sounded as though I was screeching, but it was on purpose. It wasn't a mistake."

In the Delmonico Hotel, New York, with Peter Yarrow, Paul Stookey and Mary Travers (of Peter, Paul and Mary).

Ringoisms – such as 'we've been working eight days a week' and 'it's been a hard day's night' – were an inspiration to Paul and John.

EIGHT DAYS A WEEK

John always claimed that 'Eight Days A Week' was written by Paul as a potential title track for the Beatles' follow-up film to *A Hard Day's Night*.

Director Dick Lester denied this, pointing out that 'Eight Days A Week' was recorded in October 1964, whereas filming on *Help!* didn't begin until late February 1965. It's unlikely that they were considering film music this far in advance. "The film was always supposed to be called *Help* but there was a copyright problem in that someone else had registered this title," says Lester. "So we originally called it *Beatles II* and then *Eight Arms To Hold You*, but thinking of writing a song called 'Eight Arms to Hold You' had everyone throwing their hands in the air and saying that it was impossible. It was because of this that

we thought, sod it, we'll take the chance, because the laws of registration were so vague. We decided to stick in an exclamation mark because the one that was registered didn't have one."

Paul first heard 'eight days a week' from a substitute chauffeur who drove him to John's home in Weybridge one day for a writing session. Asked by Paul if he had been busy lately the chauffeur replied, "Busy? I've been working eight days a week." When they arrvied Paul went straight in and told John that he had the title for the song they were going to write.

'Eight Days A Week', the first track to be recorded with a faded intro rather than a faded outro, was under consideration as a UK single until John came up with 'I Feel Fine'. In America, it was released as the follow-up to 'I Feel Fine' and made the Number 1 spot.

I'M A LOSER

▲ **The Beatles first became aware of Bob Dylan's music in January 1964, and met him in August that year.**

Two events during 1964 were to have a profound effect on John's writing. The first was hearing Bob Dylan's music in Paris during January, when Paul acquired *The Freewheelin' Bob Dylan* from an interviewer at a local radio station.

Paul had heard Dylan's music before through his student friends in Liverpool but it was the first time John had heard it. After hearing *Freewheelin'*, which was Dylan's second album, they went out and bought his debut album *Bob Dylan* and, according to John, "for the rest of our three weeks we didn't stop playing them. We all went potty on Dylan."

The second event to affect John in a big way was meeting journalist Kenneth Allsop, a writer for the *Daily Mail* and a regular interviewer on *Tonight*, BBC Television's news magazine programme. John first met him on March 23, when he was interviewed for four minutes on *Tonight* about his book *In His Own Write*, and then again at a Foyles Literary Luncheon at the Dorchester Hotel in London's Park Lane. Allsop, a handsome craggy Yorkshireman, was 44 years old at the time and about to become one of the best-known faces on British television. He had been in journalism since 1938, with a brief interruption caused by the war, during which he served in the Royal Air Force.

It was in the 'green room', the hospitality suite, at the BBC's Lime Grove Studios on March 23 that Allsop first spoke to John about his songwriting, encouraging him not to hide his true feelings behind the usual banalities of the pop song. It was obvious to Allsop from reading *In His Own Write* that John had much more to give if he was prepared to open up to his deeper feelings.

Years later, John told his confidant Elliot Mintz that this meeting marked a significant turning point in his

NO REPLY

songwriting. "He told me that he was very nervous that day and, because of this, became very talkative and engaged Allsop in conversation," says Mintz. "Allsop had in essence said to him that he wasn't terrible enamoured with Beatles' songs because they all tended to be 'she loves him', 'he loves her', 'they love her' and 'I love her'. He suggested to John that he try to write something more autobiographical, based on personal experience rather than these abstract images. That struck a chord with him."

Although recorded five months later, 'I'm A Loser' was the first fruit of this meeting with Allsop. It would be wrong to say it was a complete change of direction, because from the beginning John had written songs in which he exposed himself as lonely, sad and abandoned, but in 'I'm A Loser' he let a little more of his true self show. On the surface, it's another song about having lost a girl but the lines, which announce that beneath his mask he is 'wearing a frown', suggest that he considers himself a loser in more ways than one. He's not just a loser in love; he feels that he's a loser in life.

All this would be idle speculation if it wasn't for the fact that 'I'm A Loser' can now be seen as an early stage in John's tortuous journey towards candid self-revelation in his songwriting. At the time, he was quick to credit the effect Bob Dylan had on 'I'm A Loser'. "Anyone who is one of the best in his field – as Dylan is – is bound to influence people," he said at the time. "I wouldn't be surprised if we influenced him in some way."

Kenneth Allsop went on to present the television news programme *24 Hours* and then, in May 1973, he was found dead at his home. The cause of his death was an overdose of painkillers but the lack of a suicide note meant that the inquest was left to record an open verdict.

Hard Travellin', Allsop's account of the life of the American hobo which was first published in 1967, has become a classic of its kind and is still in print.

'N'o Reply' was a typical John song of betrayal and jealousy; another story of a girl taking off with another guy. It was based, he once said, not on his own experience but on 'Silhouettes', a big hit in 1957 for the Rays on Philadelphia's independent Cameo label. Written by Bob Crewe and Frank Slaye, who went on to write hits for Freddy Cannon, 'Silhouettes' put a new twist on the old love cheat story: the boy discovers he is being two-timed when he notices the silhouettes on the curtains of his lover's house.

In John's version, the boy becomes suspicious when his girl doesn't answer the door and, when he calls her on the phone, her parents tell him she's not at home. As in 'Silhouettes', he returns to her house and, watching from the shadows, sees her go in 'with another man'.

Ever since 'Please Please Me', the Beatles' compositions had been published by Northern Songs, a company set up by John, Paul, Brian Epstein and music publisher Dick James, who was a friend of George Martin. James had experience both as singer and songwriter before getting into publishing and, when he heard 'No Reply', he said to John: "That's the first complete song you've written, the first song which resolves itself. It's a complete story."

▲ **Music publisher Dick James took a great interest in the development of John and Paul as songwriters.**

I DON'T WANT TO SPOIL THE PARTY

The Beatles briefly visited America in February 1964, playing in Washington DC and New York City to promote 'I Want To Hold Your Hand'. It wasn't until August 1964 that they arrived for their first full-fledged tour, a month-long trek that would take them to 20 US cities plus three in Canada. Playing 12 songs per show, they were supported by four American acts – the Bill Black Combo, the Exciters, Jackie DeShannon and the Righteous Brothers.

Both John and Paul had to write in their hotel rooms and while flying between dates. 'I Don't Want To Spoil The Party' was one song John wrote during the tour and it was the second song the Beatles recorded on their arrival back in London. Originally intended as a country and western style track that Ringo could sing, it's a song about being stood up by a date as well as another glimpse at the frown beneath the mask. The crisis John describes is not so much the loss of the girl, which he can cope with after a few drinks, but his inability to pretend he's happy. He knows that if he lets his true feelings show, he will only prevent others from having a good time.

John said that 'I Don't Want To Spoil The Party' was a deeply-personal song and it's likely that it was inspired by his growing horror at having to be a happy, whacky Beatle in the company of record company executives, politicians and city dignitaries. The frequent photographs taken on this trip invariably showed John either forcing a smile or looking as though his mind was elsewhere.

John was not at his happiest when required to be a grinning mop top (inset). There were times on tour when he wanted to retreat, but there were few opportunities to be alone (main picture).

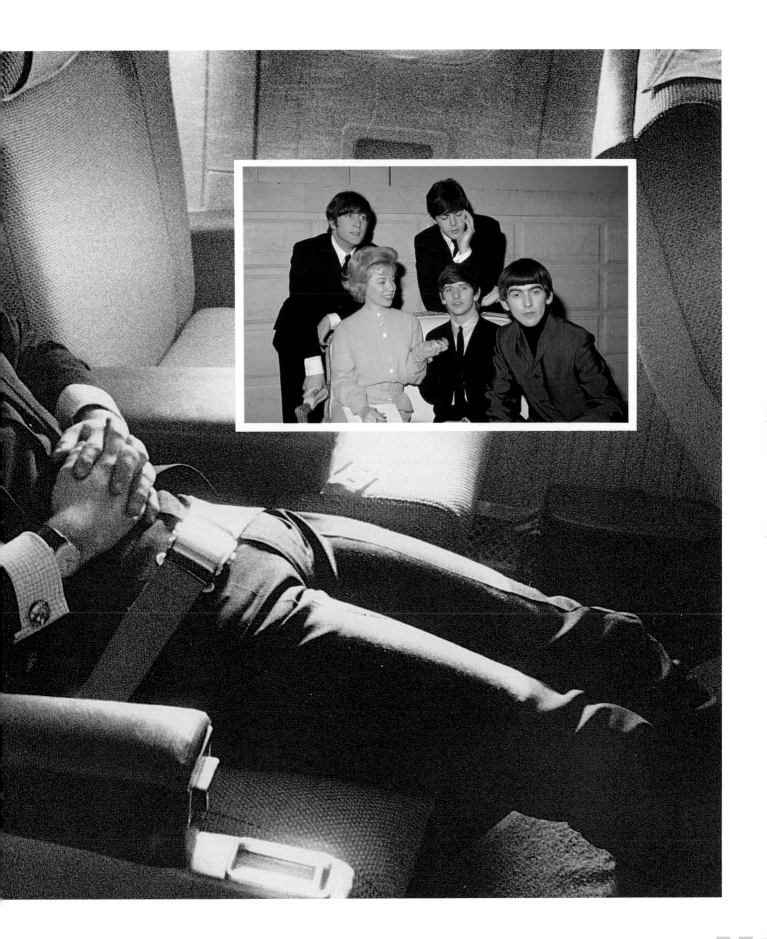

I'LL FOLLOW THE SUN

As has already been explained, the contrast between John and Paul's outlook on life and love could hardly have been greater. Whereas John usually saw himself as a victim, Paul felt himself to be in charge of life. In 'If I Fell', John demanded a guarantee that love would last. In 'I'll Follow The Sun', Paul accepts that no such promise is possible. He knows that stormy weather may hit his relationship and so he makes plans to follow the sun. A selfish song in a way because it doesn't consider how the abandoned girl might find her own sunshine, it was nonetheless an accurate reflection of Paul's romantic life in the early days.

Polished up for use when the pressure was on for the Beatles to come up with their own material, the song was originally written in 1959. There was a great wave of interest in Buddy Holly, following his death in February that year, which gave him four hit singles in Britain before the year was out. In 'I'll Follow The Sun', it's easy to detect the effect that he had on the young Paul McCartney. Holly was a decisive influence on the Beatles because, unlike Elvis, he wrote all his own songs and had a permanent, identifiable backing group. John (who was short-sighted) was encouraged that a bespectacled singer could become a rock'n'roll star and the initial naming of the group 'Beetles' was inspired by Buddy's Crickets.

Beatles For Sale eventually included a Chuck Berry track ('Rock And Roll Music'), a Leiber and Stoller ('Kansas City'), a Little Richard ('Hey, Hey, Hey'), a Buddy Holly ('Words Of Love') and two songs by Carl Perkins ('Honey Don't' and 'Everybody's Trying To Be My Baby'), all of them recorded hurriedly towards the end of the sessions. "There are still one or two of our very early numbers which are worth recording," Paul explained to *Merseybeat* at the time. "Every now and then we remember one of the good ones we wrote in the early days and one of them, 'I'll Follow The Sun', is on the LP."

In the Seventies, Paul's company MPL Communications bought Holly's publishing catalogue and has since been responsible for organizing an annual Buddy Holly Day.

BABY'S IN BLACK

A simple song with a simple story. Boy loves girl, girl loves other boy, other boy doesn't love girl. Girl feels blue and dresses in black.

By 1964, Lennon and McCartney seldom sat down together and write a song from start to finish as they had done. This usually meant that an unfinished song was given a middle eight by the other partner or awkward lines were improved. The nose-to-nose writing which had happened in Liverpool and during the early days in London was coming to an end. "It would be daft to sit around waiting for a partner to finish your song off with you," explained Paul at the time. "If you happen to be on your own, you might as well get it finished yourself. If I get stuck on the middle eight of a new number, I give up, knowing that when I see John he will finish it off for me. He'll bring a new approach to it and that particular song will finish up half and half, Lennon and McCartney."

'Baby's In Black' was a genuine joint effort, the first since 'I Want To Hold Your Hand' almost a year before, John and Paul writing the song together in the same room at Kenwood. According to Paul it was an attempt to write something "a little bit darker, bluesy..." It was the first recorded for *Beatles For Sale*.

EVERY LITTLE THING

Every Little Thing', was written by Paul for Jane Asher with much the same theme as 'Things We Said Today'. Very much of its time, it tells the tale of a lucky guy whose girl loves him so much she does everything for him.

The girl's needs are not even considered, the assumption being that she should find her fulfilment in serving her man. Ironically, it was precisely the attitudes expressed in this song that Jane Asher later challenged when she told Paul she need to find fulfilment in her acting career. It wasn't enough for her to be the girlfriend of a desirable pop star; she wanted to make her own mark in the world of the arts.

Although this song was credited solely to Paul, who had come up with the basic for the track in his room at Wimpole Street. John remembered that he might have "thrown something in" too. It was an attempt at writing a single, but it became an album track.

▲ **Paul and John in America in August 1964 with a copy of *The Freewheelin' Bob Dylan*, the album which the Beatles were given in Paris and which turned them on to Dylan.**

WHAT YOU'RE DOING

Although 'What You're Doing' tells a fairly straightforward story of a boy being given the runaround by his girl, the lyric contains some inventive rhyming in 'doing' and 'blue an'', 'running' and 'fun in'. The most memorable part of the arrangement was the Beatles shouting the first word of each verse, with Paul completing the phrases.

Tim Riley, author of a book about the Beatles' music entitled *Tell Me Why*, praised the track for its pop ingenuity, saying that the addition of piano for just the guitar solo and the final fade-out suggested a love of detail they were to develop more fully: "The Beatles' conception for what the studio allowed them to do in altering textures and changing musical colours is emerging as a stylistic trait, not just a gimmick."

'What You're Doing' was another song written by Paul specifically for *Beatles For Sale* with additions from John. The recording was quite painstaking, beginning in September 1964 and picking up again in late October, at which time the track was completely re-made. Paul's final verdict was that it was a better recording than it was a song.

It was their debut appearance on the *Ed Sullivan Show* which alerted America to the Beatles. Here they are pictured during rehearsals.

HELP!

T he Beatles' second feature was filmed between February and May 1965 at a number of locations including New Providence Island in the Bahamas, the Austrian Alps, London's Cliveden House and Twickenham Film Studios.

After accolades for his performance in *A Hard Day's Night,* Ringo was given the starring role in *Help!* He was cast as the inheritor of a magic ring pursued by members of an evil cult who are hellbent on getting hold of it. As with the first film, all songs, apart from the title track, were written without prior knowledge of the script and dropped into the film, wherever there was any excuse for the boys to start playing.

The Beatles later expressed dissatisfaction with *Help!,* saying that they'd been no more than extras in their own film. However, it marked the beginning of their most fertile period of songwriting. John wrote the film's title track, using the word 'help' to explore his own anxiety: it was to remain one of his favourite Beatles' songs. Paul's 'Yesterday', which was used on the non-soundtrack side of the album, went on to become the most covered of all the Beatles' songs and the first to become an acknowledged classic.

Having discovered pot in the autumn of 1964, the Beatles were now smoking the drug regularly and John remembered this as their 'pot period', describing how reels of film had to be scrapped because they consisted of the Beatles in fits of uncontrollable laughter.

Help!, the album, was released in August 1965 and topped the charts in Britain and America. As with *A Hard Day's Night,* the American version consisted only of the songs in the film plus a few tracks by George Martin and an orchestra.

▲ **John and Paul wearing the fawn high-collared jackets now associated with the Beatles' first New York Shea Stadium concert on August 15, 1965.**

YES IT IS

John spoke about having once written love songs purely for 'the meat market' and yet it's hard to find the songs he was referring to. 'Yes It Is', though, was one song he felt particularly embarrassed about in later years, scoffing at the line 'for red is the colour that will make me blue'. John claimed that it was nothing more than an attempt to rewrite 'This Boy' as it had the same chords, harmonies and "double-Dutch words".

The lyric is a warning to a girl not to wear red because this is the colour that the singer's 'baby' always wore. John's final verdict on the song was that "it didn't work".

It was released as the B side to 'Ticket To Ride' in both Britain and America during April 1965.

▲ **The Beatles filming a scene for *Help!* in Ailsa Avenue, Twickenham, on April 14, 1965. In the film, the modest suburban doorways opened into a single enormous luxury suite.**

I'M DOWN

The B side of the single 'Help!', 'I'm Down' is an unashamed attempt by Paul to write a Little Richard song with which to replace 'Long Tall Sally' in the Beatles' set. "We spent a lot of time trying to write a real corker – something like 'Long Tall Sally'", Paul said in October 1964. "It's very difficult. 'I Saw Her Standing There' was the nearest we got to it. We're still trying to compose a Little Richard sort of song. I'd liken it to abstract painting. People think of 'Long Tall Sally' and say it sounds so easy to write. But it's the most difficult thing we've attempted. Writing a three-chord song that's clever is not easy."

Little Richard, who'd had his first British hit with 'Rip It Up' in 1956, first met the Beatles when they shared a bill at the Tower Ballroom, New Brighton, on October 12, 1962, one week after the release of 'Love Me Do'. It was a great moment for the group, who featured 'Rip It Up', 'Good Golly Miss Molly', 'Tutti Frutti', 'Lucille' among several Little Richard numbers in their shows.

"I met them in Liverpool before the world ever knew about them," says Little Richard. "Paul especially was into my music and had been playing it since he was in high school. He was impressed with my hollerin' and when I was on stage in Liverpool, and later in Hamburg (at the Star Club the following month), he used to stay in the wings and watch me sing. I felt honoured that they liked my music. My style is very dynamic. It's full of joy, it's full of fun and it's alive. There is nothing dead about it. There's never a dull moment. It keeps you on your toes, it keeps you movin' and I think that's what everybody gets from my music. People know that if they sing one of my songs on stage, they're gonna light up the house."

Fittingly, the Beatles used 'I'm Down' to close the show during their 1965 and 1966 tours. The last song they ever played live in concert though, at San Francisco's Candlestick Park on August 29, 1966, was Little Richard's 'Long Tall Sally'.

▲ **The Beatles posing backstage at the Tower Ballroom with Little Richard in October 1962.**

HELP!

Help! sounded like another jolly Beatles' song, but was really a plea from the heart. John was overweight, lonely and insecure and ▼ waiting to be rescued.

When he embarked on his solo career in the Seventies, John would often refer to 'Help!' as one of his favourite Beatles' songs. He liked it, he said, because it was "real". His one regret was that, for commercial reasons, they had changed it from a slow Dylanesque number into a jolly Beatles' tune.

'Help!' was written with Paul at his Weybridge home, Kenwood, in April 1965. The lyric reflected John's dissatisfaction with himself. He was eating and

drinking too much, had put on weight and felt overwhelmed by the fact they were such worldwide-celebrities. The song, he would later admit, really was a cry for help, despite being written to order for their second film. "I needed the help," he said. "The song was about me."

Putting himself and his feelings at the centre of a song, wasn't a new departure but the culmination of everything he'd been working towards. The only difference was that now he seemed to be admitting that

fame, wealth and success had only increased his anxiety. At the pinnacle of pop stardom, John had started to look back with longing to what he now saw as those relatively uncomplicated days at Menlove Avenue. The idealization of his boyhood and adolescence was a theme that was to grow in significance in his songwriting.

Maureen Cleave, the London journalist who had already helped out on the lyrics for *A Hard Day's Night*, felt that John should start to use words of more than one syllable. 'Help!' was his first serious attempt to do this, and he managed to incorporate 'self-assured', 'appreciate', 'independence' and 'insecure' within the song.

In the film *Help!*, again directed by Dick Lester, the song was used in the title sequence, where black and white footage of the Beatles was projected on to a screen set up in the temple of the religious cult.

Released as a single, 'Help!', reached the Number 1 spot in Britain and America in the summer of 1965.

THE NIGHT BEFORE

As with *A Hard Day's Night,* the songs used in *Help!* owed little to the script. "I think all the songs in *Help!* were written before the screenplay was even completed," confirms Dick Lester. "I was given a demo tape with about nine songs and I chose six of them in a rather arbitrary way, thinking that they were ones which I could do something with. It was as casual as that and I fitted the songs into the film in places where I thought I could do something with them."

Composed as a song of regret over a love lost, Paul was filmed singing 'The Night Before' while surrounded by troops and tanks on Salisbury Plain. The track was recorded in February 1965 and filmed three months later.

The Beatles filming a sequence from *Help!* on Salisbury Plain, Wiltshire, during the first week of May 1965. The area is used by the British Army for military exercises and some troops were deployed as extras.

YOU'VE GOT TO HIDE YOUR LOVE AWAY

Bob Dylan's music – (the acoustic *Another Side Of Bob Dylan* was his most recent album) – directed John towards a more intense and personal style of writing. He began to write songs in which his state of mind became the immediate starting point. In the first lines of 'You've Got To Hide Your Love Away', the image of John standing facing a wall with his head in his hands was probably a perfect description of how he felt when he was writing.

The song is about a relationship that has gone wrong and John's hidden feelings for a girl he has lost. Tony Bramwell suggests that it was written for Brian Epstein, warning him to keep his homosexual rela-tionships (which, at the time, were illegal in Britain) from public view. It was also rumoured that it referred to a secret affair John was having.

Written by John at Kenwood, it was used in the film during a scene in which British actress Eleanor Bron visited the group in their terraced house to try and retrieve the missing ring.

John's childhood friend, Pete Shotton, was with him at Kenwood and remembered that in the original version he had sung that he felt 'two foot tall'. However when he sang it to Paul, he mistakenly sang 'two foot small', which Paul liked better and so it was kept. Shotton went to the recording on February 18, 1965, and added some 'heys' to the chorus.

The Beatles captured waiting for the cameras to roll during the scene in *Help!* in which John sings 'You've Got To Hide Your Love Away' to actress Eleanor Bron (seated in the middle).

I NEED YOU

ANOTHER GIRL

▲ **February 27, 1965, the first week of filming for *Help!* George and Paul are pictured here on Balmoral Island in the Bahamas during a break in miming the sequence for Paul's song, 'Another Girl'.**

A formulaic love song, 'I Need You' was written by George for his girlfriend Pattie Boyd, and was one of two of his Beatles' songs which he didn't comment on in his 1980 book *I Me Mine* (the other was 'You Like Me Too Much').

It was also the only George song to be featured in the film *Help!* (in the Salisbury Plain sequence) and the first to use a wah-wah pedal to distort the guitar sound.

Some Beatles' books have claimed that George wrote it in the Bahamas while separated from Pattie, but this can't be true as recording began on February 15, 1965, and these Bahamian scenes weren't shot until the following week.

T his was written by Paul during a ten-day holiday in Tunisia and used in a scene filmed on Balmoral Island in the Bahamas.

In this song, Paul talks about being under pressure to commit long-term to his girlfriend but how he's not going to do this, mainly because he's already got himself another girl.

John once said that the Beatles' songs were like signatures; even when they weren't trying to give anything away they would betray their most fundamental attitudes. "It was always apparent – if you looked below the surface – what was being said. Resentfulness or love or hate, it's apparent in all our work."

YOU'RE GOING TO LOSE THAT GIRL

April 30, 1965. The Beatles filming a sequence for *Help!* at Twickenham Film Studios, in which they are supposed to be at Abbey Road recording 'You're Going To Lose That Girl'.

The Beatles sang this in a scene in *Help!* set in the recording studio, which was filmed at Twickenham Film Studios. The song is interrupted when the gang chasing Ringo cut a hole around his drum kit from the ceiling of the room below.

Written mainly by John, but completed with Paul at his Weybridge home, the song is a warning to an unidentified male that if he doesn't start treating his girlfriend right, John is going to move in on her, developing a theme he first outlined in 'She Loves You'.

Ticket To Ride' was written by John and Paul as a single and described by John as "one of the earliest heavy metal records made". Although they were pipped at the post in the heavy metal stakes by the Kinks' 'You Really Got Me', which charted in Britain the previous summer, this was the first Beatles' track to feature an insistent, clanking riff underpinned by a heavy drum beat and it used a fade-out with an altered melody.

Paul confessed to his biographer Barry Miles that the apparently loopy suggestion made by some American fans at the time that the song was referring to a British Railways ticket to the town of Ryde on the Isle of Wight was partly right. Paul's cousin Betty Robbins and her husband Mike ran the Bow Bars in Union Street, Ryde, and Paul and John had visited them there. Although the song was primarily about a girl riding out of the life of the narrator, they were consicious of the potential for a double meaning.

Don Short, a show business journalist who travelled extensively with the Beatles in the Sixties, was told by John that the phrase had yet another meaning. "The girls who worked the streets in Hamburg had to have a clean bill of health and so the medical authorities would give them a card saying that they didn't have a dose of anything," says Short. "I was with the Beatles when they went back to Hamburg in June 1966 and it was then that John told me that he had coined the phrase 'a ticket to ride' to describe these cards. He could have been joking – you always had to be careful with John like that – but I certainly remember him telling me that."

'Ticket To Ride' didn't have anything to do with skiing but the single worked well when slotted into *Help!* over the Austrian snow scenes.

TICKET TO RIDE

▲ **After meeting George on the set of *A Hard Day's Night*, Pattie Boyd became his inseparable companion, and was the inspiration behind some of his best songs.**

TELL ME WHAT YOU SEE

T ell Me What You See' was another 'work song' by Paul who asks his girl to give her heart to him because he's utterly trustworthy and will brighten up her life. If she doesn't believe him, he suggests that she take a look in his eyes and tell him what she sees.

The track was recorded before the filming of *Help!* and offered to Dick Lester for the soundtrack, but was rejected. Obviously, he was not too keen on what he heard. Tim Riley, in his book about the Beatles' music, notes that it is one of the album's weaker songs, suggesting that it became a working draft for the altogether stronger track 'I'm Looking Through You'.

John, Ringo and George with an unidentified actress while filming *Help!* in Austria. Stand-ins were used for some of the more challenging snow scenes.

YOU LIKE ME TOO MUCH

Y ou Like Me Too Much' was written and recorded by George for the soundtrack and recorded before filming started on *Help!* It was eventually relegated to the B side of the album.

George chose not to discuss 'You Like Me Too Much' in his otherwise comprehensive account of his songwriting, *I Me Mine*, presumably because there was nothing much to say. A standard love story, the song describes how having been jilted, the lover feels everything will turn out alright in the end, as the girl simply loves him too much. If it had been written by John, he would undoubtedly have dismissed it as one of his throwaways.

IT'S ONLY LOVE

J ohn wrote 'It's Only Love' as an upbeat number, chock full of the most clichéd rhymes and images, so it is little wonder people think this song is completely out of character. In the lyric, he describes how his girl lights up the night for him and yet he's suffering from butterflies in his stomach. The real problem is that he is in love.

It was one of the few Beatles' songs that John really hated. "I was always ashamed of that because of the abominable lyrics," he admitted in 1969. All the songs that John regretted having written were condemned on the grounds of their lyrics rather than their melodies, because he felt that he had produced platitudes rather than expressed any real feeling.

In this case, the song's shortcomings could have been a result of the pressure to come up with a further side of songs to complete the soundtrack album or simply that John was feeling at a low ebb.

George Martin and his orchestra recorded the composition as an instrumental using John's original working title of 'That's A Nice Hat'.

YESTERDAY

Paul woke up one morning in his top floor bedroom at the Ashers' home in Wimpole Street with the tune for 'Yesterday' in his head. There was a piano by the bed and he went straight to it and started playing. "It was just all there," he said. "A complete thing. I couldn't believe it."

Although at that point it had no lyric, Paul was worried that the tune itself might have been unconsciously plagiarized, and that what had seemed like a flash of inspiration may only have been a surge of recollection. "For about a month, I went round to people in the music business and asked them whether they had ever heard it before," he said. "Eventually it became like handing something in to the police. I thought that if no-one claimed it after a few weeks then I would have it."

He then came up with the provisional title 'Scrambled Eggs' and began singing 'Scrambled eggs, Oh you've got such lovely legs', simply to get a feel for the vocal. This was a common practice and sometimes gave rise to interesting lines that were kept in the final version. "We were shooting *Help!* in the studio for about four weeks," remembers Dick Lester. "At some time during that period, we had a piano on one of the stages and he was playing this 'Scrambled Eggs' all the time. It got to the point where I said to him, 'If you play that bloody song any longer I'll have the piano taken off stage. Either finish it or give it up!' "

Paul must have conceived the tune early in 1965, but it wasn't until June when he took a brief holiday in Portugal at the villa of Shadows' guitarist Bruce Welch that he'd completed the lyric. He then hit on the idea of using a one word title – 'Yesterday'.

The music for Paul's best-known song, 'Yesterday', came to him during the night. He tumbled out of bed and went straight to the piano to work it out. The tune seemed so complete that initially he feared that it must belong to someone else.

◄ ·······························

▲ **Paul called his new song 'Scrambled Eggs' at first, and drove the others crazy during *Help!* by playing it over and over on the piano.**

I'VE JUST SEEN A FACE

I've Just Seen A Face' was a tune which Paul had been playing on piano for some time. He played it at family get-togethers back in Liverpool and his Auntie Gin loved it so much that it was dubbed 'Auntie Gin's Theme'. The George Martin Orchestra went on to record an instrumental version under this title.

Auntie Gin was the youngest sister of Paul's father Jim and would later get a mention in 'Let 'Em In' recorded by Wings, Paul's post-Beatle band.

"I was packing to leave and Paul asked me if I had a guitar," says Welch. "He'd apparently been working on the lyrics as he drove to Albufeira from the airport at Lisbon. He borrowed my guitar and started playing the song we all now know as 'Yesterday'."

Two days after returning from Portugal, Paul recorded it at Abbey Road. The song startled pop fans at the time because it featured a string quartet with Paul as the only Beatle on the session. In America, it became a single and reached the Number I spot but, in Britain, it was never released as either an A or a B side during the group's career. It rapidly became a pop standard, covered by everyone from Frank Sinatra to Marianne Faithfull. Nowadays, some 30 years on, it is still one of the most played tracks on American radio.

Although John claimed that he never wished that he had written it, he did admit that it was a "beautiful" song with "good" lyrics but argued that the lyrics were never resolved. However, others have felt that its strength lies in its vagueness. All the listener needs to know is that it's about someone wanting to turn back the clock, to retreat to a time before a tragic event. The application is universal.

There has been speculation that in Paul's case the tragedy referred to was the death of his mother and the regret was over his inability to express his grief at the time.

Iris Caldwell remembered an interesting incident in connection with the song. She had broken up with Paul in March 1963 after a silly argument over her dogs (Paul wasn't too keen on dogs at the time) and, when he later called up to speak to Iris, her mother told Paul that her daughter didn't want to speak to him because he had no feelings. Two and a half years later, on Sunday August I, 1965, Paul was scheduled to sing 'Yesterday' on a live television programme, *Blackpool Night Out*. During that week, he phoned Mrs Caldwell and said; "You know that you said that I had no feelings? Watch the telly on Sunday and then tell me that I've got no feelings."

While on holiday in Portugal with Jane Asher, Paul finally came up with the finished lyric for 'Yesterday'. The couple are pictured here on June 12, 1965, after flying back to London from Lisbon.

RUBBER SOUL

▲ Photographer Bob Whitaker encouraged the Beatles'
developing sense of surrealism – John watering
Cynthia's hat in their Weybridge garden, May 1965.

Although there had been hints of a new direction on the preceding albums, *Rubber Soul* marked a major period of transition. John would later call it the beginning of the group's 'self-conscious' period; the end of the Beatles 'tribal child-like' stage.

Despite the cover, with its deliberately distorted photograph of the Beatles suggesting the perception shifts of LSD and marijuana, this wasn't a psychedelic album. Musically however, it was an exploration of new sounds and new subject matter, introducing Paul on fuzz bass and George on sitar. When producer George Martin played the piano solo back at double-speed to create a baroque sound, it was the first time that they'd tampered with tapes to create an effect.

There was a playfulness to *Rubber Soul* that extended from the wordplay of the title down to the 'beep beeps' and 'tit tits' of the backing vocals. Paul was quoted at the time as saying that they were now into humorous songs and both 'Drive My Car', with its role reversal, and 'Norwegian Wood', with its naive seduction scene, fitted into this category. For a group which had only ever sung about love, 'Nowhere Man', a song about lack of belief, was a breakthrough: other songs like 'The Word' and 'In My Life' were only tangentially about boy-girl relationships.

The love songs of this period showed a new maturity. Paul's 'We Can Work It Out', stemming from his own troubled relationship with Jane Asher, was a long way from the simplicities expressed in 'She Loves You' or 'I Want To Hold Your Hand'. John's 'The Word' pointed in the direction of the universal love that would later be the basis of songs like 'Within You Without You' and 'All You Need Is Love'.

Recorded over a four week period in the autumn of 1965, *Rubber Soul* was released in December and became a chart-topping album in Britain and America. Four of the British tracks were left off the American album and these were replaced by two tracks from *Help!*

DAY TRIPPER

Day Tripper' was written under pressure when the Beatles needed a new single for the Christmas market. John wrote most of the lyric and the basic guitar break, coming up with a riff partly inspired by Bobby Parker's 'Watch Your Step'. Paul helped on the verses.

In the summer of 1965, John and George had been introduced to LSD by a London dentist who slipped it into their coffee after an evening meal. In August, while in America, they took a trip of their own free will and from then on John confessed that he "just ate it all the time". 'Day Tripper' was a typical play on words by John, who wanted to reflect the influence of the growing drug culture within a Beatles' song. It was his way of referring to those who couldn't, like him, afford the luxury of being almost permanently tripped out. "It's just a rock'n'roll song," commented John. "Day trippers are people who go on a day trip right? Usually on a ferryboat or something. But (the song) was kind of...you're just a weekend hippie. Get it?"

The song is about a girl who leads the singer on. His oblique description of the girl as a 'big teaser', was a knowing reference to the term 'prick teaser', a phrase sometimes used by British men about women who encouraged sexual arousal with no intention of having sex.

'Day Tripper' was released in both Britain and America as a double A sided single with 'We Can Work It Out'. It was the more popular song in Britain, reaching Number 1, but in America it peaked at five. The Beatles later said that 'We Can Work It Out' was their choice for the A side.

WE CAN WORK IT OUT

In October 1965, Jane Asher decided to join the Bristol Old Vic Company which meant that she moved away from London to the west of England just at the time the Beatles were recording tracks for *Rubber Soul*. Her departure upset Paul and caused the first major rift in their relationship. As suggested in his songs, Paul's notion of a good woman then was someone happy just to be around him. Jane's outlook was unusual. Not content to be a rock star's 'chick', she was well educated, independently minded and wanted her own career.

In 'We Can Work It Out', Paul doesn't try to argue the merits of his case, but pleads with his woman to see things his way because he believes he is right. It was typical of Paul that he didn't retreat sobbing to his room, but emerged with the positive slogan 'we can work it out'. The slightly downbeat middle eight, with its intimations of mortality, was added by John.

"You've got Paul writing 'we can work it out'," said John. " Real optimistic, and me, impatient, (with) 'Life is very short, And there's no time, For fussing and fighting my friend.'" The song was written at Paul's father's house in Heswall, Cheshire. The harmonium 'wash' was added in the studio as an after-thought and George Harrison suggested changing the middle-eight to waltz time.

Jane Asher, pictured here with Gawn Grainger in a Bristol Old Vic production of *Romeo and Juliet*, was no ordinary pop star's girlfriend. Her dedication to her own career didn't make for a smooth relationship with Paul although, at this stage, he was still determined to 'work it out'.

DRIVE MY CAR

With *Rubber Soul* came more lyrical subtlety. 'Drive My Car' sounded macho on the surface but was actually about role reversal – the car belongs to the woman, the baby being ▼ addressed is the man.

A first hearing of 'Drive My Car' might suggest that the Beatles are telling some 'baby' to drive their car, but closer inspection of the lyric reveals that it's the male narrator who is being asked to do the driving. He's trying to chat someone up, using that well-worn line, 'Well, what do you want to be?' – suggesting sexual favours in return for promises of career advancement.

The woman tells him that she wants to be a movie star – but then reverses the roles by saying that she might (and it is only might) agree to give him some love if he agrees to be her chauffeur. By the second verse it's the man who is pleading his case, arguing that his 'prospects are good'. It's a good twist, inspired perhaps by the tougher breed of woman

that the Beatles were meeting in America.

Paul remembered this song as the only one he got stuck on, the storyline being pulled together at the last minute with some help from John. When he arrived at Abbey Road on October 20, 1965, to record the song, the chorus was 'I can give you golden rings, I can give you anything, Baby I love you'. John dismissed this as "crap" and so the two of them huddled together to create an alternative and came up with 'Baby, you can drive my car', a tougher, more sexually-charged image which in turn gave rise to the playful 'Beep beep an' beep beep yeah' background vocal.

John always agreed it was Paul's song with a bit of last-minute tuning and Paul said: "The idea of the girl being a bitch was the same but (the change) made the key line better." Two days after recording 'Drive My Car', Paul told a music magazine, "We've written some funny songs – songs with jokes in. We think that comedy numbers are the next thing after protest songs."

NORWEGIAN WOOD

Although John was famous as the married Beatle he was not happily married. Nor was he faithful. He took advantage of backstage groupies, admitted to having been photographed on his hands and knees outside a Dutch brothel, and told his wife Cynthia in 1968 that he had had affairs. 'Norwegian Wood' was about one such entanglement. In language John later described as 'gobbledygook', the song details a seduction scene where again the woman appears to be the one in control.

The lyrics open with a boast about a girl John has 'had', but he quickly corrects himself by saying that it was she who 'had' him. She takes him back to her apartment and asks him to admire the furnishings which are made out of cheap Norwegian pine. After talking and drinking until two in the morning, she says it's time for bed. In the song, he makes his excuses and leaves for a night in the bathroom, but in reality the story obviously had a different ending because he said it had been written about an act of unfaithfulness, "without letting my wife know I was writing about an affair". John's friend Pete Shotton has said that it was about a female journalist that John was close to.

John began 'Norwegian Wood' in February 1965 while on a skiing holiday in St Moritz, Switzerland, with Cynthia, George Martin and George's future wife, Judy. He later asked Paul for help with the ending and Paul suggested that he develop a story about the apartment burning down. Pete Shotton thought this could have referred to John's habit of burning furniture in the fireplace at Gambier Terrace in Liverpool. While he was there, John would sometimes ask guests to sleep in the bath, the memory of which may have prompted the line in 'Norwegian Wood' about sleeping in the bath.

Paul saw the song as a complete fantasy. The Norwegian wood of the title was suggested by the decoration of Paul's room in Wimpole Street but to John it was definitely about a secret affair.

The track stood out on *Rubber Soul* for its use of sitar – it was the first time the Indian instrument had been used on a pop record. George Harrison had become fascinated with the sitar after coming across one while filming *Help!* in the Bahamas, and would later study under the Indian master, Ravi Shankar.

▲ **John wrote 'Norwegian Wood' during this Swiss holiday with Cynthia in February 1965.**

YOU WON'T SEE ME

You Won't See Me' was another song written by Paul during the crisis in his relationship with Jane Asher. He was suffering the indignity of unanswered phone calls and other rejections. The dip in his romantic fortunes raised his writing to new heights – he now found he was the vulnerable one. Paul had never seen life from this perspective. Throughout *Beatles For Sale* and *Help!*, he'd dreamt up situations for love songs but now, perhaps for the first time, he was writing from the heart.

It was written as a two-note progression and Paul had the Motown sound in mind, particularly the melodic bass playing of James Jamerson, the legendary studio musician. Ian MacDonald in *Revolution in the Head* suggests the specific model might have been 'It's The Same Old Song' by the Four Tops.

'You Won't See Me' was recorded during the last session for *Rubber Soul*, by which time Jane was playing in *Great Expectations* at the Theatre Royal, Bristol.

Paul's natural optimism was challenged by his emotionally turbulent relationship with Jane Asher. As a result, he began to write songs with more bite.

....................................▶

NOWHERE MAN

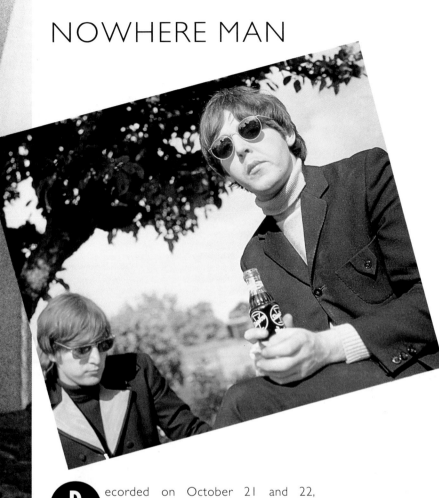

Recorded on October 21 and 22, 'Nowhere Man' has the distinction of being the first Beatles' song not to be about love. John wrote it early one morning after a night out and it marked the beginning of his overtly philosophical musings.

'Nowhere Man' was always assumed to be either about a specific person (in her Hollywood exposé *You'll Never Eat Lunch In This Town Again*, Julia Phillips speculated that it was written about an entrepreneur called Michael Brown) or about an archetypal member of 'straight' society whose life had no purpose.

John said that he was the 'Nowhere Man' in question, and that desperation had driven him to it after he'd been writing solidly for over five hours, feeling that he wouldn't be able to complete another song for the album. "I'd actually stopped trying to think of something," he told Beatles' biographer Hunter Davies. "Nothing would come. I was cheesed off and went for a lie-down, having given up. Then I thought of myself as Nowhere Man – sitting in his nowhere land."

▲ **The big change in John's lyrics came when he began chronicling his precise feelings at the time of writing. 'Nowhere Man', although interpreted by some as a comment on the erosion of belief in modern society, was said by John to be about his own lack of belief in himself when composing the song.**

THINK
FOR YOURSELF

Think For Yourself', a song written by George Harrison, is an admonition against listening to lies. Recorded just a few months before his engagement to Pattie Boyd, it was presumably not about his wife-to-be. "It must be about 'somebody' from the sound of it," he wrote in his book *I Me Mine*. "But all this time later, I don't quite recall who inspired that tune. Probably the government."

George with Pattie Boyd. As the youngest member of the Beatles and a late starter as a songwriter, George always felt he lived in the shadow of John and Paul, complaining that it was hard to get his songs on the Beatles' albums because of the Lennon-McCartney domination.

THE WORD

Recorded two years after 'She Loves You' (July 1963) and two years before 'All You Need Is Love' (June 1967), 'The Word' marks the transition between the boy-meets-girl love of Beatlemania and the peace-and-harmony love of the hippy era.

Understood at the time as just another Beatles' love song, it was sprinkled with clues pointing to a love that John was now singing about which offered 'freedom' and 'light'. It even offered 'the way'.

In *The Varieties Of Psychedelic Experience*, Masters and Houston found that LSD often produced experiences of a religious nature, and provided people with the idea that "a universal or brotherly love is possible and constitutes man's best if not only hope." It was for this reason that 'love' became such a buzz word within the drug culture of the mid- to late

Sixties, John being one of the first songwriters to catch the mood. He later recalled the song as one of the Beatles' first 'message songs' and the beginnings of the group's role as cultural leaders expected to supply answers to social and spiritual questions.

John told *Playboy* that it was a song about "getting smart", meaning the state of realization which users of marijuana and LSD were claiming as theirs. "It's love," he said. "It's the marijuana period. It's the love and peace thing. The word is 'love', right?"

When John and Paul had finished writing it at Kenwood they rolled joints and wrote out a psyche-delically decorated lyric sheet which John presented to the composer John Cage for his 50th birthday.

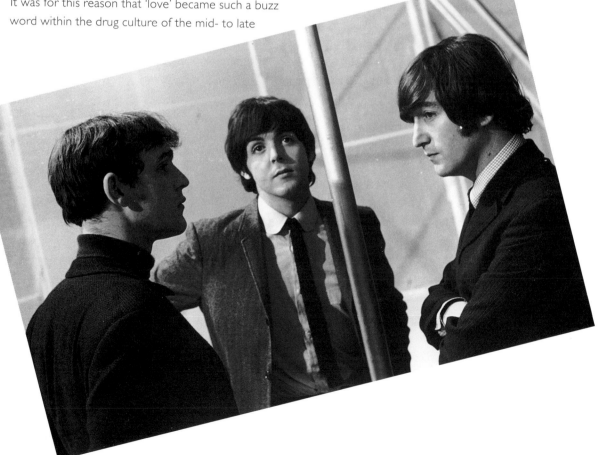

MICHELLE

Michelle' dates back to Liverpool days when Paul went to parties thrown by one of John's art tutors, Austin Mitchell. This was at a time when the intellectual life of the Parisian Left Bank was fashionable and bohemianism was signalled by berets, beards and Gitanes. "Back in those days people would point at you in the street in Liverpool if you had a beard," remembers Rod Murray, who shared the Gambier Terrace flat with John and Stuart Sutcliffe. "If you had a beret, they would call you a beatnik. We liked Juliette Greco and everyone fancied getting in with Brigitte Bardot."

At one of these parties, a student with a goatee beard and a striped T-shirt was hunched over his guitar singing what sounded like a French song. Paul worked a comical imitation to amuse his friends.

It remained a party piece with nothing more than Charles Aznavour-style Gallic groanings as accompaniment until, in 1965, John suggested that Paul should write proper words for it and include it on the album.

Radio presenter Muriel Young, then working for Radio Luxembourg, can remember Paul visiting her at her holiday home in Portugal while he was working

on it. This was probably during September 1965 when the Beatles took a month off between the American tour, which had finished on August 31, and the new album which was due to begin recording on October 12. "He sat on our sofa with Jane Asher and he was trying to find the words," Muriel says. "It wasn't 'Michelle, ma belle' then. He was singing 'Goodnight sweetheart' and then 'Hello my dear', just looking for something that would fit the rhythm."

Eventually, Paul chose to go with the French feel and to incorporate a French name and some French words. He spoke to Jan Vaughan, the wife of his old school friend Ivan Vaughan (the person responsible for introducing Paul to John), who was a French language teacher. "I asked her what sort of things I could say that were French and which would go together well," said Paul. "It was because I'd always thought that the song sounded French that I stuck with it. I can't speak French properly so that's why I needed help in sorting out the actual words."

Jan remembers that Paul first spoke to her about it when she and Ivan were visiting him at the Ashers' London home. "He asked me if I could think of a French girl's first name, with two syllables, and then a description of the girl which would rhyme. He played me the rhythm on his guitar and that's when I came up with 'Michelle, ma belle', which wasn't actually that hard to think of! I think it was some days later that he phoned me up and asked if I could translate the phrase 'these are words that go together well' and I told him that it should be 'sont les mots qui vont tres bien ensemble'."

When Paul played the song to John he suggested the 'I love you' in the middle section, specifying that the emphasis should fall on the word love each time. He was inspired by Nina Simone's recording of 'I Put A Spell On You', a hit in Britain during August 1965, where she had used the same phrase but placed the emphasis on the 'you'. "My contribution to Paul's songs was always to add a little bluesy edge to them," John said. "Otherwise 'Michelle' is a straight ballad."

GIRL

Asked who the girl was in 'Girl', John said that she was a figure from a dream, the ideal woman who had not yet appeared in his life. "I always had this dream of this particular woman coming into my life," he said. "I knew it wouldn't be someone buying Beatles' records. I was hoping for a woman who could give me what I get from a man intellectually. I wanted someone I could be myself with."

However, the girl in the song seems far from his ideal. She's heartless, she's conceited and she humiliates him. Perhaps there are two girls in the song: the dream girl in the first half, whom he appears almost addicted to, and the nightmare girl in the second half who holds him up to ridicule.

The most John ever said about the song though was not to do with his images of women but his image of the Christian Church. In 1970, he revealed to *Rolling Stone* that the verse which asks whether she had been taught that pain would lead to pleasure, and that a man must break his back to earn leisure, was a reference to, "the Catholic/Christian concept – be tortured and then it'll be alright." He added, "I was...trying to say something or other about Christianity, which I was opposed to at the time." He could have been thinking of the Genesis account of the effects of Adam and Eve's disobedience, where Eve is told that "with pain you will give birth to children" and Adam is told that "cursed is the ground because of you; through painful toil you will eat of it all the days of your life."

Christianity, and in particular Jesus Christ, seemed to bother John. At the time of writing 'Girl', he was avidly reading books about religion, a subject that preoccupied him until his death, and four months later he gave the interview to Maureen Cleave which contained his controversial comment about the Beatles having become "more popular than Jesus".

The one joke that he included was to have Paul and George repeat the word 'tit' as part of their backing vocals.

Although 'Michelle' was Paul's song, John made a contribution to the middle eight that was inspired by a version of 'I Put A Spell On You', by Nina Simone.

WHAT GOES ON

What Goes On' was actually one of the four songs which the Beatles played to George Martin on March 5, 1963, as possible follow-ups to 'Please Please Me'. (The other three were 'From Me To You', 'Thank You Girl' and 'The One After 909').

Written by John some time previously, it was the only song Martin chose not to record on that day and it was forgotten until November 4, 1965, when it was taken out and dusted down for Ringo's vocal number. A new middle eight was added by Paul and Ringo; giving Ringo his first ever credit as a composer. Asked in 1966 what exactly his contribution to the song had been, Ringo said: "About five words".

In America, it was released as the B side of 'Nowhere Man' in February 1966.

I'M LOOKING THROUGH YOU

Jane Asher's move to Bristol continued to preoccupy Paul. It meant that she was no longer readily at hand even though he was still living in her family home in Wimpole Street. As a young working-class man from Liverpool, he found it hard to come to terms with a girl who put her career before romance.

He later admitted to Hunter Davies that his whole existence so far revolved around living a carefree bachelor's life. He hadn't treated women as most people did. He'd always had a lot around him, even when he had steady girlfriends. "I knew I was selfish," he said. "It caused a few rows. Jane went off and I said, 'OK then. Leave. I'll find someone else. It was shattering to be without her. That was when I wrote 'I'm Looking Through You'."

This was Paul's most bitter song so far. Rather than question his own attitudes (as he obviously did later), Paul accuses his woman of changing and holds out the thinly veiled threat of withdrawing his affection. Love has a habit, he warns, of disappearing overnight.

IN MY LIFE

Although John had been writing more obviously autobiographical songs for over a year now, it was with 'In My Life' that he felt he'd made the breakthrough that Kenneth Allsop had encouraged him to make in March 1964, when he suggested focusing on his own interior life.

Recorded in October 1965, the song was a long time in gestation. It started, John said, as a long poem in which he reflected on favourite childhood haunts by tracing a journey from his home on Menlove Avenue down to the Docks.

Elliot Mintz, who was hired by Yoko Ono to carry out an inventory of all John's personal possessions after his death, remembers seeing the first

handwritten draft of the song. "It was part of a large book in which he kept all his original Beatles' compositions," says Mintz. "He had already told me about how the song was written and that he considered it a significant turning point in his writing."

In a later single-page draft of this rambling lyric, John listed Penny Lane, Church Road, the clock tower, the Abbey Cinema, the tram sheds, the Dutch cafe, St Columbus Church, the Docker's Umbrella and Calderstones Park. Although this fulfilled the requirement of being autobiographical, John realized that it was no more than a series of snapshots held loosely together by his feeling that once familiar landmarks were fast disappearing. "It was the most boring sort of 'what I did on my holidays' bus trip song and it wasn't working at all..." he said. "Then I lay back and these lyrics started coming to me about the places I remember."

John jettisoned all the specific place names, and worked up the sense of mourning for a disappeared childhood and youth, turning what would otherwise have been a song about the changing face of Liverpool into a universal song about confronting the facts of death and decay.

He later told Pete Shotton that when he wrote the line about friends in 'In My Life', some of whom were dead and some of whom were living, he was thinking specifically of both Shotton and former Beatle Stuart Sutcliffe, who had died of a brain tumour in April 1962.

The lyric bears a surprising resemblance to Charles Lamb's 18th-century poem 'The Old Familiar Faces' which John could well have come across in the popular poetry anthology *Palgrave's Treasury*. The poem starts:

I have had playmates, I have had companions
In my days of childhood, in my joyful schooldays –
All, all are gone, the old familiar faces.
Six verses later it ends:
How some they have died,
*   and some they have left me,*
And some are taken from me; all are departed –
All, all are gone, the old familiar faces

The source of the melody remains in dispute. John has said that Paul helped out with a section on which he was stuck. Paul still believes he wrote it all. "I

◄ ·····································
It was the streets of old Liverpool which inspired the writing of 'In My Life', one of the songs John was most proud to have written. In imagining a bus ride from his home on Menlove Avenue down to the docks, he took in all the places that held special significance for him as a boy.

remember that he had the words written out like a long poem and I went off and worked something out on the Mellotron," he said. "The tune, if I remember rightly, was inspired by the Miracles." He was almost certainly referring to 'You Really Got A Hold On Me'.

On the track itself, the instrumental break was played by George Martin who recorded himself on piano and then played it back at double speed to create a baroque effect. John's opinion on the finished result was that it was his "first real major piece of work".

WAIT

The Beatles don't appear to have had great affection for 'Wait'. It was first recorded for *Help!* in June 1965, but not used, and was taken up again as the *Rubber Soul* sessions finished – but only because the album was a song short.

Written mostly by Paul, it's an all-purpose song about a couple who separated and now that they're back together everything's going to be all right. Paul recollects it was written in the Bahamas during filming and that the late Brandon de Wilde, the child star of *Shane*, had watched as he composed it.

▲ John with art school friend Tony Carricker. 'In My Life' was a brooding reminiscence of Lennon's days in Liverpool.

IF I NEEDED SOMEONE

If I Needed Someone' was written by George for girlfriend Pattie, as a musical exercise using the D chord. "That guitar line, or variations on it, is found in many a song and it amazes me that people still find new permutations of the same notes."

When Beatles' press officer Derek Taylor moved to Los Angeles and began to represent the Byrds, George asked him to pass a message to Byrds' guitarist Roger McGuinn saying that the tune to 'If I Needed Someone' had been inspired by two Byrds' tracks – 'The Bells Of Rhymney' and 'She Don't Care About Time'.

RUN FOR YOUR LIFE

John developed 'Run For Your Life' from the line 'I'd rather see you dead little girl than see you with another man' which occurred towards the end of Elvis Presley's 1955 Sun single 'Baby, Let's Play House'. Indeed, John referred to this as "an old blues song that Presley did once" but in fact it only dates back to 1954 and was written by a 28-year-old preacher's son from Nashville named Arthur Gunter.

Gunter had based his song on a 1951 country hit by Eddy Arnold, 'I Want To Play House With You', and recorded it for the Excello label in late 1954. It wasn't a national hit but it was heard by Elvis who took it into the studios with him on February 5, 1955. When 'Run For Your Life' reached Number 10 in *Billboard*'s country chart in July 1955, it became the first Elvis record to chart nationally in America. Gunter's song was one of devotion. He wanted the girl to move in with him and the line which took John's attention was an indication of the depths of his feelings for her, not a threat.

However, in John's hands the lines become literal. If he sees his girl with anyone else she'd better run because he's going to make sure she dies. This was pure revenge fantasy, with the real Lennon showing through. The singer explains his behaviour by saying that he's 'wicked' and that he was born with 'a jealous mind'; lines which contain intimations of later songs such as 'Jealous Guy' and 'Crippled Inside'.

Although it was the first track to be recorded for *Rubber Soul*, John always picked 'Run For Your Life' as an example of his worst work. It was written under pressure, he said and, as such, was a "throwaway song".

REVOLVER

R *evolver* marked a significant development in the Beatles' sound, as well as the end of an era. After this album, all their music was sculpted in the studio, with little thought as to whether the songs could be reproduced in concert. Under the influence of the hippy movement in America and the avant-garde art scene in Britain, they had also started to write for a different audience. Encounters with the underground scene, along with the effect of psychedelic drugs, were to alter their perceptions of both themselves and their music.

In a March 1966 interview with British teenage magazine *Rave*, Paul enthused over George's interest in Indian music and his own explorations of theatre, painting, film making and electronic music. "We've all got interested in things that never used to occur to us," he said. "I've got thousands, millions, of new ideas myself."

Revolver was an album bursting with new ideas. Although variety has since become the staple of rock'n'roll, at the time it challenged all the conventions of pop. Not only did it introduce musical styles ranging from a children's singalong to a psychedelic melange of backward tape loops, it also presented a strange mix of song topics – taxation, Tibetan Buddhism, law-breaking doctors, lonely spinsters, sleep, submarines and sunshine.

Yet, despite its experimentation, *Revolver* was not inaccessible. 'Eleanor Rigby', 'For No One' and 'Here, There And Everywhere' were three of the most beautiful and popular songs Paul ever wrote. 'Taxman' and 'I Want To Tell You' were George's best compositions so far and John's dream-like 'I'm Only Sleeping' and 'She Said She Said' perfectly captured the mood of the times.

Released during what turned out to be their final tour, none of the 14 songs were to be played on stage by the Beatles. They had entered a new phase of being recording artists rather than performers, and were now happy to concentrate on the art of making records rather than having to squeeze their songwriting between touring and frequent appearances on film and television.

Revolver was released in August 1966 and made the top spot in both America and Britain. This was the last time that the British and American versions of a Beatles' album were to differ. Three of John's songs – 'I'm Only Sleeping', 'And Your Bird Can Sing' and 'Doctor Robert' – had already appeared in the US on the album *Yesterday And Today*.

Robert Whitaker, whose black and white photograph of the Beatles was used on the back cover of *Revolver*, had further sessions with the group in 1966 to capture the growing mood of experimentation.

PAPERBACK WRITER

The promotional clip for
'Paperback Writer' was
filmed on May 20, 1966 at
Chiswick House, west London.

The Beatles' first single to depart from the theme of love ('Nowhere Man' had been the first song), 'Paperback Writer' was the story of a novelist begging a publisher to take on his thousand-page book. Written by Paul in the form of a letter, it was startling at the time to hear a pop single on such a subject.

British disc jockey Jimmy Savile, who then worked for Radio Luxembourg as well as BBC Television's *Top Of The Pops*, claims he was backstage after a show when Paul first conceived the idea for the song. John had been principal writer of the Beatles' last five singles and so it was generally agreed that it was Paul's turn to come up with something. Savile recalled John asking Paul what he was going to do because there were only a few days left before they were due to record. "Paul told him that one of his aunts had just asked if he could ever write a single that wasn't about love," remembers Savile. "With that thought obviously still in his mind, he walked around the room and noticed that Ringo was reading a book. He took one look and announced that he would write a song about a book."

Paul has said that he had always liked the sound of the words 'paperback writer' and decided to build his story round them. The epistolary style of the song came to him as he drove down to Weybridge for a day's writing with John. "As soon as I arrived I told him that I wanted us to write it as if it was a letter," he said. Tony Bramwell recalls that the inspiration for much of the lyric came from an actual letter written to Paul by an aspiring novelist.

Paperbacks had caused a revolution in post-war publishing, making books available to people who would have found hardbacks too expensive to buy. Poet Royston Ellis, the first published author the Beatles had ever met when they played music backing his poetry in 1960, is convinced that Paul latched on to the phrase 'paperback writer' from his conversations with them. "Although I was writing poetry books then, if they asked me what I wanted to be I would always say 'a paperback writer' because that's what you had to be if you wanted to reach a mass market," says Ellis, who went on to become a writer of travel books and plantation novels. "My ambition was to be a writer who sold his books and made money out of it. It was my equivalent of their ambition of making a million-selling single."

As with many Beatles' songs, the lyric was driven more by the sound of the words than their logic. Taken literally, it's about a paperback writer who has written a novel based on another novel, which is also about a paperback writer. The 'man named Lear' is probably a reference to Edward Lear, the Victorian painter who, although he never wrote a novel, did write nonsense poems and songs which John loved. The *Daily Mail* gets a mention because it was John's regular newspaper and it often would be lying around the Weybridge house when they were writing. Stories from the *Daily Mail* would later be used as inspiration for two songs on *Sgt Pepper*.

The main musical innovation on 'Paperback Writer' was the boosted bass sound. Paul was now playing a Rickenbacker and, through some studio innovations made by engineer Ken Townsend, the bass became the most prominent instrument on the track, bringing it into line with recent American recordings by Otis Redding and Wilson Pickett. The harmonies were inspired by the Beach Boys' album *Pet Sounds*.

'Paperback Writer' was a Number 1 single in many countries including Britain, America, Germany and Australia.

Poet and pop music critic Royston Ellis, who the Beatles ran into in Liverpool in 1960, was the first published author they had met.

Disc jockey Jimmy Savile (seated) was with the Beatles when the idea for 'Paperback Writer' was hatched.

RAIN

a sound which accurately reflected his stoned consciousness.

'Rain' was released as the reverse side of 'Paperback Writer'.

In 'There's A Place' on the Beatles' first album, John had voiced the opinion that it's your state of mind that matters, not the events 'out there'. In 'Rain', he picked up the theme again, although by this time psychedelic drugs had influenced his thinking. On one level, it was a simple song about "people moaning because...they don't like the weather" he said. But on another level it was a song that contained a message about the need to develop a state of mind in which we transcend both the good and the bad. In the same way that we should be indifferent to the weather, he feels that there is a need for people to rise above their circumstances. The use of the phrases 'I can show you' and 'Can you hear me?' indicated that John was starting to take his role as a spokesman seriously.

'Rain' was the first Beatles' track to suggest new transcendental states of consciousness, not just in its lyric but in the music. The mournfully dragged out vocal, the slowed-down instruments and the backward tape at the end were all a taste of things to come.

Backward taping became a controversial issue in the rock industry during the Seventies and Eighties when some artists were accused of concealing hidden messages within their recordings. The Beatles, who were responsible for making the first backwards tape on this track, had done it not to conceal messages but simply to produce a new range of sounds to add extra colour to their musical palette.

George Martin said that he came up with the idea experimenting on his own after the Beatles had left the studio. He played back his new effects to them the next day. John, who wrote 'Rain' at Kenwood, always claimed that he'd discovered the process trying to thread a demo tape of the song on his home recorder while high on marijuana. He was in such a disoriented state that he got the tape twisted and when he heard what sounded like an Arabic chant coming from his headphones, he knew he had found

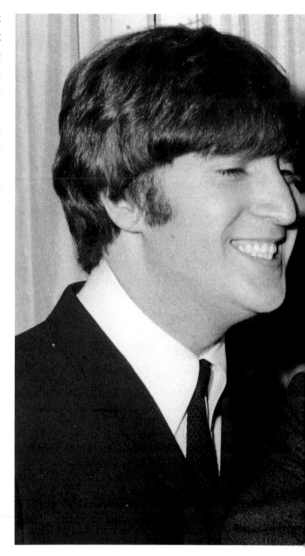

TAXMAN

'Taxman' was written by George Harrison after he found himself in the 'super-tax' bracket, which then meant paying 19 shillings and 3 pence (96p) out of every pound in tax.

Until 1966, the Beatles' touring schedule had been so hectic that there had been no time to sit down and

John, George and Paul with future Prime Minister Harold Wilson in 1964. Two years later, feeling squeezed by the punitive British tax system, the Beatles gave Mr Wilson a none-too-flattering name check in 'Taxman'.

examine the accounts. When they did get round to it, they didn't have as much money as they had imagined. "We were actually giving most (of our money) away in taxes," said George. "It was, and still is, typical. Why should this be so? Are we being punished for something we have forgotten to do?"

was rhymed with 'before you're dead' and there was none of the biting humour. Nor did the background chorus yet mention the names of the Prime Minister of Britain, Harold Wilson, and Leader of the Opposition, Edward Heath. That came later, when the song was recorded, giving them the distinction of

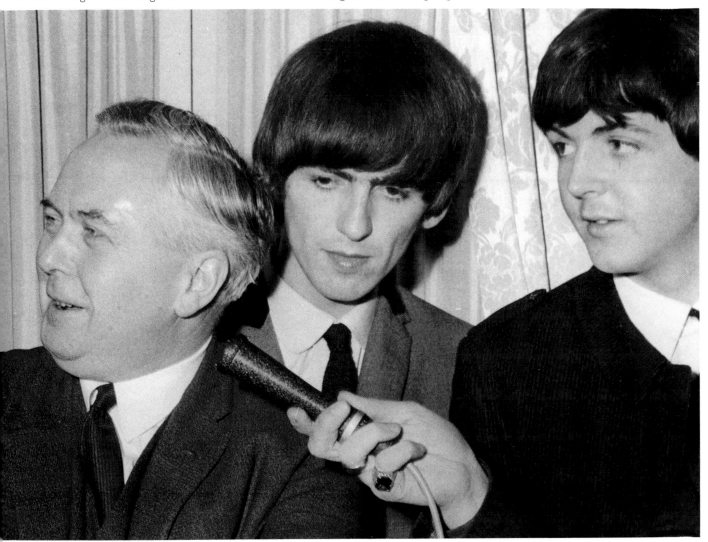

John later said that he had a hand in the writing of 'Taxman' and he was bitter that George had neglected to mention this in the account he wrote in his autobiography, *I Me Mine*. John claimed that George phoned him up as he was writing it. "I threw in a few one-liners to help the song along, because that's what he asked for," he said "I didn't want to do it... but because I loved him...I just sort of bit my tongue and said OK."

Certainly the published version is an improvement on George's rough draft, in which 'get some bread'

being the first living people to be named in a Beatles' song. Although the Beatles had never met Heath, they had met Wilson (a fellow Northerner) on several occasions and had each received MBEs in the honours list that Wilson approved after leading Britain's Labour Party to victory in 1964.

The Beatles – four enterprising young people with regional accents who came from mainly working class backgrounds – were just the sort of people Wilson wanted to encourage in his vision for a new classless Great Britain.

ELEANOR RIGBY

As in so many of his songs, the melody and first line of 'Eleanor Rigby' came to Paul as he sat playing his piano. It was through asking himself what type of person would be clearing rice up after a wedding that eventually led him to his ageing spinster whose loneliness was made worse by her job and having to clear away the debris left behind by family celebrations. "I couldn't think of any more so I put it away," he remarked.

Paul toyed with the song for a while but wasn't comfortable with the name of Miss Daisy Hawkins. He thought it didn't sound 'real' enough. Sixties folksinger Donovan remembered Paul playing him a version of the song where the protagonist was called Ola Na Tungee. "The words hadn't yet come out right for him," says Donovan."

Paul has always thought that he came up with the name of Eleanor because of having worked with Eleanor Bron in *Help!* Songwriter Lionel Bart, however, is convinced he took it from a gravestone in a cemetery close to Wimbledon Common, where they were both walking one day. "The name on the gravestone was Eleanor Bygraves," says Bart, "and Paul thought that would fit his song. He came back to my office and began playing it on my clavichord."

Paul came across the name Rigby in January 1966, while in Bristol visiting Jane Asher who was playing the role of Barbara Cahoun in John Dighton's *The Happiest Days Of Your Life*. The Theatre Royal, home of the Bristol Old Vic, is at 35 King Street and, as Paul was waiting for Jane to finish, he strolled past Rigby & Evens Ltd, Wine & Spirit Shippers, which was then on the opposite side of the road at number 22. This gave him the surname he was looking for.

The song was finally completed at Kenwood when John, George, Ringo and Pete Shotton crowded into the music room where Paul played it through. Someone suggested introducing an old man rifling

▲ **In the mid-Eighties the name Eleanor Rigby was discovered on a gravestone at St Peter's, Woolton, where John first met Paul at the church fete. Had the name been retrieved from Paul's subconscious after all these years?**

character which then became based on his memory of old people he had known as a child. Initially though, the fictional church cleaner featured in the song was to be called Miss Daisy Hawkins not Eleanor Rigby.

Paul started by imagining Daisy as a young girl but soon realized that anyone who cleaned churches after weddings was likely to be older. If she was older, he considered that she might not only have missed the wedding she was having to clear up after, she might also have missed her own. Maybe she was an through garbage cans whom Eleanor Rigby could have a romance with, but it was decided that would complicate the story. Paul had already introduced a character called Father McCartney. Ringo suggested that he could be darning his socks, an idea which Paul liked. George came up with a line about 'lonely people'. Pete Shotton suggested that it be changed from Father McCartney because people would think it was a reference to Paul's dad. A flick through the phone directory produced McKenzie as an alternative.

Paul was then stuck for an ending and it was Shotton who suggested that he bring the two lonely people together in the final verse as Father McKenzie takes Eleanor Rigby's funeral and stands by her graveside. At the time, the idea was dismissed by John who thought that Shotton had missed the point but Paul, who didn't say anything at the time, used the scene to finish off the song, and later acknowleged the help he'd received.

Extraordinarily, sometime in the Eighties the grave of an Eleanor Rigby was discovered in the graveyard of St Peter's Parish Church in Woolton, Liverpool, within yards of the spot where John and Paul had met in 1957. It's clear that Paul didn't get his idea directly from this grave, but is it possible that he saw it as a teenager and that the pleasing sound of the name lay buried in his subconscious until called up by the song? At the time he said: "I was looking for a name that was natural. Eleanor Rigby sounded natural."

In a further coincidence, the firm of Rigby and Evens Ltd, whose sign had inspired Paul in Bristol in 1966, was owned by a Liverpudlian, Frank Rigby, who established his company in Dale Street, Liverpool in the 19th century.

Paul has claimed that the name Rigby was taken from a shop front in Bristol, while Eleanor came from his former co-star Eleanor Bron, pictured here with the Beatles en route to a location for *Help!*

I'M ONLY SLEEPING

John at home in Weybridge reading the underground newspaper, *International Times*. Journalist Maureen Cleave called him "probably the laziest person in England".

The first draft of John's lyric for 'I'm Only Sleeping' was scratched on to the back of a letter from the Post Office, dated 25 March 1966, reminding him that he owed them 12 pounds and three shillings for an outstanding radio-phone bill. It's obvious from reading this early lyric that he was writing about the joys of staying in bed rather than any drug-induced dream state which the final recording, with its back-to-front guitar sounds, suggested.

John loved his bed. When he wasn't sleeping in it, he would be lying on it, or sitting propped up by pillows writing or watching television. 'I'm Only Sleeping' celebrated the bed and its value as a place for contemplation. It also prefigured 'Watching The Wheels' on the *Double Fantasy* album. The truth however was that John was losing his grip on the Beatles, spending too much time either in bed or lazing around Kenwood. Paul was now the one who was cracking the whip and making sure everyone turned up for sessions.

It was also in March 1966 that the *Evening Standard* ran Maureen Cleave's famous interview with John where he declared that "We're more popular than Jesus now; I don't know which will go first – rock'n'roll or Christianity." In the interview Cleave noted: "He can sleep almost indefinitely, is probably the laziest person in England. 'Physically lazy,' he said. 'I don't mind writing or reading or watching or speaking, but sex is the only physical thing I can be bothered with any more'. "

George being congratulated by Brian Epstein after his marriage to Pattie on January 21, 1966.

LOVE YOU TO

Although 'Norwegian Wood' had featured George on sitar, it had been as an afterthought. 'Love You To' was the first song written by George specifically for the instrument as, by now, he was studying it seriously. On this recording, he also featured tabla player Anil Bhagwat.

In his biography, *I Me Mine*, George recollected that he had used tabla and sitar on the basic track, overdubbing vocals and guitar at a later stage. However Mark Lewisohn, author of *The Complete Beatles Recording Sessions*, gained access to the original tapes and discovered that the sitar didn't appear until the third take and the tabla wasn't added until the sixth.

The song's working title was 'Granny Smith' – after the apple variety – simply because George couldn't come up with anything better. As the words 'love you to' don't appear in the song, the eventual title is rather puzzling: perhaps 'love me while you can' might have been more appropriate as this sums up what the song is saying.

HERE, THERE AND EVERYWHERE

With things starting to look up again in his romance with Jane Asher, Paul wrote what is widely regarded as his greatest love song.. Wanting to work with a structural challenge, he constructed each verse of the song around the three adverbs in the title. When he recorded it, he imagined the light voice of Marianne Faithfull.

Paul wrote 'Here, There And Everywhere' in June 1966 while sitting by John's outdoor pool. He'd heard the Beach Boys' newly-released *Pet Sounds*, which impressed him with its musical complexity and inventive vocal arrangements. Paul was particularly taken with the shimmering quality of 'God Only Knows' and wanted something which captured the same mood.

Paul pictured with Jane Asher, a fortnight before recording began on *Revolver*. With John, George and Ringo married, and Jane frequently out of town, Paul was beginning to lap up London's cultural offerings.

Lying in bed late one night, the idea of writing a children's song about different coloured submarines came into Paul's head. This was to develop into 'Yellow Submarine', the tale of a boy who listens to the tall stories of an old sailor about his exploits in the 'land of submarines' and decides to go sailing and see for himself.

Between 1962 and 1965, the Beatles had obeyed the unwritten rules for writing pop singles: they should have love as their subject; be just two minutes long, and be easily reproducible in concert. Now, gradually, they were enjoying seeing how many of these rules could be broken while still retaining the immediacy and excitement of chart music. 'Paperback Writer' was their first non-love single; 'Eleanor Rigby' and 'Rain' were the first of their songs to chart but not be played in concert, and 'Yellow Submarine' was their first singalong song.

Paul chose only short words because he wanted it to be a song which would be picked up quickly and sung by children. While writing it, he visited Donovan at his flat in Maida Vale. "We were in the habit of just dropping in on each other," remembers Donovan. "I was just waiting for the release of my album *Sunshine Superman* and so we played each other our latest songs. One of the songs Paul played me was about a yellow submarine but he said he was missing a line or two. He asked me if I'd like to make a contribution. I left the room for a bit and came back with 'Sky of blue and sea of green, In our yellow submarine'. It wasn't an earth shatter-

YELLOW SUBMARINE

'Yellow Submarine' started as a children's song and ended up three years later as the inspiration for an animated film.

ing creation but Paul liked it enough to use it on the eventual recording."

Released as the flip side of 'Eleanor Rigby' in August 1966, the same month that *Revolver* came out, the rumour quickly spread that the yellow submarine was a veiled reference to drugs. In New York, Nembutal capsules started to be known as 'yellow submarines'. Paul denied the allegations and said that the only submarine he knew that you could eat was a sugary sweet he'd come across in Greece while on holiday. These had to be dropped in water and were known as 'submarines'. "I knew 'Yellow Submarine' would get connotations," said Paul, "but it really was a children's song."

SHE SAID SHE SAID

When the Beatles visited Los Angeles in August 1965, they rented a house at 2850 Benedict Canyon for a week while they played dates in Portland, San Diego, the Hollywood Bowl and San Francisco.

All four Beatles threw a party there one afternoon, and Neil Aspinall, Roger McGuinn and David Crosby from the Byrds, actor Peter Fonda and *Daily Mirror* show business correspondent Don Short were among the guests. "Neil Aspinall was sent to escort me downstairs to the pool room," remembers Short, "because I was the only journalist on the premises. His job was to divert my attention from the fact that everyone else was taking acid."

Upstairs, out of Short's sight, everyone (except for Paul), was indeed tripping out on LSD. It was the first time John and George had deliberately taken the drug, and they were anxious to have a good experience after the hellish visions of their first, unintentional trip. Fonda had tripped out many times and saw his role as that of a guide. "I remember sitting out on the deck of the house with George, who was telling me that he thought he was dying," says Fonda. "I told him that there was nothing to be afraid of and that all he needed to do was to relax. I said that I knew what it was like to be dead because when I was 10 years old I'd accidentally shot myself in the stomach and my heart stopped beating three times while I was on the operating table because I'd lost so much blood. John was passing at the time and heard me saying 'I know what it's like to be dead'. He looked at me and said, 'You're making me feel I've never been born. Who put all that shit in your head?'"

Roger McGuinn felt that the idea had upset John because he was feeling insecure. "We were all on acid and John couldn't take it," McGuinn once said. "John said, 'Get this guy out of here'. It was morbid and bizarre. We'd just finished watching *Cat Ballou* with Jane Fonda in it and John didn't want anything to do with any of the Fondas. He was holding the movie against Peter and then what he said just added to it."

Indeed, the earliest demo of the song is far more aggressive than the final recording: 'I said, who put all that crap in your head, You know what it's like to be dead, And it's making me feel like my trousers are torn'. but John felt that as a song this was leading nowhere and abandoned it. Although it came out of a real experience it meant nothing, he said. It was just a sound. But days later he picked it up again and tried to find a middle eight. "I wrote the first thing that came into my head," said John, "and it was 'when I was a boy', in a different beat. But it was real, because it had just happened."

'She Said She Said' came together in two stages, but Fonda has no doubt of its origins. "When I heard *Revolver* for the first time I knew exactly where the song had come from, although John never acknowledged it to me and I never mentioned it to anyone."

American actor Peter Fonda was with John during his first organized acid trip in 1965. It was Fonda's comment that he knew what it was like to be dead that sparked off the lyric of the song 'She Said She Said'.

GOOD DAY SUNSHINE

Good Day Sunshine' was written by Paul at John's house on a particularly sunny day. Paul admitted in 1984 that it had been influenced by the Lovin' Spoonful, the New York-based group which had scored two American hits with 'Do You Believe In Magic?' and 'You Didn't Have To Be So Nice'. The Lovin' Spoonful were distinguished by the lyrical, folksy tunes of founder member John Sebastian who, as a solo artist, turned in a memo-

Some of the Beatles' best songs, including 'Help!', 'Paperback Writer', 'Good Day Sunshine', and 'Eleanor Rigby' were written at Kenwood, John's Surrey home.

The light folk-rock of the Lovin' Spoonful was the musical inspiration behind 'Good Day Sunshine'.

rable performance in the *Woodstock* movie.

The specific song that inspired Paul that day was 'Daydream', the Lovin' Spoonful's first British hit, which was in the Top 20 when the Beatles recorded *Revolver* in May 1966. Like 'Good Day Sunshine', 'Daydream' starts off with a choppy guitar beat before launching into a story of love-induced bliss heightened by beautiful weather: 'I'm blowin' the day to take a walk in the sun, And fall on my face on somebody's new mown lawn'.

"One of the wonderful things the Beatles had going for them," says Sebastian, "is that they were so original that when they did cop an idea from somebody else it never occurred to you. I thought there were one or two of their songs which were Spoonful-oid but it wasn't until Paul mentioned it in a *Playboy*

interview that I specifically realized we'd inspired 'Good Day Sunshine'."

'Daydream' itself was inspired by the Tamla beat on songs such as 'Where Did Our Love Go?' and 'Baby Love' that the Lovin' Spoonful heard while touring America with The Supremes. "I said, we gotta have a tune like 'Baby Love'," Sebastian remembers. "I wrote the song while trying to approximate the 'Baby Love' feel on one guitar. Sometimes you attempt to cop something and what you come up with is something very much your own."

The Lovin' Spoonful owed its foundation to a meeting between Sebastian and fellow guitarist Zal Yanovsky which took place at (Mama) Cass Elliot's house where the two men had been invited independently to see the Beatles debut on the *Ed Sullivan*

Show in February 1964. "Seeing the Beatles that night crystallized the idea for us both of wanting to be part of a self-contained unit which wrote its own music," remarks Sebastian. "I eventually got to meet them in April 1966. John, Paul and George came to see us at the Marquee Club in London's Soho and it was that night that George had his first proper meeting with Eric Clapton. Unfortunately we never got to play together because everyone was just so busy in those days. We had other meetings but we always seemed to be together because we were waiting for something else to happen."

"When they played Shea Stadium in New York in August 1966 I went backstage and had a few laughs with John who was beginning to look a lot like me. He was getting a lot of ribbing from the other Beatles about copying me. I always wished I could have spent more time with them."

AND YOUR BIRD CAN SING

It's hard to see how John could have dismissed 'And Your Bird Can Sing' as a "horror" (1971) and a "throwaway" (1980), even if the lyrics at first seem a bit impenetrable.

But John had always known how to play games. He suspected that even some of Dylan's lyrics were garbage dressed up as poetry and claimed he could do the same himself. At the time, with its talk of green birds, prized possessions and seven wonders it was assumed that with 'And Your Bird Can Sing' John was probably really on to something: that he'd had a vision of another dimension which most people couldn't fathom. Whereas in 1964 he would have knocked off a made-to-measure love song to fill out the empty spaces on an LP, by 1966, and under pressure, he was capable of coming up with a perfectly tailored piece of meaningless psychedelia.

FOR NO ONE

With its haunting melody and horn section, this was one of Paul's most beautiful songs. 'For No One' was written in a rented chalet in the Swiss ski resort of Klosters, where Paul and Jane Asher spent a brief holiday in March 1966. He then returned to work on *Revolver* and she began rehearsals for her role as the young Ellen Terry in *Sixty Thousand Nights* at the Royal Theatre, Bristol.

Through a series of flashbacks of their life together, the song captures the dawning realization that a partner's love has disappeared. In an early interview, Paul said that it was all about his own experience of living with a woman when he was fresh from leaving home. Later he was less specific, saying that he was thinking only of the character of a typical working girl.

DOCTOR ROBERT

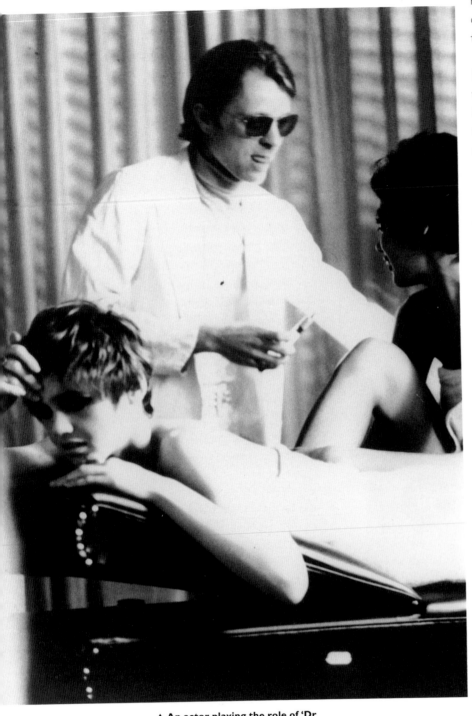

▲ **An actor playing the role of 'Dr Robert' in the Warhol movie,** *Ciao Manhattan.*

On their American visits the Beatles heard about a chic New York doctor who gave mysterious 'vitamin' injections. "We'd hear people say, 'You can get anything off him, any pills you want'," said Paul. "It was a big racket. The song was a joke about this fellow who cured everyone of everything with all these pills and tranquillizers. He just kept New York high."

Dr Robert was almost certainly Dr Robert Freymann, a 60-year-old German-born physician with a practice on East 78th Street. (The Dr Charles Roberts cited in some Beatles' books didn't exist. It was an alias used by the biographer of Warhol actress Edie Sedgwick, Jean Stein, to conceal the identity of another 'speed doctor'.) Known as Dr Robert or the Great White Father (he had a shock of white hair), Freymann was well connected with the city's arts scene. He had helped, among others, Theolonius Monk and Charlie Parker (whose death certificate he signed in 1955), and had a reputation for being generous with amphetamines. "I have a clientele that is remarkable, from every sphere of life," he once boasted. "I could tell you in ten minutes probably 100 famous names who come here." John, who wrote 'Dr Robert', was one of these famous names.

Initially prescribed as anti-depressants, amphetamines soon became a recreational drug for hip New Yorkers. One former patient of Dr Robert Freymann's, quoted in the *New York Times* in 1973, said: "If you want to make a big night of it you'd go over to Max's [Dr Max Jacobson] and then over to Freymann's and then down to Bishop's [Dr John Bishop]. It was just another kind of bar hopping." Film director Joel Shumacher, who used speed doctors in the Sixties, agrees: "We thought of them as vitamin injections but then became speed freaks."

Administering amphetamines was not illegal although regulations warned against prescribing 'excessive quantities' or giving the drug when it wasn't necessary. Dr Robert lost his licence to practise for six months in 1968 and, in 1975, was expelled from the New York State Medical Society for malpractice. Asked by the *New York Times* in March 1973 to defend his actions, he said: "the addicts killed a good drug". He died in 1987.

GOT TO GET YOU INTO MY LIFE

Got To Get You Into My Life' was written by Paul who had the idea of using brass, in an attempt to emulate the Motown sound recently developed by Holland-Dozier-Holland with The Supremes.

John believed that by mentioning 'another kind of mind' in the lyrics, Paul was alluding to his drug experiences. He has since confirmed that he was. He may have been the last Beatle to experiment with the drug, but he was the first to talk about it. His revelation, to a journalist from *Life* magazine, made headline news around the world. He later revealed that he'd already tripped on acid four times.

On June 19, 1967, a British TV reporter asked whether it would have been better to keep his drug-taking private. "I was asked a question by a newspaper and the decision was whether to tell a lie or tell the truth," he said. "I decided to tell him the truth but...if I'd had my way, I wouldn't have told anyone because I'm not trying to spread the word about this...I'll keep it a personal thing if he does too. But he wanted to spread it, so it's his responsibility for spreading it. Not mine."

I WANT TO TELL YOU

I Want To Tell You' was a song, written by George, about the frustrations of having things to say but being unable to articulate them. "It's about the avalanche of thoughts that are so hard to write down or say or transmit", he later said, adding that if he were to write the song again he would amend the bridge section which says: 'But if I seem to act unkind, It's only me, it's not my mind, That's confusing things' so that it was clear that his

mind *was* responsible for the confusion. "The mind is the thing that hops about telling us to do this and do that. What we need is to lose the mind," explained George.

Appropriately for a song which was about not knowing what to say, 'I Want To Tell You' was recorded under the nonsensical title 'Laxton's Superb'; a name of an English apple, first suggested by engineer Geoff Emerick. It later became known as 'I Don't Know', after George Martin had asked George what he wanted to title it and had been given this negative answer.

TOMORROW NEVER KNOWS

As 'Tomorrow Never Knows' is the last track on the album, and the clearest signpost of things to come, it's often assumed that it was the last track recorded. In fact, it was the first track laid down for *Revolver*. Certainly the weirdest and most experimental track to appear under the Beatles' name at the time, this was John's attempt to capture something of the LSD experience in words and sounds.

The words were borrowed, adapted and embellished from Timothy Leary's 1964 book *The Psychedelic Experience*, which was itself a poetic reinterpretation of the ancient Tibetan *Book Of The Dead*. John had been sent the book by Barry Miles, who ran Indica Books in Southampton Row and was an influential figure on the British underground scene in the Sixties. He had an arrangement with the Beatles to send them significant books, magazines and newspapers to keep them up-to-date.

Leary, known as the High Priest of LSD, had spent seven months in the Himalayas studying Tibetan Buddhism under Lama Govinda. *The Psychedelic Experience* was a direct result of this period of study. "I would ask Lama Govinda questions," says Leary, "and then I tried to translate what he said into something useful for people. *Book Of The Dead* really means 'Book Of The Dying' but it's your ego rather than your body which is dying. The book is a classic. It's the bible of Tibetan Buddhism. The concept of Buddhism is of the void and of reaching the void – that is what John captured in the song."

The working title of the track was in fact 'The Void', taken from Leary's line "Beyond the restless flowing electricity of Life is the ultimate reality – the void." Its eventual title was a Ringoism which John snatched at because it added some deceptive levity to what otherwise might have sounded like a bleak journey into nothingness. The actual sound of the piece, which consists of 16 tape loops made by each of the Beatles fading in and out, grew out of Paul's home experimentation on his tape recorder. "He had this little Grundig," says George Martin. "He found by moving the erase head and putting a loop on he could actually saturate the tape with a single noise. It would go round and round and eventually the tape couldn't absorb any more and he'd bring it in and play it."

For the vocal track, John wanted it to sound like a chorus of Tibetan monks chanting on a mountain top." He said he wanted to hear the words but he didn't want to hear him," says George Martin. The result, which sounds as if John is singing at the end of a long tunnel, was achieved by feeding his voice through a Leslie speaker.

Timothy Leary, known as the 'High Priest of LSD', referred to the Beatles as messengers from God – "inspired revealers of the great vibration."

..............................▶

SGT PEPPER'S LONELY HEARTS CLUB BAND

▲ **Paul was the brains behind *Sgt Pepper*, the Beatles' most experimental album.**

The fruitful period which produced the singles 'Penny Lane' and 'Strawberry Fields Forever' as well as the *Sgt Pepper* album was the first in which the Beatles were totally devoted to the studio. They took an unprecedented 105 hours to record both sides of the single and then a further five months to complete the album.

Sgt Pepper was the brainchild of Paul, who conceived the album as a show staged by a fictional Edwardian brass band transported through time into the psychedelic age and played, of course, by the electronically equipped Beatles. Released in June 1967, *Sgt Pepper* was *the* album of what became known as 'The Summer Of Love' – a brief season when the hippie ethic that radiated from San Francisco seemed to pervade the whole of the Western world. For anyone who was young at the time, the music automatically evokes the sight of beads and kaftans, the sound of tinkling bells and the aroma of marijuana masked by joss sticks. Despite this, there were only four songs on *Sgt Pepper* – 'Lucy

By virtue of the Beatles' song, Penny Lane has become one of the best known street names in Britain. The original signs have long since been stolen by zealous fans – those that exist today are firmly fixed in vandal-proof positions.

In The Sky With Diamonds', 'She's Leaving Home', 'Within You Without You' and 'A Day In The Life' – that made specific reference to the social upheaval caused by the changing youth culture.

The rest of the songs were very British pop songs, tackling a range of domestic subjects from neighbourliness ('A Little Help From My Friends') and self-improvement ('Getting Better'), through suburban living ('Good Morning, Good Morning') and home decoration ('Fixing A Hole'), to Victorian entertainment ('Being For The Benefit Of Mr Kite'). The language of the songs was often deliberately old-fashioned – 'guaranteed to raise a smile', 'may I inquire discreetly', 'meeting a man from the motor trade', 'a splendid time is guaranteed for all', 'indicate precisely what you mean to say' – as if this really was an Edwardian production staged by the good Sergeant Pepper and his men from the local Lonely Hearts club.

Yet, the spirit of 1967 did shape the album in other significant ways. It encouraged the belief that limits to the imagination were culturally imposed and should therefore be challenged. Anything that appeared artistically possible was attempted, including a frenetic orchestral climax on 'A Day In The Life' and a special high note that only a dog could hear on the playout groove.

Almost all the conventions of album-making were overturned. *Sgt Pepper* was one of the first records to have a gatefold sleeve, printed lyrics, decorated inner bag, free gift and an elaborately staged cover photograph. It was also one of the first albums to present itself as a total concept rather than a simple collection of songs. "Basically *Sgt Pepper* was McCartney's album, not Lennon's," says Barry Miles, who was the group's main contact on the London underground scene at the time. "People make the mistake of thinking it must have been Lennon's because he was so hip. Actually, he was taking so many drugs and trying to get rid of his ego that it was much more McCartney's idea."

Sgt Pepper was a tremendous commercial and critical success, reaching Number 1 in the album charts in Britain and America. Almost 30 years later, it still regularly tops critics' polls as the greatest rock album ever made.

PENNY LANE

Although Penny Lane is a Liverpool street it's also the name given to the area that surrounds its junction with Smithdown Road. None of the places mentioned in 'Penny Lane' exists in the lane itself. Indeed to anyone not raised in this area of Liverpool it is, as musician and art critic George Melly once put it, a "dull suburban shopping centre". But to Paul and John, who had spent their early years in the neighbourhood, it was a symbol of glorious childhood innocence when everyone seemed friendly and the sun shone for ever in a clear blue sky.

John had been the first to refer to Penny Lane in song, having tried to incorporate it into 'In My Life', but it was Paul who eventually picked it up and made it work. He created a Liverpool street scene that could have been taken from a children's picture book with a pretty nurse, a jolly barber, an eccentric banker, a patriotic fireman and some friendly passers by. "It's part fact," he admitted. "It's part nostalgia."

There was a barber's shop in Penny Lane, run by

The 'shelter in the middle of the round-about' has changed since this picture of Penny Lane was taken, but the bank on the corner looks the same as it did when Paul wrote the song in 1966.

a Mr Bioletti who claimed to have cut hair for John, Paul and George as children; there were two banks, a fire station in Allerton Road and, in the middle of the roundabout, a shelter. The banker without a mac and fireman with a portrait of the Queen in his pocket never really existed. They were Paul's embellishments. "I wrote that the barber had photographs of every head he'd had the pleasure of knowing," said Paul. "Actually he just had photos of different hairstyles. But all the people who come and go do stop and say hello."

Finger pie was a Liverpudlian sexual reference included in the song to amuse the locals. "It was just a nice little joke for the Liverpool lads who like a bit of smut," said Paul. "For months afterwards, girls serving in local chip shops had to put up with requests for 'fish and finger pie'."

Liverpool poet Roger McGough, who was in the Sixties group Scaffold with Paul's brother Mike, believes that 'Penny Lane' and 'Strawberry Fields' were significant because it was the first time that places other than Memphis, and roads other than Route 66 or Highway 61, had been celebrated in rock. "The Beatles were starting to write songs about home," McGough says. "They began to draw on things like the rhymes we used to sing in the streets and old songs our parents remembered from the days of the music halls. Liverpool

didn't have a mythology until they created one."

Today, Penny Lane has become an important landmark on any Beatles' tour of Liverpool and yet the success of the song has meant that many of its features have changed. All the original street signs were stolen and so those that remain are screwed down tightly and very high up. The barber's shop has become a unisex salon with a picture of the Beatles displayed in the window. The shelter on the roundabout has been renovated and re-opened as Sgt Pepper's Bistro. The Penny Lane Wine Bar has the song's lyrics painted above its windows.

Both 'Strawberry Fields Forever' and 'Penny Lane' were intended for the new album, but Capitol Records in America were pushing for a single, and it was released as a double A side. In America it took the top spot but in Britain it was kept at Number 2 by Engelbert Humperdinck's hit, 'Please Release Me'.

STRAWBERRY FIELDS FOREVER

In the autumn of 1966, John went to Spain after accepting the part of Gripweed in Dick Lester's film of How I Won The War. While relaxing on the beach at Almeria, John started work on 'Strawberry Fields Forever', a song he imagined as a slow-talking blues number. He completed it in a large house he was renting in nearby Santa Isabel.

It started out as a nostalgic view of a Salvation Army orphanage in Woolton, where he, Pete Shotton and Ivan Vaughan used to play amongst the trees, and ended up, like so many of John's songs, as a rumination on states of consciousness. Strawberry Field (John added the 's') was a large Victorian building with extensive wooded grounds in Beaconsfield Road, a five-minute walk from John's home in Menlove Avenue. Since 1936, it had been a children's home with an annual fete, which Aunt Mimi regularly took him to.

The gothic grandeur of the building and the mystery of the woods fascinated John. He recognized it as a place where he could be alone and let his imagination run free. He soon discovered that there was a more direct route from his garden into the grounds and it became one of his places of escape.

Because of these romantic associations, Strawberry Field became a symbol of his desire to be alone, of his feeling that he was somehow set apart from his contemporaries. If 'Strawberry Fields Forever' is a song about John seeing the world in a different way to everyone around him, the meaning is clearer in the earliest version of the lyric, where he wrote that no-one is on his wavelength, they're either 'too high or too low'. By the time he came to record it, he had deliberately obscured this meaning — perhaps for fear of being labelled pretentious — by singing that no-one was in his 'tree', as this was either too high or low.

▲ **The original Strawberry Field building has since been replaced by a modern block.**

SGT PEPPER'S LONELY HEARTS CLUB BAND

One of the problems of success was that people had begun to expect so much from the Beatles. To deflect this pressure, Paul came up with the idea of taking on the personae of Sgt Pepper and his musicians. As Beatles they had become self-conscious but as the Lonely Hearts Club Band they had no expectations to live up to.

Paul conceived the idea on a flight home to London from Nairobi in November 1966. During an earlier part of this holiday when he was in France he had used a disguise to get around and do ordinary things without being spotted. This had led him to consider how free the Beatles would be if they as a group could adopt a disguise.

The aliases, however, were never sustained beyond the opening and closing tracks and the segue into 'A Little Help From My Friends', where Ringo is introduced as Billy Shears. The plan still helped because it gave the impression that *Sgt Pepper's Lonely Hearts Club Band* was a 'concept album'. "The songs, if you listen to them, have no connection at all," George Martin admits. "Paul said ' Why don't we make the band 'Pepper' and Ringo 'Billy Shears' because it gives a nice beginning to the thing? It wasn't really a concept album at all. It was just a question of me trying to make something coherent by doing segues as much as possible."

Sgt Pepper and his band achieved the seemingly impossible feat of being quintessentially English at the same time as being very West Coast 1967. Paul had intended to play it both ways, writing old-fashioned lyrics delivered with a satirical psychedelic intensity, and using a title that appealed to the late Sixties vogue for long and surreal band names – Jefferson Airplane, Quicksilver Messenger Service, Incredible String Band, Big Brother and the Holding Company. "They're a bit of a brass band in a way," Paul said at the time, "but they're also a rock band because they've got that San Francisco thing."

The origin of the name Sgt Pepper is disputed. The Beatles' former road manager Mal Evans is sometimes cited as having created it as a jokey substitute for 'salt 'n' pepper'. Others suggest the name was derived from the popular American soft drink 'Dr Pepper'.

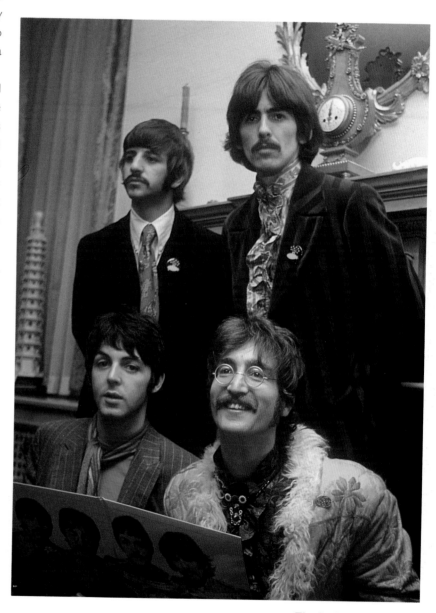

▲ The *Sgt Pepper* album was launched to the media on May 19, 1967, from Brian Epstein's Belgravia home.

WITH A LITTLE HELP FROM MY FRIENDS

Journalist Hunter Davies was granted a unique insight into the Beatles' writing methods while working on their authorized biography. On the afternoon of March 29, 1967, Davies went to Paul's house and watched as Paul and John worked out 'With A Little Help From My Friends'. It was one of the first times a journalist had witnessed a Lennon and McCartney song in the process of creation. "They wanted to do a Ringo-type song," remembers Davies. "They knew it would have to be for the kids, a sing-along type of song. That was what they thought was missing on the album so far. I recorded them trying to get all the rhymes right and somewhere I've got a list of all the ones they didn't use."

At the beginning of the afternoon, all the writers had was a chorus line and a bit of a melody. For the first two hours, they thrashed away on guitars, neither of them getting very far. It was John who eventually suggested starting each verse with a question. The line, 'Do you believe in love at first sight?' didn't have enough syllables and so it became 'a love at first sight'. John answer to this was 'Yes, I'm certain that it happens all the time'. This was then followed by 'Are you afraid when you turn out the light?' but rephrased to 'What do you see when...'.

Cynthia Lennon then came in and suggested 'I'm just fine' as an answer, but John dismissed it saying that 'just' was either a filler or a meaningless word. Instead he tried 'I know it's mine', eventually coming up with the more substantial 'I can't tell you, but I know it's mine'.

After a few hours of playing around with words, their minds began to wander. They began fooling around, singing 'Can't Buy Me Love' and playing 'Tequila' (a 1958 hit for the Champs) on the piano. "When they got stuck, they would go back and do a rock'n'roll song," remembers Davies. "Sometimes they would sing an Englebert Humperdinck song and just bugger around and then get back to the job in hand."

A recording session was due to begin at seven o'clock and they called Ringo to tell him that his song was ready, even though the lyrics weren't quite there yet. The lyrics were completed in the studio, where ten takes of the song were recorded that night. As John had an injured finger at the time it was initially known as 'Bad Finger Boogie' but was later changed to the rather apt 'With A Little Help From My Friends'.

LUCY IN THE SKY WITH DIAMONDS

Lucy O' Donnell pictured around the time that she inspired Julian Lennon's painting – which, in turn, instigated the writing of 'Lucy In The Sky With Diamonds'.

···············➤

One afternoon early in 1967, Julian Lennon came home from his nursery school with a painting that he said was of his classmate, four-year-old Lucy O'Donnell. Explaining his artwork to his father, Julian described it as Lucy – 'in the sky with diamonds'.

This phrase stuck in John's mind and triggered off the stream of associations that led to the writing of the dream-like 'Lucy In The Sky With Diamonds', one of three tracks on the *Sgt Pepper* album which received

special media attention because it was thought to be 'about drugs'. Although it's unlikely that John would have written such a piece of reverie without ever having experimented, this song was equally affected by his love of surrealism, word play and the works of Lewis Carroll.

The suggestion that the song was a description of an LSD trip appeared to be substantiated when it was noted that the initials in the title spelt LSD. Yet John consistently denied this, going into great detail in interviews about the drugs he *had* taken. He insisted that the title was taken from what Julian had said about his painting. Julian himself recalls, "I don't know why I called it that or why it stood out from all my other drawings but I obviously had an affection for Lucy at that age. I used to show dad everything I'd built or painted at school and this one sparked off the idea for a song about Lucy in the sky with diamonds."

Lucy O'Donnell (now 36 and working as a teacher with special needs' children) lived near the Lennon family in Weybridge and she and Julian were pupils at Heath House, a nursery school run by two old ladies in a rambling Edwardian house. "I can remember Julian at school," says Lucy, who didn't discover that she'd been immortalized in a Beatles' song until she was 13. "I can remember him very well. I can see his face clearly ... we used to sit alongside each other in proper old-fashioned desks. The house was enormous and they had heavy curtains to divide the classrooms. Julian and I were a couple of little menaces from what I've been told."

John claimed that the hallucinatory images in the song were inspired by the 'Wool And Water' chapter in Lewis Carroll's *Through The Looking Glass*, where Alice is taken down a river in a rowing boat by the Queen, who has suddenly changed into a sheep.

As a child, *Alice's Adventures In Wonderland* and *Through The Looking Glass* were two of John's favourite books. He said that it was partly through reading them that he realized the images in his own mind weren't indications of insanity. "Surrealism to me is reality," he said. "Psychedelic vision is reality to

me and always was."

For similar reasons, John was attracted to *The Goon Show*, the British radio comedy programme. *The Goon Show* scripts, principally written by Spike Milligan, lampooned establishment figures, attacked post-war stuffiness and popularized a surreal form of humour. The celebrated Beatle 'wackiness' owed a lot to the Goons, as did John's poetry and writing. He told Spike Milligan that 'Lucy In The Sky With Diamonds' and several other songs had been partly inspired by his love of *Goon Show* dialogue. "We used to talk about 'plasticine ties' in *The Goon Show* and this crept up in Lucy as 'plasticine porters with looking glass ties'," says Milligan who, as a friend of George Martin, sat in on some of the *Sgt Pepper* sessions. "I knew Lennon quite well," he said. "He used to talk a lot about comedy. He was a *Goon Show* freak. It all stopped when he married Yoko Ono. Everything stopped. He never asked for me again."

When Paul arrived at Weybridge to work, John had only completed the first verse and the chorus. For the rest of the writing they traded lines and images; Paul coming up with 'newspaper taxis' and 'cellophane flowers', John with 'kaleidoscope eyes'.

▲ **Published for the first time, this is the drawing which Julian Lennon told his father was of "Lucy – in the sky with diamonds".**

GETTING BETTER

Much of *Sgt Pepper* was written on the hoof as the album was being recorded, with John and Paul snatching ideas from whatever was happening around them. Hunter Davies was with Paul on one such occasion – when he was struck by the phrase which became the basis of 'Getting Better'. "I was walking around Primrose Hill with Paul and his dog Martha," he says. "It was bright and sunny – the first spring-like morning we'd had that year. Thinking about the weather Paul said, 'It's getting better'. He was meaning that spring was here but he started laughing and, when I asked him why, he told me that it reminded him of something."

The phrase took Paul's mind back to drummer Jimmy Nicol, who briefly became a Beatle in June 1964, substituting on tour for a sick Ringo. Nicol was an experienced musician who had worked with the Spotnicks and Georgie Fame's Blue Flames, but he had to learn to be a Beatle overnight. Called in by George Martin on June 3, he met John, Paul and George that afternoon and was on stage with them in Copenhagen the following night. A week later in Adelaide, after playing just five dates, Nicol was given his fee, together with a jokey 'retirement present', a gold watch. "After every concert, John and Paul would go up to Jimmy Nicol and ask him how he was getting on," says Hunter Davies. "All that Jimmy would ever say was, 'It's getting better'. That was the only comment they could get out of him. It ended up becoming a joke phrase and whenever the boys thought of Jimmy they'd think of 'it's getting better'."

After the walk on Primrose Hill, Paul drove back to his home in St John's Wood and sang the phrase over and over, while picking out a tune on his guitar. Then he worked it out on the piano in his music room which had a strange tone which sounded almost out of tune. "That evening John came round," remembers Davies. "Paul suggested writing a song called 'It's Getting Better'. Now and again, they'd write whole songs individually, but mostly one of them had half a song and the other one would finish it off. That's how it was with this one. Paul played what he'd come up with to John and together they finished it."

'Getting Better' proved an interesting example of how they curbed each other's excesses when they worked together. The optimism of Paul's chorus, where everything is improving because of love, is counterbalanced by John's confession that he was once a schoolboy rebel, an angry young man and a wife beater. When Paul sings that things are getting better all the time, John chimes in with 'it couldn't get much worse'.

Asked about the song years later, John admitted it referred to his aggressive tendencies, "I sincerely believe in love and peace. I am a violent man who has learned not to be violent and regrets his violence."

Jimmy Nicol became a Beatle overnight in June 1964, but he only occupied the drum seat until Ringo was well enough to return. His most lasting contribution to the group was his phrase 'it's getting better'.

FIXING A HOLE

Paul was advised by his accountant to invest his earnings in more property. In June 1966, without having seen it, he bought a semi-derelict farm house called High Park near Campbeltown on the west coast of Scotland with 400 acres of grazing land around it. The house hadn't been lived in for five years and was in poor condition from the regular battering of rain and sea winds. The brown walls were dark with damp, the only furniture consisted of potato boxes and there was no bath. When Paul eventually visited High Park with Jane Asher he found that it provided a welcome release from the pressures of London. The farm was too remote for even the keenest of fans to bother him and few locals knew who owned it.

'Fixing A Hole' was another *Sgt Pepper* song pounced on for its drug associations. People just couldn't believe that Paul was talking about fixing holes in the DIY sense. That was too simple. They assumed that he was talking about fixing a hole in his arm – in other words, a heroin fix. But the song really was about renovation and fixing a hole in the roof where the rain gets in. Paul had recently performed this simple task in the most primitive of conditions at his new Scottish property, a job which had the effect of refocusing his thinking and making him re-assess his immediate priorities.

This newfound practicality did not stop Paul doing up his property 'in a colourful way' as remembered by Alistair Taylor, Brian Epstein's assistant who accompanied Paul and Jane on their first visit to High Park. "The brown paint made the farmhouse look like the inside of an Aero bar," he wrote in his book *Yesterday: My Life With The Beatles*. "Paul decided he'd had enough of it so he went into Campbeltown and bought lots of packets of coloured pens. The three of us spent the next few hours just doodling in all these colours, spreading them all over the wall and trying to relieve the gloom."

In 1967, in an interview with artist Alan Aldridge, Paul was probed on the drug associations: "If you're a junky sitting in a room and fixing a hole then that's what it will mean to you, but when I wrote it I meant if there's a crack, or the room is uncolourful, then I'll paint it."

SHE'S LEAVING HOME

In February 1967, Paul came across a newspaper article about a 17-year-old schoolgirl studying for her A level exams who'd been missing from home for over a week. Her distressed father was quoted as saying, "I cannot imagine why she should run away. She has everything here."

The subject of teenage runaways was a topical one in 1967. As part of the creation of an alternative society, counter-culture guru Timothy Leary had urged his followers to drop out, to abandon education and 'straight' employment.

The story of teenage runaway Melanie Coe was published in London's *Daily Mail* on February 27, 1967.

▲ Melanie Coe, pictured standing behind the Beatles during a *Ready Steady Go!* rehearsal in October 1963, later became a teenage runaway and the subject of one of Paul's most poignant songs.

hand-made clothes in silk and cashmere and even my own car.

"Then there was the line 'after living alone for so many years', which really struck home to me because I was an only child and I always felt alone," Melanie continues. "I never communicated with either of my parents. It was a constant battle. I left because I couldn't face them any longer. I heard the song when it came out and thought it was about someone like me but never dreamed it was actually about me. I can remember thinking that I didn't run off with a man from the motor trade, so it couldn't have been me! I must have been in my twenties when my mother said she'd seen Paul on television and he'd said that the song was based on a story in a newspaper. That's when I started telling my friends it was about me."

As a result, streams of young people headed for San Francisco, centre of Flower Power, leading the FBI to announce a record number of 90,000 runaways that year.

With only the newspaper's facts to guide him, Paul created a haunting song of a young girl sneaking away from her claustrophobically respectable home in search of fun and romance in the swinging Sixties. What he didn't know at the time was how accurate his speculation was. He also had no idea that he had met the girl in question just three years before.

The girl in the newspaper report Paul had read was Melanie Coe, the daughter of John and Elsie Coe who lived in Stamford Hill, north London. The only differences between her story and the story told in the song are that she met a man from a gambling casino rather than from 'the motor trade' (the song's reference to the Beatles' Liverpool friend Terry Doran), and that she walked out in the afternoon while her parents were at work, rather than in the morning while they were asleep. "The amazing thing about the song was how much it got right about my life," says Melanie. "It quoted the parents as saying 'we gave her everything money could buy' which was true in my case. I had two diamond rings, a mink coat,

Melanie's case was a good example of how the Sixties' alternative culture caused a clash of values between generations, and expanded the gulf between them. Melanie wanted a freedom she'd heard about but could not find at home. Her father was a fairly well-off executive and her mother a hairdresser, but their marriage was dry and brittle. The family was not religious: to them the most important things in life were respectability, cleanliness and money. "My mother didn't like any of my friends," says Melanie. "I wasn't allowed to bring anyone home. She didn't like me going out. I wanted to act but she wouldn't let me go to drama school. She wanted me to become a dentist. She didn't like the way I dressed. She didn't want me to do anything which I wanted to do. My father was weak. He just went along with whatever my mother said, even when he disagreed with her."

It was through music that Melanie found consolation. At the age of 13, she began clubbing in the West End of London and, when the legendary live television show *Ready Steady Go!* began transmission in late 1963, she became a regular dancer on the programme. Her parents would often scour the clubs and drag her back home. If she came back late, she would be hit. "When I went out, I could be *me*," she said. "In fact, in the clubs I was encouraged to be myself and to have a good time. Dancing was my passion. I was crazy for the music of the time and couldn't wait until the next single came out. When the song says 'Something was denied', that something was *me*. I wasn't allowed to be me. I was looking for excitement and affection. My mother wasn't affectionate at all. She never kissed me."

On Friday, October 4, 1963, Melanie won a *Ready Steady Go* mime competition. By coincidence, it happened to be the first time the Beatles were on the show and she was presented with her award by Paul McCartney. Each of the Beatles then gave her a signed message. "I spent that day in the studios going through rehearsals," she says, "so I was around the Beatles most of that time. Paul wasn't particularly chatty and John seemed distant but I did spend time talking to George and Ringo."

Melanie's flight from home took her into the arms of David, a croupier she had met in a club. They rented a flat in Sussex Gardens near Paddington Station and, while out walking one afternoon, they saw her photo on the front page of an evening newspaper. "I immediately went back to the flat and put on dark glasses and a hat," she said. "From then on, I lived in terror that they'd find me. They did discover me after about ten days, because I think I'd let it slip where my boyfriend worked. They talked to his boss who persuaded me to call them up. When they eventually called to see me, they bundled me into the back of their car and drove me home."

In order to finally escape from her parents, Melanie married at 18. The marriage didn't last much more than a year and by the age of 21 she had moved to America to live in an ashram, and tried to make it as an actress. Melanie now lives outside London with two young children and a partner, buying and selling Fifties Hollywood jewellery. "If I had my life to live over again, I wouldn't choose to do it the same way," Melanie remarks. "What I did was very dangerous but I was lucky. I suppose it is nice to be immortalized in a song but it would have been nicer if it had been for doing something other than running away from home."

BEING FOR THE BENEFIT OF MR KITE!

John standing beside the Victorian poster which provided almost all of the names and phrases for 'Being For The Benefit Of Mr Kite!'. The poster now hangs in the bedroom of his younger son, Sean Lennon.

In January and February of 1967, the Beatles went to Knole Park near Sevenoaks in Kent to make a film to accompany 'Strawberry Fields Forever'. "There was an antique shop close to the hotel we were using in Sevenoaks," says former Apple employee Tony Bramwell. "John and I wandered in and John spotted this framed Victorian circus poster and bought it."

Printed in 1843, the poster proudly announced that Pablo Fanque's Circus Royal would be presenting the 'grandest night of the season' at Town Meadows, Rochdale, in the north of England. The production was to be 'for the benefit of Mr Kite' and would feature 'Mr J Henderson the celebrated somerset (sic) thrower' who would 'introduce his extraordinary trampoline leaps and somersets over men and horses, through hoops, over garters and lastly through a hogshead of real fire. In this branch of the profession Mr H challenges the world'. Messrs Kite and Henderson were said to assure the public that 'this night's production will be one of the most splendid ever produced in this town, having been some days in preparation'.

Inspired by the finely-wrought language and the evocative names of the performers, John began to

▲ **The real Pablo Fanque, photographed around 1855, 16 years before his death in Stockport, Lancashire. As a celebrated Victorian circus owner, he employed all of the famous performers of his day, including the Hendersons and William Kite.**

compose a song based on the poster. By now it was hanging on the wall of his music room and Pete Shotton can remember him squinting at the words while he picked out a tune on his piano. John changed a few facts when composing the song. On the poster it was Mr Henderson who offered to challenge the world, not Mr Kite: the Hendersons weren't 'late of Pablo Fanque's Fair' anyway, it was Kite who was 'late of Wells's Circus'. In order to rhyme with 'don't be late', John had events moved from Rochdale to Bishopsgate and to rhyme with 'will all be there' he changed the circus to a fair. The original horse was named Zanthus rather than Henry.

Pablo Fanque, Mr Kite and the Hendersons were never more than colourful names to John but records show that, 150 years ago, they were stars in the circus world. Mr Kite was William Kite, son of circus proprietor, James Kite, and an all-round performer. In 1810 he formed Kite's Pavilion Circus and 30 years later he was with Wells's Circus. He is believed to have worked in Pablo Fanque's Circus from 1843 to 1845.

Pablo Fanque was a multi-talented performer, who became the first black circus proprietor in Britain. His real name was William Darby and he was born in Norwich in 1796 to John and Mary Darby. He started calling himself Pablo Fanque in the 1830s.

The Hendersons were John (wire-walker, equestrian, trampolinist and clown) and his wife Agnes, who was the daughter of circus owner Henry Hengler. The Hendersons travelled all over Europe and Russia during the 1840s and 1850s. The 'somersets' which Mr Henderson performed on 'solid ground' were somersaults, 'garters' were banners held between two people and a 'trampoline' in those days was a wooden springboard rather than stretched canvas.

At the time, John saw 'Being For The Benefit Of Mr Kite!' as a throwaway, telling Hunter Davies, "I wasn't proud of that. There was no real work. I was just going through the motions because we needed a new song for *Sgt Pepper* at that moment." By 1980, he had radically revised his opinion. He told *Playboy* interviewer David Sheff: "It's so cosmically beautiful... The song is pure, like a painting, a pure watercolour."

WITHIN YOU WITHOUT YOU

George first became interested in Eastern thought as a consequence of discovering the sitar in 1965 and, having studied the instrument under Ravi Shankar, made his first explicit statement of his new-found philosophy in 'Within You Without You'.

Written as a recollected conversation, the song put forward the view that Western individualism – the idea that we each have our own ego – is based on an illusion that encourages separation and division. In order for us to draw closer and get rid of the 'space between us all', we need to give up this illusion of ego and realize that we are essentially 'all one'. Although the view expressed in 'Within You Without You' was drawn from Hindu teaching, it touched a chord amongst those experimenting with acid at the time. Through a chemically-induced destruction of ego, acid trippers often felt as if they had been

absorbed into a greater 'cosmic consciousness'.

George began to compose the song one night after a dinner party at the home of Klaus Voormann, a German artist and musician he had first met in Hamburg and who had designed the cover for *Revolver*. Voormann was now in living in London, married to former *Coronation Street* actress Christine Hargreaves and playing bass for Manfred Mann. Also present at the party were Tony King and Pattie Harrison. King had known the Beatles since they first arrived in London in 1963 and he would later work for Apple in London. "Klaus had this pedal harmonium and George went into an adjoining room and started fiddling around on it," remembers King. "It made these terrible groaning noises and, by the end of the evening, he'd worked something out and was starting to sing snatches of it to us. It's interesting that the eventual recording of 'Within You Without You' had the same sort of groaning sound that I'd heard on the harmonium because John once told me that the instrument you compose a song on determines the tone of a song. A number originally written on the piano sounds totally different to one worked out on a guitar."

King's recollection of the evening is of a typical hip Sixties affair with joints being smoked and lots of cosmic ideas floating around: "We were all on about the wall of illusion and the love that flowed between us but none of us knew what we were talking about. We all developed these groovy voices. It was a bit ridiculous really. It was as if we were sages all of a sudden. We all felt as if we had glimpsed the meaning of the universe.

"When I first met George in 1963, he was Mr Fun, Mr Stay Out All Night," King continues. "Then all of a sudden, he found LSD and Indian religion and he became very serious. Things went from rather jolly weekends, where we'd have steak and kidney pie and sit around giggling, to these rather serious weekends where everyone walked around blissed out and talked about the meaning of the universe. It was never really my cup of tea but we all got caught up in it because we were young, easily influenced, and around famous people. I remember when the Dutch artists Simon and Marijke, who later painted the Apple shop front, were at George's, I got fed up with it all and went down the pub. Just as I was walking down George's drive, Simon and Marijke floated past

▲ **Paul, John, George and partners listen attentively to the Maharishi Mahesh Yogi speaking at the London Hilton on August 24, 1967. The Beatles' interest in Indian religion stemmed principally from George and Pattie and was first explicitly stated in George's song 'Within You Without You'.**

in yards of chiffon and said in their groovy voices 'Ooh. Where are you going man?' I told them I was going for a Guinness. They said. "Oh. Say something beautiful for me, will you?"

In an interview with *International Times* in 1967, George said: "We're all one. The realization of human love reciprocated is such a gas. It's a good vibration which makes you feel good. These vibrations that you get through yoga, cosmic chants and things like that, I mean it's such a buzz. It buzzes you out of everywhere. It's nothing to do with pills. It's just in your own head, the realization. It's such a buzz. It buzzes you right into the astral plane."

None of the other Beatles were present when 'Within You Without You' was recorded. George and Neil Aspinall played tambouras while session musicians played an assortment of instruments including dilruba, tabla, violin and cello. "The Indian musicians on the session weren't hard to organize," remembers George Martin. "What was difficult, though, was writing a score for the cellos and violins that the English players would be able to play like the Indians. The dilruba player, for example, was doing all kinds of swoops and so I actually had to score that for strings and instruct the players to follow."

"The laugh at the very end of the track was George Harrison. He just thought it would be a good idea to out on it," recalls Martin.

Paul's relationship with his father was characterized by mutual respect and admiration. 'When I'm Sixty-Four' was an affectionate tribute not only to McCartney Senior's most recent birthday, but to the music he loved as a young man.

................................▶

WHEN I'M SIXTY-FOUR

Paul has said that the melody to 'When I'm Sixty-Four' was composed on the piano at Forthlin Road, Liverpool, "when I was about 15". This places it in either 1957 or 1958, shortly after he joined John in the Quarry Men. By 1960, Paul was playing a version of it in performance. At the time, he thought of it as "a cabaret tune", written out of respect for the music of the Twenties and Thirties, which his father had played as a young man.

In the midst of psychedelia, the fashions of Jim McCartney's younger days were being revived and it made sense for Paul to dust off his teenage song.

Twenties pastiche 'Winchester Cathedral' had been a UK hit for The New Vaudeville Band in September 1966, and *Bonnie and Clyde*, the movie that started a craze for Thirties clothing, was released in 1967.

Although the song was written with his father in mind, it was coincidental that he was 64 when it was eventually released. "My dad was probably only 56 when I wrote it," Paul said, "Retirement age in Britain is 65, so maybe I thought 64 was a good prelude. But probably 64 just worked well as a number."

The song is written as a letter from a socially inept young man who seems to be trying to coax a female he hardly knows into promising him long term devotion. The official tone of the letter ('drop me a line, stating point of view') paints a convincing picture of this formal young gent who wants to get it all in writ-

LOVELY RITA

An American friend was visiting Paul and, noticing a female traffic warden, a relatively new British phenomenon, commented: "I see you've got meter maids over here these days." Paul was taken with this alliterative term and began experimenting with it on the piano at his father's home. "I though it was great," he said. "It got to be 'Rita meter maid' and then 'lovely Rita meter maid'. I was thinking it should be a hate song...but then I thought it would be better to love her." Out of this came the idea for a song about a shy office worker who, having been issued with a parking ticket, seduces the warden in an attempt to get let off the fine. "I was imagining the kind of person I would be to fall for a meter maid," Paul remarked.

Some years later, a traffic warden by the name of Meta Davies, who operated in the St John's Wood area of London, claimed she had inspired the song. Not that she had been seduced by a Beatle but, in 1967, she had booked a certain P McCartney who had, apparently, asked about her unusual name. "His car was parked on a meter where the time had expired," says Meta, "I had to make out a ticket which, at the time, carried a ten shilling fine. I'd just put it on the windscreen when Paul came along and took it off. He looked at it and read my signature which was in full, because there was another M Davies on the same unit. As he was walking away, he turned to me and said, 'Oh, is your name really Meta?' I told him that it was. We chatted for a few minutes and he said, 'That would be a good name for a song. Would you mind if I use it?' And that was that. Off he went."

It may be that Paul had already written 'Lovely Rita' and was flattering her a little, although Meta herself was 22 years his senior and the mother of a teenage daughter. "I was never a Beatles' fan," admits Meta. "But you couldn't help hearing their music. My own daughter used to wait outside the Abbey Road Studios to see them."

ing before he signs on the dotted line. "It was a kind of pastiche," says George Martin. "It was a send-up of the old stuff. The words are slightly mocking. It was also something of his father's music coming out because his father had been a musician in the Twenties. Paul always had that sneaking respect for the old rooty-tooty music."

John claimed that he wouldn't have dreamt of writing anything like 'When I'm Sixty-Four'. "John sneered at a lot of things," says Martin. "But that was part of the collaborative style. They tended to be rivals. They were never Rodgers and Hart. They were more like Gilbert and Sullivan. One would do one thing and the other would say, yeah, I can do better than that and go and do better than that. At the same time, he was thinking – that was bloody good. I wish I could do it."

GOOD MORNING, GOOD MORNING

Paul dominated *Sgt Pepper* mainly because John had become lazy as a songwriter, never venturing from home if he could help it and only drawing inspiration from things immediately to hand such as the television, newspapers, a child's painting or a poster on the wall. Anything that came into the house.

As a result, 'Good Morning, Good Morning' was a song about having nothing to say – "a piece of garbage" as John later described it. A song about his life of indolence, it was the result of too many drugs, a cold marriage and days measured from meal to meal and in banal television programmes such as *Meet The Wife*. "When he was at home, he spent a lot of his time lying in bed with a notepad," remembers Cynthia of this period. "When he got up he'd sit at the piano or he'd go from one room to the other listening to music, gawping at television and reading newspapers. He was basically dropping out from everything that was happening. He was thinking about things. Everything he was involved in outside the home was pretty high-powered."

While sitting around in this state of mind, odd sounds and scraps of conversation would trigger ideas. It was a television commercial for Kellogg's Corn Flakes that gave John the title and chorus of 'Good Morning, Good Morning'. The black and white commercial featured nothing more than corn flakes being tipped into a bowl. The four-line jingle went: 'Good morning, good morning, The best to you each morning, Sunshine breakfast, Kellogg's Corn Flakes, Crisp and full of fun'.

This could have sounded very mundane if George Martin hadn't spiced up the backing track with Sounds Incorporated and tagged a series of animal sounds to the end of the track.

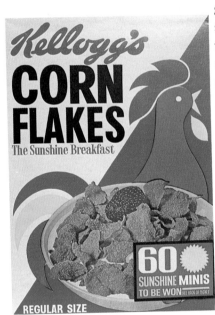

The press photo of Tara Browne's crushed Lotus Elan provoked John to write about the 'man who blew his mind out in a car'.

When the Beatles stopped touring, John used the opportunity to act in Dick Lester's *How I Won The War* and made reference to the movie in 'A Day In The Life'.

A DAY IN THE LIFE

For 'She Said She Said', John had combined two of his unfinished songs but here, for the first time, he put together an unfinished song of his own with one of Paul's to create 'A Day In The Life', the track that many regard as the most outstanding on *Sgt Pepper*.

John's part of the finished song was drawn from his interminable newspaper reading. The reference to the 4000 holes in Blackburn, Lancashire, came from the Far And Near column in the *Daily Mail* dated January 17, 1967. This reported that a Blackburn City Council survey of road holes had revealed the mind-boggling fact that there was one twenty-sixth of a hole in the road for each Blackburn resident. When John was stuck for an ending to the line 'Now they know how many holes it takes to fill', needing something that rhymed with 'small', Terry Doran (his friend from the motor trade) suggested the Albert Hall.

The film about the English army winning the war referred to in the lyric was *How I Won The War*, which John had himself acted in. Although the subject of several articles, the film wasn't premiered until October 1967.

The man who 'blew his mind out in a car' was Tara Browne, an Irish friend of the Beatles and a well-known socialite, who met his death in a car accident

Tara Browne was a young 'gentleman of independent means' who sought out the company of pop stars and models.

Edward Cecil Guinness and son of Lord Oranmore and Browne, was part of the new young aristocracy who loved to mingle with pop stars. Although only 21 at the time of his death, he would have inherited a £1,000,000 fortune at the age of 25 and was described on his death certificate as a man "of independent means" with a London home in Eaton Row, Belgravia. After schooling at Eton, Browne married at 18 and fathered two boys before separating from his wife and taking up with Suki Potier. He frequented London nightspots such as Sibylla's and the Bag O'Nails and had become particularly friendly with Paul and Mike McCartney and Rolling Stone Brian Jones. For his 21st birthday, he had the Lovin' Spoonful flown to his ancestral home in County Wicklow, Ireland. Mick Jagger, Mike McCartney, Brian Jones and John Paul Getty were amongst the guests.

Paul's unfinished song, a bright and breezy piece about getting out of bed and setting off for school, was spliced between the second and third verses of John's song. "It was another song altogether but it happened to fit," Paul said. "It was just me remembering what it was like to run up the road to catch a bus to school, having a smoke and going into class. It was a reflection of my schooldays. I would have a Woodbine (a cheap unfiltered British cigarette), somebody would speak and I'd go into a dream."

The references to having a smoke, dreams and 'turn-ons' meant that the track was banned from the airwaves in many countries. There were even some who were convinced that the holes in Blackburn, like the holes Paul had been keen to fix, were heroin addicts' track marks.

In 1968 Paul admitted that 'A Day In The Life' was what he called 'a turn-on song'. "This was the only one on the album written as a deliberate provocation," he said. "But what we want to do is to turn you on to the truth rather than on to pot." George Martin comments: "The woke up, got out of bed bit was definitely a reference to marijuana but 'Fixing A Hole' wasn't about heroin and 'Lucy In The Sky With Diamonds' wasn't about LSD. I had a strong suspicion that 'went upstairs and had a smoke' was a drug reference. They always used to disappear and have a little puff, but not in front of me. They used to go down to the canteen and Mal Evans used to guard it."

on December 18, 1966. The coroner's report was issued in January 1967. "I didn't copy the accident," John told Hunter Davies. "Tara didn't blow his mind out. But it was in my mind when I was writing that verse." The details of the accident in the song – not noticing traffic lights and a crowd forming at the scene – were similarly part of the fiction. In fact, Paul, who contributed lines to this part of the song, says that he didn't envisage Tara Browne, but a politician.

In real life, Browne was driving down Redcliffe Gardens in Earls Court during the early hours, when a Volkswagen pulled out of a side street into his path. In swerving to avoid it, his Lotus Elan ploughed into a stationary van and he was pronounced dead on arrival at a local hospital. The autopsy revealed that his death was the result of "brain lacerations due to fractures of the skull." His passenger, model Suki Potier, escaped with bruises and shock.

Tara Browne, great grandson of the brewer

With *Sgt Pepper* behind them, the Beatles immediately plunged into recording soundtracks for two very different film projects – *Yellow Submarine* and *Magical Mystery Tour*.

Yellow Submarine, a feature length animation project, wasn't initiated by the group but that didn't stop them from taking a keen interest in how it developed. The Beatles were happy to see themselves turned into cartoon characters and they set about thinking up storylines as well as supplying four original songs. The script was put together by a team of screenwriters, one of whom was Erich Segal, author of the best-selling novel, *Love Story*. A psychedelic fantasy, *Yellow Submarine*'s plot concerns a happy kingdom called Pepperland, which is taken over by the villainous Blue Meanies. The fab four ride to the rescue in a yellow submarine from Liverpool, eventually conquering the Meanies through the combined power of Love and Music.

Magical Mystery Tour was a pioneering 50-minute colour feature for television. It started off as Paul's project but soon all the Beatles were heavily involved in every aspect of production. They financed, directed, cast and scripted the film, as well as appearing in it themselves.

Including the single 'All You Need Is Love'/'Baby You're A Rich Man', the songs from this period are the wildest, most psychedelic collection the Beatles put together, though they were never released together on one record. *Magical Mystery Tour* was released in Britain as a double extended play disc in December 1967 and as a single album in the US in November that year. The *Yellow Submarine* soundtrack, which included an orchestral side from George Martin, wasn't released until January 1968, shortly after *The Beatles*.

If the Beatles had wished to release an album straight after *Sgt Pepper* in the Summer of Love, this eclectic bunch of songs would have made a fitting final fanfare for 1967 – before the more sober reflections of the following year. 1968 marked a new period in the Beatles' songwriting, when cleaning up, straightening out and getting back to basics became the order of the day.

Magical Mystery Tour, which was first seen on British television on December 26, 1967, was a critical failure, which consequently received only limited exposure in America. The music was much more successful; the British double EP reached Number 2 in the singles charts and the American album went to Number 1.

The *Yellow Submarine* film was released in July 1968 and was a commercial success in America, although it was never put on full release in Britain. The album, which featured other artists as well as the Beatles, reached the Number 3 spot in Britain and Number 2 in America.

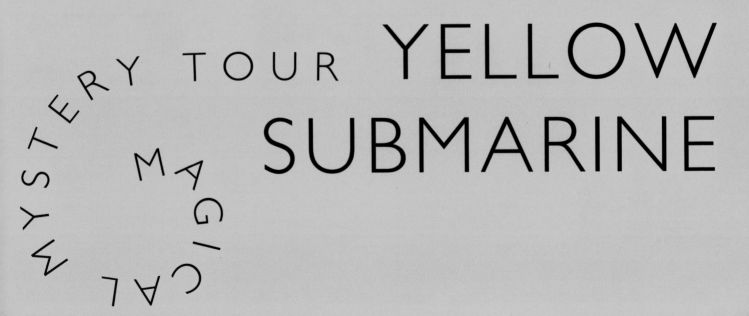

MYSTERY TOUR YELLOW SUBMARINE MAGICAL

ALL YOU NEED IS LOVE

Early in 1967, the Beatles were approached by the BBC to take part in what would be the first ever live global television link: a 125-minute programme broadcast to 26 countries with contributions from national broadcasting networks in Europe, Scandinavia, North America, Central America, North Africa, Japan and Australia.

To mark the occasion, the Beatles were asked to write a simple song that would be understood by viewers of all nationalities. Writing began in late May, with Paul and John working on separate compositions, until John's 'All You Need Is Love' emerged as the obvious choice. The song not only had simple words and an uncomplicated tune but it perfectly captured the aspirations of international youth in the summer of 1967. This was the time when the war in Vietnam reached its height and the 'love generation' showed their opposition by staging a number of peaceful protests. "It was an inspired song and they really wanted to give the world a message," said Brian Epstein. "The nice thing about it is that it cannot be misinterpreted. It is a clear message saying that love is everything."

In its call for universal love, 'All You Need Is Love' extended the message that John had first tried to put across in 'The Word' in 1965 to a worldwide audi-

John was never afraid to create art out of propaganda. An admirer of political slogans, revolutionary songs and even advertising jingles, he drew on his knowledge of all these to create an anthem for the Summer of Love.

The global link-up for the *Our World* telecast was a forerunner of events such as **Live Aid** (1985), where the power of music was linked to the latest in satellite technology.

ence. He was fascinated by the power of slogans to unite people and was determined to write something of his own with the timelessness of 'We Shall Overcome' (a labour union song popularized in the Sixties by folk singer Pete Seeger). "I like slogans," John once said. "I like advertising. I love the telly." When asked in 1971 whether songs like 'Give Peace A Chance' and 'Power To The People' were propaganda songs, he answered, "Sure. So was 'All You Need Is Love'. I'm a revolutionary artist. My art is dedicated to change."

What viewers saw in *Our World* on June 25, 1967, was actually a re-creation of a Beatles recording session: rhythm tracks had been laid down on June 14 and the live input was instantaneously added and mixed for transmission. A party atmosphere was

created in Abbey Road's Studio One by inviting celebrity friends such as Mick Jagger, Marianne Faithfull, Eric Clapton and Keith Moon to sit around, hold balloons, wave placards and join in on the chorus. George Martin helped accentuate the message of international unity by opening the song with bars from the French national anthem, and closing it with snatches from Glenn Miller's 'In The Mood', Bach and 'Greensleeves'.

The single was released on July 7, and became the soundtrack song for the Summer of Love, a paeon to peace, love and understanding. "We had been told that we'd be seen recording it by the whole world at the same time," said Paul. "So we had one message for the world – love. We need more love in the world."

BABY YOU'RE A RICH MAN

A s with 'A Day In The Life', two unfinished songs were sewn together to create 'Baby You're A Rich Man', which opens with John's section, originally titled 'One Of The Beautiful People', and then moves up a gear for Paul's chorus about the rich man.

'The beautiful people' was then a term for a generation of hippies who, with their long hair, free love and dope, created an alternative to 'straight' society. They used the word 'beautiful' freely in their conversations to describe anything of which they approved. "At the back of my mind somewhere...there is something which tells me that everything is beautiful," said Paul in a stoned rap of an interview with *International Times* in January 1967. "Instead of opposing things like 'Oh, I don't like that television show' or 'No I don't like the theatre' I know really that it's all great and that everything's great and there's no bad ever if I can think of it all as great."

In 1967, San Francisco was regarded as the city of the beautiful people because it was here that the hippy movement was first noticed by the media and where the first psychedelic 'happenings' and mass open-air 'tribal gatherings' had taken place. Although the Beatles played San Francisco in 1964, 1965 and 1966, they didn't really get to explore the city until 1967. Paul was the first to visit, on April 4, when he dropped in on a Jefferson Airplane rehearsal and jammed on guitar. George was next on August 7, when he descended on Haight Ashbury, the district in San Francisco that had given birth to underground newspapers, psychedelic poster art, communes, crash pads, head shops, free clinics and legions of exotic street people. "You are our leader, George," one hippy shouted as he set off walking from the corner

> Readers of the UK weekly *Disc and Music Echo* are let in on the secrets of 'the beautiful people'.

This is how it feels to be a beautiful person

by PENNY VALENTINE

BEAUTIFUL PEOPLE have existed for years. It's nothing to do with what you look like or the clothes you wear. It's what goes on in your mind and your approach to life.

Beautiful people, as a phrase, has come into the foreground today because of the emergence of the flower movement, the emergence of the hippies, Sgt. Pepper and the Beatles and Scott McKenzie's "San Francisco."

But even the hippiest hippy, surely, has harboured some pretty evil thoughts and some pretty anti-feelings. Has been unkind, insensitive, thoughtless. Not noticed things around him.

It's been borrowed by the hippies. But even if you don't wear kaftans, beads, bells and granny green glasses take heart, you can **STILL** be a beautiful person. Read on and find out how.

YOU ARE BEAUTIFUL IF YOU:

● Like dancing on cool grass in your bare feet (even if there are no pipes of Pan and the grass is in your own back garden);
● Read Professor Tolkein's "The Hobbit" or 'Lord Of The Rings" and love Bilbo Baggins;
● Have watched the dawn come up and actually realised what was happening;
● Dream;
● Love your dog, the postman, the blind man who sells matches on the corner, your neighbours (even when they bang on the wall when you put Sgt Pepper on full volume);
● Dislike war, the Government, anti-people;
● Think the countryside is a gas and ought to stay wild;
● Enjoy splashing through the rain, laughing, children, colours, poetry, people;
● Refuse to tread on ants, spiders and beetles;
● Know where "Granny Takes A Trip" is;
● Give a daisy to the policeman who tells you your party is too noisy, drags you away from Wanstead Flats when you are merely admiring the view or pulls you feet first up a dirty road to a waiting van during a sit-down protest;
● Harbour a burning desire to visit Mexico or India.

● Beautiful People: Paul and Jane at the Beatles' "All You Need Is Love" recording session.

of Haight and Masonic with Pattie, Neil Aspinall and Derek Taylor beside him. "You know where it's at."

George was taken aback at the drug-glazed adoration of those who began to push flowers, poems, posters and drugs at him. "It's you who should be leading yourself," he told his would-be followers. "You don't want to be following leaders – me or anyone else." When he arrived at a park, George sat on the grass, listened to other people's songs and then started to sing 'Baby You're A Rich Man'.

The rich man in Paul's section is reputed to be manager Brian Epstein and in a demo version of the song, John maligns him by singing 'Baby, you're a rich fag Jew'. "The point was," said John, "stop moaning. You're a rich man and we're all rich men."

> **On November 10, 1967, the Beatles were filmed performing 'Hello Goodbye' at a London theatre for promotional use all over the world.** ▼

HELLO GOODBYE

Alistair Taylor, who worked for Brian Epstein, remembered once asking Paul how he wrote his songs, and Paul taking him into his dining room to give a demonstration on a hand-carved harmonium. He told Taylor to shout out the opposite of whatever he sang as he struck the keys. And so it went – black and white, yes and no, stop and go, hello and goodbye. "I've no memory at all of the tune," Taylor later recounted. "You have to remember that melodies are as common around the Beatles as bugs in May. Some grow into bright butterflies and others shrivel and die. I wonder whether Paul really made up that song as he went along or whether it was running through his head already. Anyway, shortly afterwards, he arrived at the office with a demo tape of the latest single – 'Hello Goodbye.'"

The last part of the record, where the Beatles repeat the line 'Hela, hey, aloha' came about spontaneously in the studio. ('Aloha' is an affectionate form of Hawaiian greeting.)

If 'Hello Goodbye' was nothing more than a word game set to music, in the mystical climate of 1967, Paul was expected to offer a deeper interpretation. In an interview with *Disc*, he gallantly tried to produce an explanation: "the answer to everything is simple. It's a song about everything and nothing...If you have black you have to have white. That's the amazing thing about life."

'Hello Goodbye' was released as a single in November 1967 and topped the charts in both Britain and America. The final 'aloha' chorus was used in the *Magical Mystery Tour* film.

ONLY A NORTHERN SONG

Originally recorded in February 1967 as George's contribution to *Sgt Pepper's Lonely Hearts Club Band*, 'Only A Northern Song' first saw the light of day in *Yellow Submarine*. The song was a sly dig at the business arrangements of the Beatles. Their songs had always been published by Northern Songs Ltd, 30 per cent of whose shares belonged to John and Paul, with Ringo and George owning only 1.6 per cent each. This meant that John and Paul, in addition to being the group's main songwriters, were twice benefiting as prime shareholders in the publishing company. As far as Northern Songs was concerned, George was only a contracted writer.

In 'Only A Northern Song', George complained that it didn't really matter what he wrote because the bulk of the money was going into other people's pockets. Underlying this was his feeling, only expressed publicly after the group had broken up, that his songs were not being judged on merit and that he was effectively only being offered a token showcase for his work. "At first it was just great (to get one song on each album), it was like, hey, I'm getting in on the act too!" George commented. "After a while I did (come to resent this), especially when I had good songs. Sometimes I had songs that were better than some of theirs and we'd have to record maybe eight of theirs before they'd *listen* to mine."

It's not surprising that George, who in 1964 claimed "security is the only thing I want. Money to do nothing with, money to have in case you want to do something", ultimately became the Beatle least keen to resurrect the Beatles.

ALL TOGETHER NOW

All Together Now' was written in the studio in May 1967 with Paul as main contributor. It was intended as a singalong in the style of 'Yellow Submarine' and John was delighted later, when he heard British soccer crowds singing it.

It was the closest that the Beatles ever came to writing a nursery rhyme, probably echoing a rhyme remembered from childhood or a Liverpool skipping song. Folklorist Iona Opie, editor of *The Oxford Dictionary of Nursery Rhymes*, believes that as the lines sound so familiar, it draws more on a shared memory: "I can't distinguish any particular influence on 'All Together Now'," she says. "So many ABC rhymes exist and there are counting rhymes like 'One, two, three, four, Mary at the cottage door...' which come pretty close." Paul has confirmed that he saw it in the tradition of children's songs ("It's a play away command song") but that he was also playing with the dual meaning of 'all together now' which could be either a music hall-style invitation to participate or a slogan for world unity. Paul Horn remembers the song being sung in India but instead of singing 'H, I, J, I love you' they would sing 'H, I, Jai Guru Dev' in honour of Maharishi's spiritual master.

HEY BULLDOG

Hey Bulldog' was recorded on February 11, 1968, when the Beatles were at Abbey Road to make a promotional film for 'Lady Madonna'. Paul suggested that instead of wasting time pretending to record 'Lady Madonna', they should tape something new and so John produced some unfinished lyrics he'd written for *Yellow Submarine*. John explained to the others how he heard the song and they all threw in suggestions for the words. One line John had written – 'Some kind of solitude is measured out in news' – was misread and came out as 'Some kind of solitude is measured out in you'. They decided to keep it.

The bulldog of the title never existed before the recording. The original lyric mentioned a bullfrog but, to everyone's amusement, Paul started to bark at the end of the song. Because of this, they retitled it..

Erich Segal, the author of *Love Story*, was one of the screenwriters on *Yellow Submarine*. Years later, he claimed that 'Hey Bulldog' had been written for him because the bulldog was the mascot of Yale University where he was a lecturer in classics.

▲ **Erich Segal was a Professor of Classics at both Oxford and Yale, but received greater popular acclaim as the author of the weepie novel *Love Story* and as one of the writers of the *Yellow Submarine* screenplay.**

IT'S ALL TOO MUCH

George was the Beatle who most often spoke in spiritual terms about his experience of LSD. 'It's All Too Much', recorded in May 1967, was written, George said, "in a childlike manner from realizations that appeared during and after some LSD experiences and which were later confirmed in meditation".

Through images of silver suns and streaming time, the song attempted to articulate the overwhelming illusion of someone having his identity swallowed up by a benign force. Three months after this recording, George met the Maharishi Mahesh Yogi and began to view his LSD experience as a signpost rather than a destination. "LSD isn't a real answer," he said in September 1967. "It doesn't give you anything. It enables you to see a lot of possibilities that you may never have noticed before but it isn't the answer. It can help you go from A to B, but when you get to B you see C, and you see that to get really high, you have to do it straight. There are special ways of getting high without drugs – with yoga, meditation and all those things."

MAGICAL MYSTERY TOUR

F lying home to London on April 11, 1967, after visiting Jane Asher in Denver for her 21st birthday party, Paul began to work on an idea for a Beatles television special. The group felt that they had outgrown the 'caper' format and now Paul was fascinated with the process of making films himself, working with an 8mm camera and composing electronic soundtracks.

Encouraged by the experimental mood of the times, Paul envisaged making an unscripted film where characters and locations were decided upon beforehand, but the story would unfold spontaneously during shooting. His plan was to put the Beatles alongside an assorted collection of actors and colourful characters on a strange coach journey.

As Hunter Davies reported in the *Sunday Times* the day before *Magical Mystery Tour* was shown on British television: "(They had decided that the film) would be Magical, so that they could do any ideas which came to them, and Mysterious in that neither they nor the rest of the passengers would know what they were going to do next.

There were two main sources of inspiration behind *Magical Mystery Tour*. The first was the British working-class custom of the 'mystery tour', the organized day trip by coach, where only the driver knows the route. The second was American novelist Ken Kesey's idea of driving through America on a psychedelically painted bus. On the front of Kesey's bus it said 'Furthur'(sic) and on the back – 'Caution: Weird Load'. Kesey's idea was to fill a coach full of counter-culture 'freaks', turn up the music, put LSD in the drinks and just set off to see what would happen. His driver was Neal Cassady, the model for Dean Moriarty in Jack Kerouac's *On The Road;* the story of their adventures was eventually told in Tom Wolfe's book *The Electric Kool-Aid Acid Test*.

On April 25, Paul arrived at Abbey Road studios with nothing more than the song title, the first line and a general idea for the tune. He said he wanted his

The *Magical Mystery Tour* coach negotiates a narrow bridge on its way over Dartmoor on September 13, 1967. This television film was to be the first project the Beatles touched that didn't turn to gold.

new song to be like a commercial for the television programme, letting viewers know what was in store. Mal Evans was dispatched to find some real mystery tour posters from which they could lift phrases but, after a tour of coach stations, he returned empty-handed. When the backing track had been recorded, Paul asked everyone to shout out words connected with mystery tours which Mal wrote down. Although they came up with 'invitation', 'reservation', 'trip of a lifetime' and 'satisfaction guaranteed', it wasn't enough and so the vocal track was filled with make-do nonsense until Paul returned two days later with a completed lyric.

Paul's words were a mixture of traditional fair-

THE FOOL ON THE HILL

Paul started work on 'The Fool On The Hill' in March 1967 while he was writing 'With A Little Help From My Friends', although it wasn't recorded until September.

Hunter Davies observed Paul singing and playing "a very slow, beautiful song about a foolish man sitting on the hill", while John listened staring blankly out of the window at Cavendish Avenue. "Paul sang it many times, la la-ing words he hadn't thought of yet. When at last he finished, John said he'd better write the words down or he'd forget them. Paul said it was OK. He wouldn't forget them," says Davies.

The song was about an *idiot savant;* a person everyone considers to be a fool but whose foolishness is actually an indication of wisdom. Paul was thinking of gurus like the Maharishi Mahesh Yoga who were often laughed at by the general public.

An experience which is said to have contributed to Paul's image of the fool standing on the hill is recounted by Alistair Taylor in his book *Yesterday.* Taylor recalls an early morning walk on Primrose Hill with Paul and his dog Martha, where they watched the sun rise before realizing that Martha was missing. "We turned to go and suddenly there he was standing behind us," wrote Taylor. "He was a middle-aged man, very respectably dressed in a belted raincoat. Nothing in that, you may think, but he'd come up behind us over the hill in total silence." Both Paul and Taylor were sure that the man hadn't been there seconds earlier because they'd been searching the area for the dog. He seemed to have appeared miraculously. The three men exchanged greetings, the man commented on the beautiful view and then walked way. When they looked around, he'd vanished.

"There was no sign of the man," said Taylor. " He'd just disappeared from the top of the hill as if he'd been carried off into the air! No-one could have run to the thin cover of the nearest trees in the time we had turned away from him, and no-one could have run over the crest of the hill."

ground barking and hidden drug references. To the majority of the audience 'roll up, roll up' was the ring master's invitation to the circus. To Paul it was also an invitation to roll up a joint: the Magical Mystery Tour was going to 'take you away', on a trip. Even the phrase 'dying to take you away' was a conscious reference to the *Tibetan Book Of The Dead.*

The track was used over an opening sequence made up of scenes from the film with an additional spoken section which declared: "When a man buys a ticket for a magical mystery tour, he knows what to expect. We guarantee him the trip of a lifetime, and that's just what he gets – the incredible Magical Mystery Tour."

Like the street signs in Penny Lane and Abbey Road, the sign for Blue Jay Way has become a collector's item, much to the annoyance of local residents.

What added to the mystery was that immediately before the man's appearance Paul and Taylor had, provoked by the beautiful view over London and the rising of the sun, been mulling over the existence of God. "Paul and I both felt the same weird sensation that something special had happened. We sat down rather shakily on the seat and Paul said, 'What the hell do you make of that? That's weird. He was here wasn't he? We did speak to him?'

"Back at Cavendish, we spent the rest of the morning talking about what we had seen and heard and felt," continues Taylor. "It sounds just like any acid tripper's fantasy to say they had a religious experience on Primrose Hill just before the morning rush hour, but neither of us had taken anything like that. Scotch and Coke was the only thing we'd touched all night. We both felt we'd been through some mystical religious experience, yet we didn't care to name even to each other what or who we'd seen on that hilltop for those few brief seconds."

In *Magical Mystery Tour*, the song was used over a sequence with Paul on a hilltop overlooking Nice.

George waiting to be filmed for the 'Blue Jay Way' sequence.

FLYING

The Beatles had recorded two previous instrumentals – 'Cry For A Shadow' in Germany in 1961 (when backing Tony Sheridan as the Beat Brothers) and the unreleased '12-Bar Original' in 1965. 'Flying' was the only instrumental to be released on a Beatles' record.

Required as incidental music for *Magical Mystery Tour*, 'Flying' emerged out of a studio jam. Originally titled 'Aerial Tour Instrumental', it was registered as a group composition and featured a basic rhythm track with additional mellotron, backwards organ and vocal chanting. The cloud scenes over which 'Flying' was heard in the film, were originally shot by Stanley Kubrick for *2001 Space Odyssey* but never used.

BLUE JAY WAY

Blue Jay Way' was written by George in August 1967 during his visit to California with Pattie, Neil Aspinall and Alex Mardas. On arrival in Los Angeles on August 1, they were driven to a small rented house with a pool on Blue Jay Way, a street high in the Hollywood Hills above Sunset Boulevard. It belonged to the manager of singer Peggy Lee, who was on vacation in Hawaii at the time.

Derek Taylor, formerly the Beatles' press officer and now a publicist working in Los Angeles, was due to visit them on their first night in town, but got lost in the narrow canyons on his way to the house, and was badly delayed. There was a small Hammond organ in the corner of the room and George whiled away the time by composing a song about being stuck in a house on Blue Jay Way while his friends were lost in the fog.

Blue Jay Way is a notoriously hard street to find – you can be geographically close and yet separated by a ravine. "By the time we got there the song was virtually intact," says Derek Taylor. "Of course, at the time I felt very bad. Here were these two wretchedly jet-lagged people, and we were about two hours late. But here, indeed, was a song which turned up in *Magical Mystery Tour* (the film) through a prism with about eight images, with George in a red jacket sitting and playing piano on the floor."

Taylor was amused by what people made of the song. One critic thought the line in which George urged his guest not to 'be long' was advice to young people telling them not to 'belong' (to society, that is). Another acclaimed musicologist believed that, when George said that his friends had 'lost their way', he meant that a whole generation had lost direction. "It's just a simple, little song," laughs Taylor.

YOUR MOTHER SHOULD KNOW

Your Mother Should Know' by Paul could have been written as early as May 1967, when both John and Paul were working on songs for the *Our World* television special. Like 'When I'm 64', the song was a throwback to the music his father enjoyed singing when he was a young man in Jim Mac's Jazz Band. Jim McCartney formed his own ragtime band in 1919 and played in Liverpool, performing songs like 'Birth Of The Blues' and 'Stairway To Paradise'. One day, Paul surprised his dad by recording one of his songs under the title 'Walking In The Park With Eloise', under the alias of the Country Hams.

Paul wrote it at Cavendish Avenue and thinks it was affected by the fact that his Auntie Gin and Uncle Harry were staying there. It was the sort of song they would have liked. Paul also had in mind 'mother knows best', a lament for those no longer close to their parents. Strictly speaking, any hit Paul's mother would have known would have been a hit before she was born in 1909, when hits were not determined by record sales but by sales of sheet music.

I AM THE WALRUS

The sprawling, disjointed nature of 'I Am The Walrus' owes much to the fact that it is an amalgamation of at least three song ideas that John was working on, none of which seemed quite enough in its own right. The first, inspired by hearing a distant police siren while at home in Weybridge, started with the words 'Mis-ter c-ity police-man' and ran to the rhythm of the siren. The second was a pastoral melody about John in his Weybridge garden. The third was a nonsense song about sitting on a corn flake.

John told Hunter Davies, who was still researching the Beatles' official biography at the time: "I don't know how it will all end up. Perhaps they'll turn out to be different parts of the same song." According to Pete Shotton, the final catalyst was a letter received from a pupil of Quarry Bank School, which mentioned that an English master was getting his class to analyze Beatles' songs. The letter from the Quarry Bank pupil was sent to John by Stephen Bayley who received an answer dated September 1, 1967 (which

'I Am The Walrus' was partly a wind-up on John's part but it was taken very seriously by some fans who were anxious to find a key to its symbolism.

was sold at auction by Christie's of London in 1992). This amused John, who decided to confuse such people with a song full of the most perplexing and incoherent clues. He asked Shotton to remind him of a silly playground rhyme which English schoolchildren at the time delighted in. John wrote it down: 'Yellow matter custard, green slop pie, All mixed together with a dead dog's eye, Slap it on a butty, ten foot thick, Then wash it all down with a cup of cold sick'.

John proceeded to invent some ludicrous images ('semolina pilchards, elementary penguins') and nonsense words ('texpert, crabalocker'), before adding some opening lines he'd written down during an acid trip. He then strung these together with the three unfinished songs he'd already shown Hunter Davies. "Let the fuckers work that one out", he apparently said to Shotton when he'd finished.

The 'elementary penguin' which chanted Hare Krishna was John having a dig at Allen Ginsberg who, at the time, was chanting the Hare Krishna mantra at public events. The walrus itself came from Lewis Carroll's poem 'The Walrus and The Carpenter'.

The 'eggman' was supposedly a reference to the Animals' vocalist Eric Burdon who had an unusual practice of breaking eggs over his female conquests while making love and became known amongst his musical colleagues as the 'egg man'. Marianne Faithfull believes that 'semolina pilchard' referred to Det. Sgt. Norman Pilcher, the Metropolitan police officer who made a name for himself by targeting pop stars for drug possession.

The recording of 'I Am The Walrus' began on September 5. It lasted on and off throughout the month because George Martin was trying to find an equivalent to the flow of images and word play in the lyrics by using violins, cellos, horns, clarinet and a 16-voice choir, in addition to the Beatles themselves. On

John as the Egg Man at West Malling Air Station, Kent, in September 1967, during the filming of *Magical Mystery Tour.* In the distance is his psychedelically-painted Rolls Royce.

LADY MADONNA

Lady Madonna' was the first single to show that the way forward for the Beatles now lay in going back to basic rock'n'roll. After *Sgt Pepper's Lonely Hearts Club Band* and *Magical Mystery Tour,* it was assumed that musical progression would mean more complexity, but the Beatles again defied expectations.

The piano line was taken from Johnny Parker's riff on 'Bad Penny Blues', a 1956 hit in Britain for jazz trumpeter Humphrey Lyttelton, which had been produced by George Martin. "We asked George how they got the sound on 'Bad Penny Blues'," said Ringo. "George told us they used brushes. So I used brushes and we did a track with just brushes and piano and then we decided we needed an off-beat, so we put an off-beat in." Lyttelton didn't mind, as he had taken the riff from Dan Burley anyway. "You can't copyright a rhythm and rhythm was all they had borrowed," he said. "I was very complimented. Although none of the Beatles cared for traditional jazz, they all knew and liked 'Bad Penny Blues' because it was a bluesy, skiffley thing rather than a trad exercise."

The song was intended by Paul to be a celebration of motherhood, starting with an image of the Virgin Mary and child but moving on to consider all mothers. "How do they do it?", he asked when interviewed by *Musician* in 1986. "Baby at your breast – how do they get the time to feed them? Where do they get the money? How do you do this thing that women do?" American singer Richie Havens remembered being with Paul in a Greenwich Village club watching Jimi Hendrix perform when a girl asked whether 'Lady Madonna' had been written about America. "No," said Paul. "I was looking through this African magazine and I saw this African lady with a baby. And underneath the picture it said 'Mountain Madonna'. But I said, oh no – *Lady* Madonna – and I wrote the song."

Released as a single in March 1968, 'Lady Madonna' went to Number 1 in Britain but stalled at Number 4 in America.

Jazz trumpeter,
Humphrey Lyttelton
(centre) who helped
to establish Afro-
American music in
▼ Britain in the Fifties.

THE INNER LIGHT

On September 29, 1967, John and George were guests of David Frost on the live late night television show *The Frost Report*. The subject of this particular edition was Transcendental Meditation and it included an interview with the Maharishi Mahesh Yogi, filmed earlier the same day at London Airport.

In the invited audience at the studio in Wembley, north London was Sanskrit scholar Juan Mascaró, a Cambridge professor. The following month, Mascaró wrote to George enclosing a copy of *Lamps Of Fire*, a collection of spiritual wisdom from various traditions which he had edited. He suggested that George might consider putting verses from the Tao Te Ching to music, in particular a poem titled 'The Inner Light'.

In his preface to *Lamps Of Fire*, first published in 1958, Mascaró wrote: "The passages of this book are lamps of fire. Some shine more and some shine less, but they all merge into that vast lamp called by St John of the Cross 'the lamp of the being of God'."

'The Inner Light' was the first song of George's to appear on a single when it became the B side of 'Lady Madonna'.

HEY JUDE

As John and Yoko started living together, not surprisingly divorce proceedings began between John and Cynthia. An interim agreement was reached whereby Cynthia and Julian were allowed to stay at Kenwood while the two respondents took up residence in a Montagu Square flat in central London.

Paul had always enjoyed a close relationship with John's son Julian, then five years old and, to show his support for mother and child during the break-up, he drove down to Weybridge from his home in St John's Wood bearing a single red rose. Paul often used driving time to work out new songs and, on this day, with Julian's uncertain future on his mind, he started singing 'Hey Julian' and improvising lyrics on the theme of comfort and reassurance. At some point during the hour-long journey, 'Hey Julian' gave way to 'Hey Jules' and Paul developed the lines 'Hey Jules, don't make it bad, Take a sad song and make it better.' It was only later, when he came to flesh out the lyric, that he changed Jules to Jude, feeling that Jude was a name which sounded stronger.

The song then became less specific. John always felt it was addressed to him and was Paul encouraging him to make the break from the Beatles and build a new future with Yoko. Paul felt that, if anything, it was addressed to himself and the adjustments he knew that he was going to have to make as old bonds

When John took up
with Yoko in 1968, he
saw much less of his
son Julian, who
continued to live with
▼ Cynthia.

A firm believer in family life, Paul was concerned for Julian when his parents' marriage broke up in 1968.

were broken and new ones forged. As with so many of Paul's songs, it was the music that drove the lyric, with sound taking precedence over sense.

One line in particular – 'the movement you need is on your shoulder' – was only seen as a temporary filler. When Paul played the song to John on July 26, 1968, he pointed out that this line needed replacing, saying he knew that it sounded as if he was singing about his parrot. "It's probably the best line in the song," said John. "Leave it in. I know what it means."

Julian Lennon grew up knowing the story behind 'Hey Jude' but it wasn't until 1987 that he heard the facts of the composition first-hand from Paul, whom he bumped into while staying at the same hotel in New York. "It was the first time in years that we'd sat down and talked to each other," says Julian. "He told me that he'd been thinking about my circumstances all those years ago, about what I was going through and what I would have to go through in the future. Paul and I used to hang out quite a bit – more than dad and I did. Maybe Paul was into kids more at the time. We had a great friendship going and there seem to be far more pictures of me and Paul playing together than there are pictures of me and dad."

It's only fairly recently that Julian has started asking questions about his past. Paul was right to anticipate that he would have a hard time growing up. "I've never really wanted to know the truth about how dad was and how he was with me," Julian admits. "I didn't want to know the truth and so I kept my mouth shut. There was some very negative stuff talked about me – like when he said that I'd come out of a whisky bottle on a Saturday night. Stuff like that. That's tough to deal with. You think, where's the love in that? It was very psychologically damaging and for years that affected me. I used to think, how could he say that about his own bloody son!"

Julian hasn't studied the words of 'Hey Jude' for some time but finds it hard to get away from the song. He'll be in a restaurant when he'll hear it played, or it'll come on the car radio.

"It surprises me whenever I hear it," he says. "It's strange to think someone has written a song about you. It still touches me."

THE BEATLES

The Beatles, or the White Album as it is commonly known, surprised people by being sparse and simple. It seemed as if the group had decided to produce the exact opposite of *Sgt Pepper*. Long album title? Let's just call it *The Beatles*. Multi-coloured cover? Let's use plain white. Clever overdubs and mixes? Let's use acoustic guitars on a lot of the tracks. Profound lyrics? Let's sing about cowboys, piggies, chocolates and doing it in the road.

The album's most significant new ingredient was the influence of Indian guru, Maharishi Mahesh Yogi. Pattie Harrison had attended a lecture by the Maharishi in February 1967 and she encouraged George and the rest of the Beatles to attend a similar event in August 1967 at the Hilton Hotel in Park Lane, London. As a result of this meeting, they all began a ten-day course on Transcendental Meditation, held at University College, Bangor, in North Wales.

It was while they were on this course, on Sunday, August 27, 1967, that they heard that Brian Epstein had been found dead at his Belgravia flat – news that precipitated their return to London. The loss of Epstein, who had managed their career since early 1962 and had become something of a father figure, may well have made the Beatles even more open to the guidance of the Maharishi, whom they visited in India in February 1968.

The trip to India not only brought a period of calm into their fraught lives, when for the first time in ages they had time to reflect, but also brought them back together as longstanding friends, able to fool around with their acoustic guitars. Paul Horn, an American flautist who was there at the same time, believes that meditation was a great stimulus for the Beatles. "You find out more about yourself on deeper levels when you're meditating," he said. "Look how prolific they were in such a relatively short time. They were in the Himalayas away from the pressures and away from the telephone. When you get too involved with life, it suppresses your creativity. When you're able to be quiet, it starts coming up."

On their return from India, the Beatles claimed that they had brought back 30 songs which they would be using on their next album. There were indeed 30 new songs on *The Beatles* but not all of them were written in India, and some of the Indian songs (like George's 'Sour Milk Sea' and 'Circles') were never recorded by the Beatles. It's probably accurate to say that around half of the album was written or started while they were away. This meant that because they had no access to electric guitars or keyboards, many of these songs were acoustically based.

John would later refer to *The Beatles* as being the first unselfconscious album after the Beatles' great period of self-consciousness beginning with *Rubber Soul* and ending with *Magical Mystery Tour* and *Yellow Submarine*. *The Beatles* was released as a double album in November 1968 and rose to the Number 1 spot on both sides of the Atlantic.

The time spent in India under the guidance of Maharishi Mahesh Yogi provided the Beatles with the necessary breathing space to write a follow-up album to *Sgt Pepper*.

BACK IN THE USSR

F riendly rivalry existed between the Beatles and the Beach Boys, and between 1965 and 1968 each new effort by either band spurred the other on to greater heights. When Brian Wilson heard *Rubber Soul*, he reported that it blew his mind to hear an album of such variety and consistency. "It flipped me out so much," he said, "that I determined to try the same thing – to make an entire album that was a gas." His reply was *Pet Sounds*, the Beach Boys' crowning achievement, which contained such songs as 'Sloop John B', 'Caroline No', 'Wouldn't It Be Nice' and 'God Only Knows'. When Paul heard *Pet Sounds*, he was equally impressed and went on to mastermind *Sgt Pepper*.

Although they were mutual admirers, the two groups had little social contact. Carl Wilson and Mike Love had seen the Beatles play in Portland, Oregon, on August 22, 1965, and called by the dressing room after the show. In April 1967, Paul dropped by the studios in LA where Brian Wilson was working on the Beach Boys track 'Vegetables'.

The most prolonged contact came in February 1968, when all four Beatles and their partners travelled to Rishikesh, India, to study Transcendental Meditation under the Maharishi Mahesh Yogi. On the course were three other professional musicians –

Scottish singer Donovan, American flautist Paul Horn and Beach Boy Mike Love. The musicians spent a great deal of time together talking, jamming and song-writing.

One of the songs that came out of this encounter was 'Back In The USSR', written by Paul as a pastiche of the Beach Boys and Chuck Berry. The genesis of the song was a comment made by Love to Paul one morning over breakfast in Rishikesh. "Wouldn't it be fun to do a Soviet version of 'Back In The USA'," Love suggested, referring to Berry's jingoistic 1959 single in which the singer expressed how mighty glad he was to be back home in civilized America with its cafes, drive-ins, skyscrapers, hamburgers and juke boxes. The Beach Boys had earlier drawn on this song and Berry's 'Sweet Sixteen' for their tracks 'California Girls' and 'Surfin' USA', in which they extolled the virtues of local ladies and surf beaches.

for Paul acted on Love's suggestion and came up with a parody that did for the USSR what Berry had done the USA and for Soviet women what the Beach Boys had done for the girls of California. After a decade of songs which had made poetry out of the names of places such as Memphis, Chicago and New Orleans, it was striking to hear Moscow mentioned in rock'n'roll. "I just liked the idea of Georgia girls and talking about places like the Ukraine as if it was California," said Paul. As a tribute to Love, the Beatles' eventual recording imitated the vocal sound of the Beach Boys.

'Back In The USSR' was thought shocking by conservative Americans, because it appeared to be celebrating the enemy in the midst of the Cold War, at a time when America was at war with the Russian-backed Viet Cong. Having admitted to drug taking, were these long-haired boys now embracing communism? American anti-rock campaigner David A Noebel, author of *Communism, Hypnotism and the Beatles*, while unable to produce their party membership cards, was sure that they were furthering the cause of revolutionary socialism. "John Lennon and the Beatles were an integral part of the revolutionary milieu and received high marks from the Communist press," he wrote, "especially for the White Album which contained 'Back In The USSR' and 'Piggies'. One line from 'Back In The USSR' left the anti-

Communists speechless: 'You don't know how lucky you are boy, Back in the USSR.'"

Through more diligent research, Noebel would have discovered that the official Soviet line was that the Beatles were evidence of capitalism's decadence. Just as the Nazis had seized on jazz music and abstract painting as examples of degeneracy which had to be countered with officially sanctioned art, so the Communists railed against the evil of rock'n'roll and instead encouraged a love of folk music that extolled the virtues of the State. Young people in the Soviet Union were just as excited by the Beatles' music as their Western counterparts but had to rely on bootleg recordings, smuggled imports and radio broadcasts from America and Britain. In 1988, with the Cold War about to be consigned to history, Paul paid tribute to his Soviet fans by recording an album of rock'n'roll standards on the official government recording label, Melodia.

"Back In The USSR is a hands-across-the-water song," said Paul. "They like us out there. Even though the bosses in the Kremlin may not, the kids do."

DEAR PRUDENCE

Prudence was Prudence Farrow (younger sister of American actress Mia Farrow) who attended the same course with the Beatles in India. The song was a plea to her to come out from her excessively long periods of meditation and relax with the rest of the group.

At the end of the demo version of 'Dear Prudence', John continues playing guitar and says: "No-one was to know that sooner or later she was to go completely berserk, under the care of Maharishi Mahesh Yogi. All the people around were very worried about the girl because she was going insane. So, we sang to her." Later, John was to explain that Prudence had gone slightly 'barmy', locked in her room meditating for three weeks, "trying to reach God quicker than anyone else."

Paul Horn, the American flautist, remembers events in much the same way. He says that Prudence was a highly sensitive person and that, by jumping straight into deep meditation, against the Maharishi's advice, she had allowed herself to fall into a catatonic state. "She was ashen-white and didn't recognize anybody," he says. "She didn't even recognize her own brother, who was on the course with her. The only person she showed any slight recognition towards was Maharishi. We were all very concerned about her and Maharishi assigned her a full-time nurse."

Prudence, whose living quarters were in the same building as the four Beatles and their partners, denied that she went mad but agreed that she was more fanatical about meditating than the Beatles were. "I'd been meditating since 1966 and had tried to get on the course in 1967, so it was like a dream come true for me," she explains. "Being on that course was more important to me than anything in the world. I was very focused on getting in as much meditation as possible, so that I could gain enough experience to teach it myself. I knew that I must have stuck out because I would always rush straight back to my

Prudence Farrow (second from left, front row) had to be coaxed out of her bungalow by fellow meditators in Rishikesh. John wrote 'Dear Prudence' for her while they were there.

room after lectures and meals so that I could meditate. It was all so fascinating to me. John, George and Paul would all want to sit around jamming and having a good time and I'd be flying into my room. They were all serious about what they were doing but they just weren't as fanatical as me. The song that John wrote was just saying, 'Come out and play with us. Come out and have fun.'"

This she eventually did and got to know the Beatles well. The Maharishi put her in an after-lecture discussion group with John, and George – who he thought would be good for her. "We talked about the things we were all going through," she says. "We were questioning reality, asking questions about who we were and what was going on. I liked them and I think they liked me."

Although the song was written in India, and Prudence overheard various jam sessions between the Beatles, Mike Love and Donovan, John never played the song to her. "George was the one who told me about it," she recalls. "At the end of the course, just as they were leaving, he mentioned that they had written a song about me but I didn't hear it until it came out on the album. I was flattered. It was a beautiful thing to have done."

Prudence is now married and lives in Florida where she teaches meditation. In October 1983, Siouxie and the Banshees had a British Top 10 hit with their version of 'Dear Prudence'.

GLASS ONION

In an age of rapid social change, the Beatles were often regarded as prophets and every song was scrutinized for symbols and allusions that might contain a message. Who was the egg man in 'I Am The Walrus'? Was the tea that was mentioned in 'Lovely Rita' really marijuana? Was 'Henry The Horse' street slang for heroin?

The Beatles had perhaps laid themselves open to wild misinterpretation by mixing up the languages of poetry and nonsense. John, in particular, had enjoyed obfuscating his point of view beneath layers of imagery. However, by 1968, John was trying to write more directly and most of the work he brought back from India was simpler and less self-conscious. When a pupil from his old school wrote and asked him to explain the motives behind his songwriting, John replied that the work was done for fun and laughs. "I do it for me first," he said. "Whatever people make of it afterwards is valid, but it doesn't necessarily have to correspond to my thoughts about it, OK? This goes for anyone's 'creations', art, poetry, song etc. The mystery and shit that is built around all forms of art needs smashing anyway."

'Glass Onion' was a playful response by John to those who pored over his work looking for hidden meanings. He started to piece together the song using odd lines and images from some of the most enigmatic Beatles' songs – 'Strawberry Fields Forever', 'There's A Place', 'Within You Without You', 'I Am The Walrus', 'Lady Madonna', 'The Fool On The Hill' and 'Fixing A Hole'. In 'Glass Onion', he jokingly claimed that the walrus, from 'I Am The Walrus', was really Paul. (In some primitive cultures the walrus is a symbol of death and this new information was later used as confirmation by those who believed that Paul had been killed in a road accident in 1966, to be replaced by a double.) Finally, he came up with four new tantalizing images for his 'literary' fans to pore over – bent back tulips, a glass onion, the Cast-Iron Shore and a dovetail joint.

The bent back tulips, explains former Apple press officer Derek Taylor, was a reference to a particular flower arrangement in Parkes, a fashionable London restaurant in the Sixties. "You'd be in Parkes sitting around your table wondering what was going on with the flowers and then you'd realize that they were actually tulips with their petals bent all the way back, so that you could see the obverse side of the petals and also the stamen. This is what John meant about 'seeing how the other half lives'. He meant seeing how the other half of the flower lives but also, because it was an expensive restaurant, how the other half of society lived."

There were simple explanations for the other perplexing references: the Cast-Iron Shore was Liverpool's own beach (also known as the Cassie); a dovetail joint referred to a wood joint using wedge-

OB-LA-DI OB-LA-DA

shaped tenons, and Glass Onion was the name John wanted to use for The Iveys, the band that signed with Apple in July 1968.

The Iveys didn't like the name Glass Onion and, instead, called themselves Badfinger after 'Badfinger Boogie', the original title of 'A Little Help From My Friends'.

Paul first heard the words 'Ob-la-di Ob-la-da' uttered by Nigerian conga player Jimmy Scott, whom he met at the Bag o' Nails club in Soho, London. A flamboyant and unforgettable character in dark glasses and African clothing, Scott was renowned for his catch phrases: "He used these phrases every day of his life," says Doug Trendle (aka Buster Bloodvessel) who later worked

'Ob-La-Di Ob-La-Da' has a distinctively Jamaican flavour to it and yet Jimmy Scott, who supplied the catchy phrase the song was built around, was born in Nigeria.

with him in the band Bad Manners. "He walked around using them. He was from the Yoruba tribe and if you find someone from the Yoruba they will tell you that 'Ob-la-di Ob-la-da' means 'Life goes on'."

Jimmy Anonmuogharan Scott Emuakpor was born in Sapele, Nigeria, and came to England in the Fifties, where he found work in the jazz clubs of Soho. He played with Georgie Fame and the Blue Flames in the Sixties, backed Stevie Wonder on his 1965 tour of Britain and later formed his own Ob-la-di Ob-la-da Band.

The fact that Paul used his catch phrase as the basis of a song became a matter of controversy. "He got annoyed when I did a song of it because he wanted a cut," Paul told *Playboy* in 1984. "I said 'Come on, Jimmy. It's just an expression. If you'd written the song, you could have had the cut.'"

'Ob-la-di Ob-la-da' has been cited as the first example of white reggae; although the phrase was Yoruba, the song Paul created around it and the characters he invented were from Jamaica. When recording the vocals, Paul made a mistake in singing that Desmond, rather than Molly, "stayed at home and did his pretty face". The other Beatles liked the slip and so it was kept. Paul loved the song and wanted it to be a single. John always hated it.

▲ Marmalade had a British hit with Ob-La-Di Ob-La-Da after John refused to consider the song as a potential Beatles' single.

Jimmy Scott played congas on the session (July 5, 1968) – the one and only time he worked with the Beatles. Later that year, he appeared on the Rolling Stones' *Beggars Banquet* album and in 1969 at the Stones' free concert in Hyde Park. Around this time he was arrested and taken to Brixton prison to await trial on a charge of failing to pay maintenance to his ex-wife. He asked the police to contact the Beatles' office to see if Paul would foot his huge outstanding legal bill. This Paul did, on condition that Scott dropped his case against him over the song.

Scott left England in 1969 and didn't return until 1973 when he immersed himself in the Pyramid Arts project in east London, giving workshops on African music and drumming. In 1983, he joined Bad Manners and was still with them when he died in 1986. "We'd just done this tour of America and he caught pneumonia," remembers Doug Trendle. "When he got back to Britain he was strip-searched at the airport because he was Nigerian. They left him naked for two hours. The next day he was taken into hospital and he died. Nobody is too sure how old he was because he lied about his age when he got his first British passport. He was supposed to be around 64."

In July 1986, a concert featuring Bad Manners, Hi Life International, the Panic Brothers, Lee Perry and the Upsetters as well as many others was mounted at the Town and Country Club, London to raise money for the Jimmy Scott Benevolent Fund. He left a widow Lurcrezia and an estimated 12 children from two marriages. "Jimmy was essentially a rhythmic, charming, irresistible man with the gift of the gab," Lurcrezia Scott wrote in the benefit's programme. "If life was sometimes dull, it shouldn't have been, for his stories of people, of places, of incidents, were an endless stream bubbling with fun."

Paul, who kept in contact with Jimmy, also contributed a quote. "He was a great friend of mine," he wrote. "In the Sixties we used to meet in a lot of clubs and spent many a happy hour chatting until closing time. He had a great positive attitude to life and was a pleasure to work with."

Two British cover versions of 'Ob-la-di Ob-la-da' were recorded and the one by Scottish group Marmalade went to Number 1. The Beatles' version was only released in America, but not until 1976.

WILD HONEY PIE

The shortest and most repetitive of any Beatles' lyric, 'Wild Honey Pie' emerged from a spontaneous singalong in Rishikesh. "It was just a fragment of an instrumental which we were not sure about," said Paul. "But Pattie Harrison liked it very much, so we decided to leave it on the album."

Coincidentally Mike Love had recently co-written a Beach Boys' track entitled 'Wild Honey'.

THE CONTINUING STORY OF BUNGALOW BILL

Bungalow Bill, the song says, 'Went out tiger hunting with his elephant and gun. In case of accidents he always took his mum.' Written by John while in India, it recounts the true story of Richard Cooke III, a young American college graduate, who visited his mother Nancy while she was on the course in Rishikesh.

John described Bungalow Bill as "the all-American bullet-headed Saxon mother's son" and Cooke agrees that it was an accurate description of him when he first met the Beatles. Cooke is over 6ft tall and was, on this occasion, dressed in white and sporting a crew cut. "The other Beatles were always real nice to me but John was always aloof", he says. "They epitomized the counter culture and I was the classic good American boy and college athlete. There wasn't a whole bunch that we got to connect on."

The tiger hunt itself took place about three hours away from Rishikesh and involved Cooke and his mother travelling by elephant and then hiding in a tree on a wooden platform known as a marchand.

"Rik sat down and I stood behind him," remembers Nancy. "It wasn't long before I saw this flash of yellow and black. I let out a yell and Rik twirled and shot the tiger right through the ear."

"I was pretty excited that I had shot a tiger," remembers Cooke. "But the Texan who organized the shoot came over and said, 'You shot it, but don't say a word. As far as the world is concerned you didn't shoot this tiger.' He wanted to be the one who went back home with the skin as his trophy."

It was when they arrived at the ashram that Cooke began to feel remorse, wondering whether the killing of the animal would bring him 'bad karma'. He and his mother had a meeting with Maharishi which was also attended by John and Paul.

"It was a fluke that they happened to be sitting there when I had this conversation with Maharishi,"

says Cooke. "My mother was talking excitedly about killing the tiger and Maharishi looked aghast that his followers could actually go out and do something like this. It was the only time I ever saw him almost angry."

"Rik told him that he felt bad about it and said that he didn't think he'd ever kill an animal again," recalls Nancy. "Maharishi said – 'You had the desire Rik and now you no longer have the desire?' Then John asked, 'Don't you call that slightly life destructive?' I said, 'Well John, it was either the tiger or us. The tiger was right where we were'. That came up in the lyric as 'If looks could kill it would have been us instead of him.'"

John came up with the name Bungalow Bill for Cooke as a play on Buffalo Bill, the performing name of showman William Frederick Cody (1846-1917) who was a hero in post-war schoolboy comics. He chose 'Bungalow' because all the accommodation in Rishikesh was in bungalows. Ian MacDonald points out in *Revolution In The Head* that the tune appears to be based on 'Stay As Sweet As You Are' which was written by Mack Gordon and Henry Revel and was used in the 1934 film *College Rhythm*.

Cooke knew nothing of 'Bungalow Bill' until he started getting postcards saying 'Hey Bungalow Bill. What did you kill?' from friends who recognized him in the song. He now divides his time between Hawaii and Oregon and is a photographer for *National Geographic* magazine. Nancy lives in Beverley Hills.

WHILE MY GUITAR GENTLY WEEPS

George was reading the *I Ching*, the Chinese book of changes, and decided to apply its principles of chance to his songwriting. At his parents' Lancashire home, he picked a novel off the shelf with the intention of writing a song based on the first words that he came across. The words were 'gently weeps' and so George began to write.

He started recording in July 1968 but felt that the other Beatles weren't showing sufficient interest in the song. In September, he brought in his friend Eric Clapton to play lead guitar while he played rhythm.

▲ John dubbed all-American Richard A Cooke III 'Bungalow Bill' and in his song mocked the fact that he went on a tiger hunt with his mother.

HAPPINESS
IS A WARM GUN

The idea for this song came to John after he discovered a gun magazine belonging to George Martin that had been left lying around the studio. On the cover was the line 'Happiness Is A Warm Gun In Your Hand'. It was too good a phrase to let go and he began to toy with it. "I thought, what a fantastic thing to say!" John later remarked. "A warm gun means you've just shot something."

John had recently started living with Yoko Ono, the Japanese artist he'd first met at an exhibition of her art in 1966. By his own admission, he felt "very sexually oriented" during this period, so before long the idea for a song about a warm gun had taken on sexual connotations, and gave rise to phrases about itchy trigger fingers and discharged loads.

If it was a song about anybody, it was a song about Yoko. She was the girl he held in his arms, the girl who was so smart that she didn't miss a trick and the one he always called Mother — in this case, Mother Superior.

But tagged on to the original lines were random images picked up from a night of acid tripping with Derek Taylor, Neil Aspinall and Pete Shotton at a house Taylor was renting from Peter Asher in Newdigate near Dorking in Surrey. "John said he had written half a song and wanted us to toss out phrases while Neil wrote them down," says Taylor. "First of all, he wanted to know how to describe a girl who was really smart and I remembered a phrase of my father's which was 'she's not a girl who misses much'. It sounds like faint praise but on Merseyside, in those days, it was actually the best you could get.

"Then I told a story about a chap my wife Joan and I met in the Carrick Bay Hotel on the Isle of Man. It was late one night drinking in the bar and this local fellow who liked meeting holiday makers and rapping to them suddenly said to us , 'I like wearing moleskin gloves you know. It gives me a little bit of an unusual sensation when I'm out with my girlfriend.' He then

said, 'I don't want to go into details.' So we didn't. But that provided the line, 'She's well acquainted with the touch of the velvet hand'. Then there was 'like a lizard on a window pane'. That, to me, was a symbol of very quick movement. Often, when we were living in LA, you'd look up and see tiny little lizards nipping up the window," continues Taylor.

"'The man in the crowd with multi-coloured mirrors on his hobnail boots' was from something I'd seen in a newspaper about a Manchester City soccer fan who had been arrested by the police for having mirrors on the toe caps of his shoes so that he could look up girls' skirts. We thought this was an incredibly complicated and tortuous way of getting a cheap thrill and so that became 'multi-coloured mirrors' and 'hobnail boots' to fit the rhythm. A bit of poetic license," adds Taylor. "The bit about 'lying with his eyes while his hands were working overtime' came from another thing I'd read where a man wearing a cloak had fake plastic hands, which he would rest on the counter of a shop while underneath the cloak he was busy lifting things and stuffing them in a bag around his waist.

"I don't know where the 'soap impression of his wife' came from but the eating of something and then donating it 'to the National Trust' came from a conversation we'd had about the horrors of walking in public spaces on Merseyside, where you were always coming across the evidence of people having crapped behind bushes and in old air raid shelters. So to donate what you've eaten to the National Trust (a British organization with responsibilities for upkeeping countryside of great beauty) was what would now be known as 'defecation on common land owned by the National Trust.' When John put it all together, it created a series of layers of images. It was like a whole mess of colour," Taylor concludes.

The Beatles had just started to record this track on the day Linda Eastman arrived in London to begin life with Paul.

Paul's first meeting with Linda Eastman was in June 1967. By the time they started living together, the Beatles were recording the White Album.

◀ ·····································

MARTHA MY DEAR

Martha may have been the name of Paul's two-year-old Old English Sheepdog, but this song was not an account of canine love. 'Martha My Dear' is a plea to a girl who has always been the singer's muse: he asks her to remember him because he still believes that they were meant for each other. In January 1968, Paul and Jane Asher had announced that they were going to get married during the year but Paul began dating other girls while Jane was away acting and in July she called off the engagement. "We still see each other and love each other, but it hasn't worked out," Jane said at the time. "Perhaps we'll be childhood sweethearts and meet again and get married when we're about 70."

The song began as a two-handed piano exercise, something that was deliberately beyond his level of competence at the time and designed to stretch him musically. 'Martha My Dear' was recorded in October 1968 – by which time Linda Eastman had become Paul's girlfriend.

Paul's old English sheepdog Martha, with whom he could often be seen in Hyde Park or on Primrose Hill.

John pictured below composing while at Rishikesh.

I'M SO TIRED

During the Beatles' stay in Rishikesh, there were two 90-minute lectures each day and much of the rest of the time was taken up with meditating. Students were expected to build up their periods of meditation slowly as their technique improved. One person on the course reportedly claimed to have clocked up a 42-hour session. John found that this life of stillness and inner absorption meant that he couldn't sleep at night and consequently he began feeling tired during the day.

'I'm So Tired', written after three weeks in India, was also about the things he was beginning to miss. The Academy of Meditation was alcohol- and drug-free and John's mind was turning to his beloved cigarettes and the possibility of a drink. Sometimes a friend of his would smuggle some wine in.

Most of all he was missing Yoko Ono. The couple had not yet begun an affair because John was unsure how to end his marriage. He had briefly entertained the idea of inviting her to India but realized that the complications of having both Cynthia and Yoko under the same roof would be too great.

PIGGIES

BLACKBIRD

There are two conflicting stories surrounding the creation of 'Blackbird'. One story simply says that Paul woke early one morning in Rishikesh to hear a blackbird singing. The other suggests that he was inspired by news reporting of racial tension in America.

Paul's step-mother, Angie McCartney, says it was written for her mother, Edith Stopforth, and that she has a copy of a studio take where Paul says, "This one's for Edie" before recording it. "My mother was staying with Jim and I after a long illness," she says. "During that time Paul spent some time sitting on mum's bed. She told him she would often listen to a bird singing at night. Paul eventually took the tape recorder up and recorded the sound of this bird."

Paul has said the tune was not based on a blackbird singing but on a piece by Bach which he had learned as a teenager. He was partly thinking of the racial situation in America and wrote it for the typical black woman facing oppression.

One night in summer 1968, Paul serenaded the fans gathered outside his home with an acoustic version of 'Blackbird'. Margo Bird, a former Apple Scruff (the term for fans who used to congregate outside the Apple offices) remembers: "I think he had a young lady round, Francie Schwartz. We'd been hanging around outside and it was obvious she wasn't going to be leaving. He had a music room right at the top of the house and he opened the sash window, sat on the edge and played it to us.'

Paul often cites 'Blackbird' as evidence that the best of his songs come spontaneously.

George referred to 'Piggies' as "a social comment" although the song did little more than mock the middle-classes by calling them pigs, a Sixties term of derision usually reserved for the police.

The song became notorious in 1971 when it was revealed that Charles Manson, the self-appointed leader of the notorious Manson 'family', had interpreted the words as a warning to the white establishment that they were to get ready for an uprising.

Particularly significant, in Manson's disturbed mind, was the suggestion that the piggies were in need of "a damn good whacking". According to witnesses, this was one of Manson's favourite lines, and one that he quoted frequently before his imprisonment for involvement in the murders which many saw as the

final dark chapter in the hippie era.

The clue that eventually linked the eight murders – five at the residence of film-star Sharon Tate, two at Leno LaBianca's and one at Gary Hinman's – was the painting of the word 'pig', 'pigs' or 'piggy' in the victims' blood. The LaBiancas were even stabbed with knives and forks, apparently because these utensils are mentioned in the last verse.

George was horrified at Manson's maniacal interpretation of what he felt was a rather tame song, pointing out that the 'damn good whacking' line had been suggested by his mother when he was looking for something to rhyme with 'backing' and 'lacking'. "It was nothing to do with American policemen or Californian shagnasties," he said.

ROCKY RACCOON

R ocky Raccoon' was a musical Western, written by Paul while in India. Set in the mountains of Dakota, it tells the tale of young Rocky whose girl, Nancy Magill, runs off with Dan. Rocky pursues Dan and attempts to shoot him down but is beaten to the draw. Afterwards, Rocky is treated in his hotel room by a doctor stinking of gin. "We were sitting on the roof at Maharishi's just enjoying ourselves when I wrote this one," said Paul. "I started laying the chords and originally the title was 'Rocky Sassoon'. Then me, John and Donovan started making up the words and they came very quickly and eventually it became Rocky Raccoon because it sounded more cowboyish."

Apple Scruff, Margo Bird, heard that the character of the doctor was drawn from real life. "Paul had a moped which he came off one day in May 1966. He was a bit stoned at the time and cut his mouth and chipped his tooth," she says. "The doctor that came to treat him was stinking of gin and because he was a bit worse for wear he didn't make a very good job of the stitching which is why Paul had a nasty lump on his lip for a while."

DON'T PASS ME BY

A ppropriately, 'Don't Pass Me By' became Ringo's first complete Beatles' song. Until then, his only contribution to the Beatles' compositions had been the titles for 'A Hard Day's Night', 'Eight Days A Week' and 'Tomorrow Never

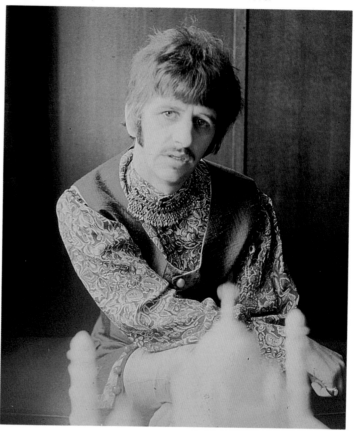

Knows', as well as musical contributions to 'Flying' and 'What Goes On'.

Asked in December 1967 whether he had aspirations as a songwriter, Ringo replied: "I try. I have a guitar and a piano and play a few chords, but they're all just chinga-lingas. No great tune comes out as far as I'm concerned."

The truth is he'd been trying to get the Beatles to record 'Don't Pass Me By' for years. During an interview for radio in New Zealand on their June 1964 tour of Australasia, Ringo could be heard urging the others to "sing the song I've written, just for a plug".

▲ **It took Ringo four years to get his first composition on a Beatles' album. Ironically, the song was entitled 'Don't Pass Me By'.**

Paul responded by saying: "Ringo has written a song called 'Don't Pass Me By'. A beautiful melody. This is Ringo's first venture into songwriting."

After Paul and John had sung a verse, Ringo was asked more about it: "It was written as a country and western but Paul and John singing it with that blues feeling has knocked me out. Are the Beatles going to record it? I don't know. I don't think so actually. I keep trying to push it on them every time we make a record."

It was to remain unrecorded for another five years. "Unfortunately there's never enough time to fit Ringo's song on an album," Paul explained in 1964. "He never finishes it."

WHY DON'T WE DO IT IN THE ROAD?

One of the great strengths of the Lennon and McCartney team was that, although they now rarely sat down and created a song from scratch together, they did egg each other on to greater extremes in what was increasingly to become solo work.

They always sought to wind the other up, particularly by composing in a style more often associated with the other. This explains why the White Album contains the sensitive 'Julia' and sentimental 'Goodnight' by John in Paul's style, as well as gritty rock'n'roll numbers like 'Helter Skelter' and 'Why Don't We Do It In The Road?' from Paul à la Lennon. John was upset by 'Why Don't We Do It In The Road?' because Paul recorded it with Ringo in a separate studio at Abbey Road. What probably irritated John most though was that Paul's chosen style – a risque lyric and sparse arrangements – was recognized as his own trademark.

Paul had the idea for the song while in India when he saw two monkeys copulating in the open.

He was struck by the apparently uncomplicated way in which animals mate compared with the rules, rituals and routines of human sex. "The Beatles have always been a rock group," Paul explained in November 1968. "It's just that we're not completely rock'n'roll. That's why we do 'Ob-La-Di Ob-La-Da' one minute, and this the next. When we played in Hamburg we didn't just play rock'n'roll all evening because we had these fat old businessmen coming in – and thin old businessmen as well – and they would ask us to play a mambo or a samba. So we had to get into this kind of stuff. "

I WILL

Paul spent 67 takes getting 'I Will' right on September 16, 1968, with Ringo playing on cymbal and maracas and John tapping the rhythm with a piece of wood. It was the first of Paul's songs to be written about Linda and he was still adding and changing lines as it was being recorded.

Unsurprisingly, there's a sense of anticipation in the lyric, provoked no doubt by the knowledge that Linda and her daughter were arriving in London the very next week. Paul had previously only met Linda in London during the *Sgt Pepper* period and on two subsequent visits to America, but he obviously felt he knew enough about her to be confident in offering her his love 'forever and forever'.

JULIA

Although many of John's songs were shaped by the trauma of losing his mother as a teenager, 'Julia' was the first time he directly introduced his mother into a Beatles' song.

Julia Stanley was born in Liverpool in 1914 and married Frederick Lennon in 1938. John was the only child they had together. By the time John was five, Julia gave birth to another man's child, and John was taken into the care of Julia's sister Mimi. His mother was attractive and unconventional. From her John inherited his sense of humour and also his interest in music. She taught him to play banjo and it was through her that John heard his first Elvis Presley records.

Julia's sudden death in a road accident in 1958 came just when John was becoming close to her again. He'd started using her home in Blomfield Road for band practices with the Quarry Men because Aunt Mimi didn't like loud music in her house.

Although 'Julia' was addressed to his mother, it was also a coded message to his new love, Yoko Ono. The 'ocean child', who John writes is calling him, is clearly a reference to Yoko whose name in Japanese means 'child of the ocean'. "It was in India that she began writing to me," John said. "She would write things like 'I am a cloud. Watch for me in the sky.' I would get so excited about her letters."

The first two lines of the song are taken from *Sand And Foam*, a collection of proverbs by the Lebanese mystic, Kahlil Gibran, first published in 1927. Gibran wrote: "Half of what I say is meaningless; but I say it so the other half may reach you." The rest of the song, John said, was finished with help from Yoko herself when they met up back in England because, besides being an artist and film maker, she was a poet who specialized in minimalist haiku-like verse.

The guitar work on 'Julia' was influenced by Donovan. "John would take particular interest in the finger-style guitar parts I was playing in my songs," says Donovan, "he wanted to know the patterns I was using and I told him I would teach him. John was a diligent student and mastered the complex pattern in a few days. In common with most songwriters, learning a new style meant composing in a different way. In his deep meditation sessions, John had opened up feelings for his mother. He found release for these emotions in 'Julia', the tune he had learned with the new finger style."

BIRTHDAY

The songs on *The Beatles* composed in India tended to be guitar-based because the Beatles only had stringed instruments with them while they were away.

However 'Birthday', was written in Abbey Road Studios, on September 18, 1968 with Paul thumping out the basic tune on a piano. According to John, Paul had been thinking of 'Happy, Happy Birthday', a 1957 hit in America for the Tuneweavers, but wanted to produce something which sounded contemporary and rock'n'roll. It was also Linda Eastman's 26th birthday in six days' time and Paul knew that she was arriving in London the following week, just in time to celebrate.

Paul went in the studio during the late afternoon of the 18th and worked out the basic keyboard riff. Later, George, John and Ringo came in and added a backing track. During the evening, the four of them took a break and went round to Paul's house to watch the British television premiere of *The Girl Can't Help It* (1956), which starred Jayne Mansfield and featured music by Fats Domino, Gene Vincent, the Treniers, the Platters, Little Richard and Eddie Cochran.

Perhaps inspired by this dose of early rock'n'roll, the Beatles returned to the studio around 11pm and completed the vocals. Each of the Beatles threw in lines and Yoko Ono and Pattie Harrison helped with the backing. "We just made up the words in the studio," said Paul. "It's one of my favourite tracks on the album because it was instantaneous. It's a good one to dance to."

John's opinion, volunteered 12 years later, was par for the course: "It's a piece of garbage."

Folk singer Donovan wrote his hit single 'Jennifer Juniper' about Pattie's sister Jenny Boyd while they were all in India. During this time, Donovan also taught John some finger-style guitar techniques.

◄ ·······································

YER BLUES

Yer Blues' was the most despairing song John had written to date, representing an anguished cry to Yoko for help. John felt he was at a crossroads in his life: his career as a concert performing Beatle was nearly over; his manager was dead; and now he was contemplating bringing an end to his marriage.

He felt loyalty to Cynthia and yet he knew that in Yoko he'd met his artistic and intellectual match. She was, he later said, the girl he had always dreamed of meeting; the girl he had imagined when he wrote 'Girl'.

During the stay in Rishikesh, John and Cynthia were often separated because of their different meditation routines and it wasn't until the flight back to London from Delhi that John first mentioned his indiscretions during their six-year marriage. Cynthia was shocked: "I never dreamt that he had been unfaithful to me during our married life. He hadn't revealed anything to me. I knew of course that touring abroad and being surrounded by all the temptations any man could possibly want would have been impossible to resist. But even so my mind just couldn't and wouldn't accept the inevitable. I had never had anything concrete to go on, nothing telltale."

John later said that this dilemma had made him feel suicidal. In this song, he jokingly compares himself to 'Mr Jones', the witless central character in Dylan's 'Ballad Of A Thin Man'. Musically, 'Yer Blues' was indicative of the direction he would be taking with his solo work.

MOTHER NATURE'S SON

Both John and Paul wrote songs after hearing a lecture by the Maharishi about the unity of man and nature, but it was to be Paul's 'Mother Nature's Son' that made the album's final selection. John's song, 'A Child Of Nature', made similar observations about sun, sky, wind and mountains but, whereas Paul fictionalized his resp-onse by writing in the character of a 'poor young country boy', John wrote about himself 'on the road to Rishikesh'.

Paul had always been a lover of the countryside and when he wrote 'Mother Nature's Son' he had in mind a song he had heard when he was younger called 'Nature Boy', presumably the standard made popular by Nat 'King' Cole. Although the song was started in India it was completed at his father's house.

EVERYBODY'S GOT SOMETHING TO HIDE EXCEPT ME AND MY MONKEY

Initially known as 'Come On, Come On', the song was built up from the line which eventually became its title. John said it was a clear reference to his relationship with Yoko. "That was just a nice line which I made into a song," he said. "Everybody seemed to be paranoid except for us two, who were in the glow of love...everybody was sort of tense around us."

It hadn't been until his return from India that the friendship turned into an affair. It was then that Cynthia discovered what was happening. Yoko started to attend recording sessions for the new album, much to the annoyance of the other Beatles. The British press also found it difficult to accept Yoko and this irked John and was to play a part in his eventual move to America. "In England they think I'm someone who has won the pools and gone off with a Japanese Princess," he once said. "In America, they treat her with respect. They treat her as the serious artist she is."

SEXY SADIE

John's honeymoon period with the Maharishi didn't last long. By the end of his stay in India, he had rejected the guru's leadership and channelled his feelings of disappointment into 'Sexy Sadie'.

Sexy Sadie' appears to be a song about a girl who leads men on, only to make fools of them, but was actually written about the Maharishi Mahesh Yogi, with whom John had become disillusioned. Knowing that he could never record a potentially libellous song called Maharishi, he titled it 'Sexy Sadie', but on the demo recording of the track he let rip with a string of obscenities directed towards his real quarry.

There were two reasons why the Beatles decided to leave Rishikesh. One was that they had been told

that the Maharishi was only after their money and the other was the rumour going around that he had made a sexual advance to one of the females on the course. Although there was never any concrete evidence behind these accusations, it was enough to unnerve them and the three Beatles arranged a meeting with the guru where they informed him that they were leaving. Pressed to explain their decision, John reportedly said, "Well, if you're so cosmic, you'll know why."

Paul Horn, who remembered them leaving, believes it was partly because they expected too much of the Maharishi and partly because of jealousies amongst some hangers-on at the camp. "These courses were really designed for people who wanted to become teachers themselves and who had a solid background in meditation," Horn says. "The

Beatles didn't really have the background and experience to be there and I think they were expecting miracles. George was obviously really interested but Ringo wasn't into Eastern philosophy at all. John was on his own trip and always sceptical about anything until it had been proven to him. Paul was easy-going and could have gone either way.

"The big fuss came because there were some people there who were more interested in the Beatles than learning to meditate and they became hangers-on," continues Horn. "There was one girl, a school teacher from New York, who was really into the Beatles and she started all this crap about the Maharishi making passes at her. She told the Beatles this and they got upset about it and left. Basically, there were a lot of rumours, jealousies and triangles going on and she got back at the Beatles through saying this about the Maharishi. The bottom line though is that it was time for them to go home anyway. This was just the catalyst."

HELTER SKELTER

The concept for 'Helter Skelter' came from a music paper's rave review of a new single by the Who. At the time, Paul hadn't heard the single in question, but the paper's comments made him want to create something which could provoke an equally powerful description.

The single was 'I Can See For Miles', which was released in October 1967, and the most likely review was written by Chris Welch in *Melody Maker*. "Forget Happy Jack sitting in sand on the Isle of Man," wrote Welch. "This marathon epic of swearing cymbals and cursing guitars marks the return of the Who as a major freak-out force. Recorded in America, it's a Pete Townshend composition filled with Townshend mystery and menace, and delivered by the emphatic Mr Roger Daltry."

However, it's impossible to be sure that this was in fact the review, because Paul's description has changed over the years. In 1968, he reported that this review had said "the group really goes wild with echo and screaming and everything," but 20 years later his memory of it was more fanciful, claiming that it described the Who single as, "the loudest, most raucous rock'n'roll, the dirtiest thing they'd ever done." However Paul's account of the effect that the review had on him hasn't changed: "I thought 'That's a pity. I would like to do something like that.' Then I heard it and it was nothing like it. It was straight and sophisticated. So we did this. I like noise."

Despite being described as having 'swearing cymbals' and 'cursing guitars', 'I Can See For Miles' had a discernible melody throughout and could not properly be described as raucous. Paul wanted to write something that really did 'freak people out' and, when the Beatles first recorded 'Helter Skelter' in July 1968, they did it in one take which was almost half an hour long. They returned to it in September, by all accounts 'out of their heads', and produced a shorter version. At the end of it, Ringo can be heard shrieking, "I've got blisters on my fingers."

Most British listeners were aware that a helter skelter was a spiral fairground slide but Charles Manson, who heard the White Album in December 1968 thought that the Beatles were warning America of a racial conflict that was 'coming down fast'. In the scenario that Manson had developed, the Beatles were the four angels mentioned in the New Testament book of Revelation who, through their songs, were telling him and his followers to prepare for the coming holocaust by escaping to the desert. Manson referred to this future uprising as 'Helter Skelter' and it was the daubing of these words in blood at the scene of one of the murders that became another vital clue in the subsequent police investigation. It was because of the song's significance that Vincent Bugliosi, the Los Angeles District Attorney who prosecuted at Manson's trial, named his best-selling account of the murders *Helter Skelter*.

▲ Although Paul was regarded as the ballad writer of the Beatles, he was responsible for three of the group's dirtiest rock numbers – 'I'm Down', 'Why Don't We Do It In The Road' and 'Helter Skelter'.

LONG LONG LONG

More than any other Beatle, George was inspired to write by hearing other songs. The chords of 'Long Long Long' were suggested to him by Bob Dylan's haunting track 'Sad Eyed Lady Of The Lowlands', which had taken up one whole side of Dylan's 1966 double album *Blonde On Blonde*. George was fascinated with the movement from D to E minor to A and back to D and wanted to write something which sounded similar. He scribbled the lyric out in the pages of an empty 'week at a glance' diary for 1968 and called it 'It's Been A Long Long Long Time' which then became the working title in the studio.

'Long Long Long' sounds like a straightforward love song written by someone who has lost and regained the object of his affections but, according to George, the 'you' in question here is God. This is hardly surprising because he was the first Beatle to show an interest in Eastern religion and the only one to carry on with it after the others became disenchanted with the Maharishi following their visit to India. George did, however, alter his allegiances, distancing himself from Maharishi and Transcendental Meditation and becoming publicly identified with the International Society for Krishna Consciousness, later producing their Hare Krishna mantra as a hit single.

There was a time when George's devotion to religion conflicted with his devotion to his wife Pattie. In the end, this was to play a part in the couple's divorce.

REVOLUTION

The Summer of Love was followed by the Spring of Revolution. In March 1968, thousands marched on the American Embassy in London's Grosvenor Square, a rally which ended in violence between police and revolutionaries. In May, French students rioted in Paris and barricades were erected. Unlike Mick Jagger, who made an appearance at Grosvenor Square, John surveyed these events from the comfort of his Weybridge home, keeping in touch through the news media and the underground press. He began work on 'Revolution' while in India and completed it at home when Cynthia was away in Greece. He took it to Paul as a potential single but Paul said the song wasn't commercial enough.

As with 'Back In The USSR', the title was deceptive. It wasn't the song of a revolutionary but rather the song of someone under pressure from revolutionaries to declare his allegiance. Easily the most politically conscious of the Beatles and unapologetically left wing in outlook, John had become a target for various Leninist, Trotskyist and Maoist groups, who felt he should lend both moral and financial support to their causes.

'Revolution' was John's reply to these factions, informing them that, while he shared their desire for social change, he believed that the only worthwhile revolution would come about through inner change rather than revolutionary violence. However, he was never absolutely sure of his position, hedging his bets on the slow version of the song released on the album. After talking about the destruction that might come with revolution, he changed the phrase 'count me out' to 'count me in'. On the fast version, released as the B side of 'Hey Jude', he omitted the word 'in'.

The omission provoked much hand-wringing in the underground press. The American magazine *Ramparts* called it a 'betrayal' and the *New Left Review*: "a lamentable petty bourgeois cry of fear". *Time* magazine, on the other hand, devoted a whole article to the song which it said, "criticized radical activists the world over".

The nature of John's dilemma is revealed in an exchange of letters published in a Keele University magazine. In an open letter, student John Hoyland said of 'Revolution': "That record was no more revolutionary than *Mrs Dale's Diary* (a BBC radio soap).

In order to change the world, we've got to understand what's wrong with the world. And then — destroy it. Ruthlessly. This is not cruelty or madness. It is one of the most passionate forms of love. Because what we're fighting is suffering, oppression, humiliation – the immense toll of unhappiness caused by capitalism. And any 'love' which does not pit itself against these things is sloppy and irrelevant. There is no such thing as a polite revolution."

In his reply, John wrote: "I don't remember saying that 'Revolution' was revolutionary. Fuck Mrs Dale. Listen to all three versions of Revolution – 1, 2 and 9 and then try again, dear John (Hoyland). You say 'in order to change the world, we've got to understand what's wrong with the world and then destroy it. Ruthlessly'. You're obviously on a destruction kick. I'll tell you what's wrong with it – people. So, do you want to destroy them? Ruthlessly? Until you/we change your/our heads – there's no chance. Tell me one successful revolution. Who fucked up communism, Christianity, capitalism, Buddhism etc? Sick heads, and nothing else. Do you think all the enemy wear capitalist badges so that you can shoot them? It's a bit naive, John. You seem to think it's just a class war."

Interviewed later by journalists from the magazine, John (Lennon) said: "All I'm saying is I think you should do it by changing people's heads, and they're saying we should smash the system. Now the system smashing scene has been going on forever. What's it done? The Irish did it, the Russians did it and the French did it and where has it got them? It's got them nowhere. It's the same old game. Who's going to run this smashing up? Who's going to take over? It'll be the biggest smashers. They'll be the ones to get in first and, like in Russia, they'll be the ones to take over. I don't know what the answer is but I think it's down to people."

It was a position John was to hold to. In 1980, he said that 'Revolution' still stood as an expression of his politics. "Count me out if it's for violence. Don't expect me on the barricades unless it's with flowers."

HONEY PIE

Honey Pie' was a tribute to Jim McCartney from his son. "My dad's always played fruity old songs like this, and I like them," Paul said. "I would have liked to have been a writer in the Twenties because I like the top hat and tails thing."

Just as he believed 'Helter Skelter' was written for him personally, Charles Manson found further instructions in 'Honey Pie'. After all, it was addressed to people in the USA, inviting them to display the magic of their 'Hollywood song'? Manson lived near Los Angeles. What could be clearer?

SAVOY TRUFFLE

By now, George was seeing a lot of Eric Clapton and 'Savoy Truffle' was a playful song about Clapton's love of chocolate. This habit contributed to Clapton's tooth decay and George was warning him that one more soft-centred chocolate and he'd have to have his teeth pulled out.

The song's lyric is made up of the exotic names then given to individual chocolates in Mackintosh's *Good News* assortment such as Creme Tangerine, Montelimart, Ginger Sling and Coffee Dessert. Savoy Truffle was another authentic name, whereas Cherry Cream and Coconut Fudge were invented to fit the song.

Derek Taylor helped with the middle eight by suggesting the title of a film he'd just seen called *You Are What You Eat* which was made by two American friends, Alan Pariser and Barry Feinstein. It didn't scan properly so George changed it to 'you know that what you eat you are'.

CRY BABY CRY

In 1968, as Hunter Davies was finishing his biography of the Beatles, John told him: "I've got another (song) here, a few words, I think I got them from an advert – 'Cry baby cry, Make your mother buy'. I've been playing it over on the piano. I've let it go now. It'll come back if I really want it."

The lines came back to him while he was in India where Donovan remembered him working on it. "I think the eventual imagery was suggested by my own songs of fairytales. We had become very close in exchanging musical vibes."

Partly based on the nursery rhyme 'Sing A Song Of Sixpence', the song includes John's own creations the Duchess of Kirkaldy and the King of Marigold. Kirkaldy is in Fife, Scotland, and the Beatles played there at the Carlton Theatre on October 5, 1963, just as Beatlemania was breaking.

REVOLUTION 9

'Revolution 9' was neither a Lennon and McCartney song nor a Beatles' recording but an 8 minute and 15 second-long amalgamation of taped sounds which John and Yoko mixed together.

The album track of 'Revolution' originally clocked in at over 10 minutes; more than half of it consisting of John and Yoko screaming and moaning over a range of discordant sounds, created to simulate the rumblings of a revolution. Subsequently, they decided to clip the chaotic section and use it as the basis of another track, which turned into 'Revolution 9'.

At this point, home-made tapes of crowd disturbances were brought in and other sound effects were found in EMI's library. Due to the lack of sophisticated multi-track recording, all three Abbey Road studios had to be commandeered, with machines being specially linked together and tape loops held in place with pencils. John operated the faders to create a live mix.

With so many overlapping sounds, it is almost impossible to identify all the individual noises and spoken comments. Mark Lewisohn, who studied the original four-track recording, divided these into: a choir; backwards violins; a backwards symphony; an orchestral overdub from 'A Day In The Life'; banging glasses; applause; opera; backwards mellotron; humming; spoken phrases by John and George, and a cassette tape of Yoko and John screaming the word 'right' from 'Revolution'.

The most memorable tape, (which supplied part of the title), was the sonorous voice intoning 'Number Nine, Number Nine'. This was apparently discovered on a library tape, which may have formed part of a taped examination question for students of the Royal Academy of Music.

Once again, Charles Manson thought that John was speaking personally to him through the hubbub, taking the number 9 as a reference to Revelation chapter 9 with its vision of the coming apocalypse. Manson thought John was shouting 'rise', rather than 'right', and interpreted it as an incitement to the black community to rise against the white middle class. 'Rise' became one of Manson's key phrases and was found painted in blood at one of the murder scenes.

Paul was in America when 'Revolution 9' was put together and was disappointed at its inclusion on *The Beatles*, particularly as he had been making sound collages at home since 1966 and realized that John would now be seen as the innovator.

◄ ....
Although Cynthia accompanied John to India, it was Yoko who was becoming his spiritual companion.

Perhaps aware that his family was about to break up, John wrote 'Good Night' as a lullaby for Julian.

GOOD NIGHT

Good Night' is certainly the most schmaltzy song ever written by John. If it had been one of Paul's songs, he would probably have dismissed it as "garbage" but his final comment was only that it was possibly "over-lush".

John wrote it, he said, for Julian as a bedtime song just as, 12 years later, he would write 'Beautiful Boy' for his second son Sean.

Julian wasn't aware that John had written the song for him until he was interviewed for this book. This was probably due to the fact that his parents split up within a few weeks of its composition.

DON'T LET ME DOWN

John had always expressed fears of being let down by those he had put his trust in. 'If I Fell' was the template for a number of songs in which he confessed his need for love and his anxiety over being rejected.

Written about Yoko and released as the B side of 'Get Back' in April 1969, this same old worry was expressed as an agonizing cry having found someone who loved him more than anyone had ever done before. Influenced by Yoko's minimalist approach to art, he has cut out all embellishments, reducing his perennial plea to the form of an urgent telegram.

LET IT BE

LET IT BE

The Beatles pictured with Yoko listening to a track for *Let It Be*. **At one time they all stood together, now they sat apart, barely able to conceal the differences** ▼ **between them.**

Committed to completing one last movie for United Artists, but with no inclination to perform in another romp, the Beatles fulfilled their contract with *Let It Be*, an 80-minute colour documentary of the group rehearsing at

LIB-1

Twickenham Film Studios, recording at Apple Studios and playing live on the roof of the Apple office in London. These three strands were filmed in January 1969 but the film wasn't premiered until May 1970, when a boxed album and book set was tied into the release. The album wasn't available on its own until November 1970.

The original plan had been to make an album called 'Get Back' and to film the recording process for a television documentary. There was also the possibility of performing live for the programme and a number of venues were considered – the Roundhouse in London, Liverpool Cathedral and a Roman amphitheatre in Tunisia.

The film and album that finally did emerge involved compromises. Instead of being a document of how a group created, *Let It Be* became a record of how a group fell apart. In order to get the album finished, Paul assumed control, pushing and prodding where necessary, while John and George sulked, openly displaying their resentment.

Rows over the album contributed to the group's final break-up. American Allen Klein, now acting as their manager, wasn't happy with the quality of the tapes which engineer Glyn Johns had edited down, and so he brought in a fellow American, producer Phil Spector, to beef up the production. When Paul heard what Spector had done to 'The Long And Winding Road', he requested that it be restored to its original form. After this request was ignored, Paul announced his departure from the Beatles.

The *Let It Be* album was scrappy. Because it was the last album released, it's often assumed that it was the last album recorded. The amazing fact is that after the squabbling that characterized *Let It Be* the Beatles still went on to record *Abbey Road*, an album which George Martin still ranks as his favourite.

By the time *Let It Be* was released the Beatles had ceased to exist. Paul had already released his first solo album, although it wasn't until December 1970 that their union was officially dissolved following Paul's lawsuit. *Let It Be* reached the top of the British and American album charts after its release in May 1970. The advance orders of almost 4 million in the US were the largest for any album ever.

TWO OF US

Sung in the documentary *Let It Be* by John and Paul, both playing acoustic guitars, 'Two Of Us' sounds like a song about their Liverpool teenage years together – burning matches, lifting latches and going home to play more music together. But, by this time, the 'two of us' were not Paul and John but Paul and Linda. One of the most attractive things to Paul about his new girlfriend was her unpretentious 'hang-loose' approach to life. As his life became increasingly restricted by schedules and contractual obligations, he relished being with someone who seemed consistently laid-back, some-

It was Linda who helped Paul through his "hour of darkness" as the Beatles broke up. She introduced him to simple pleasures – such as Sunday driving and getting lost in the countryside.

one with whom he could forget he was a Beatle.

Soon after they met in London during the autumn of 1968, Linda taught Paul the delights of getting completely lost. She would drive him out of the city with no destination in mind and with the sole intention of ending up miles from anywhere. To a Beatle, who had become reliant on being constantly told where and when he was needed, and having his life organized for him with military precision, this was an exhilarating return to freedom. "As a kid I loved getting lost," explains Linda. "I would say to my father – let's get lost. But you could never seem to be able to get really lost. All signs would eventually lead back to

New York or wherever we were staying! Then, when I moved to England to be with Paul, we would put Martha in the back of the car and drive out of London. As soon as we were on the open road I'd say 'Let's get lost' and we'd keep driving without looking at any signs. Hence the line in the song 'two of us going nowhere'.

"Paul wrote 'Two Of Us' on one of those days out," Linda explains. "It's about us. We just pulled off in a wood somewhere and parked the car. I went off walking while Paul sat in the car and started writing. He also mentions the postcards because we used to send a lot of postcards to each other."

DIG A PONY

Dig A Pony' was largely made up in the studio and the words make very little sense. At one point it was called 'Con A Lowry' (possibly a reference to a make of organ used in the studio) but John changed it to 'Dig A Pony', "because 'I con a Lowry' didn't sing well...It's got to be d's and p's, you know."

Similarly, the line 'I do a road hog' started as 'I dig a skylight' and then became 'I did a groundhog'. "It had to be rougher," John argued. "I don't care if skylight was prettier." The chorus was taken from a separate song of John's written about Yoko called 'All I Want Is You'. The original song listing for the album used this title rather than 'Dig A Pony'.

In January 1969 when the song was recorded, John explained the secret of its composition, "I just make it up as I go along". In September 1980, he laconically concluded, "(just) another piece of garbage".

ACROSS THE UNIVERSE

The oldest song on the *Let It Be* album, 'Across The Universe' was recorded in February 1968 and first featured on a charity album for the World Wildlife Fund in December 1969.

A song about writing songs, or at least about the wonders of the creative process, John was often to refer to it as one of his favourite Beatles' songs because of the purity of the lyric. The words had come to him while in bed at Kenwood. He had been arguing with Cynthia and, as he lay there trying to sleep, the phrase 'pools of sorrow, waves of joy' came to him and wouldn't leave until he got up and started writing the words down. "It drove me out of bed," John said. "I didn't want to write it. I was just slightly irritable and I couldn't go to sleep."

Written after having met the Maharishi Mahesh Yogi in England but before studying with him in India the chorus makes mention of Guru Dev, who was Maharishi's guru. John wanted this to be the single that the Beatles put out while they were away in India but it lost out to 'Lady Madonna'. David Bowie later recorded a cover version on his *Young Americans* album (1975) on which John played guitar.

David Bowie got to know John in New York during the Seventies. They collaborated as writers on Bowie's hit single 'Fame'.

◄ ·····························

I ME MINE

As George became more deeply involved in Eastern thought, he tried to reconcile his position as a rock star with the religious demands of relinquishing his ego in order to attain enlightenment.

It was his belief that it is our preoccupation with our individual egos – what 'I' want, what belongs to 'me', what's 'mine' – which prevents us from being absorbed into the universal consciousness, where there is no duality and no ego. "There is nothing that isn't part of the complete whole," George said. "When the little 'i' merges into the big 'I', then you are really smiling!"

The waltz tune of 'I Me Mine' was inspired by music he heard being played by an Austrian marching band on a television broadcast.

George, pictured here recording in Bombay, fought to reconcile his belief in the value of humility with the growing demands of rock superstardom

DIG IT

Credited to all four Beatles, 'Dig It' started as a fledgling song by John called 'Can You Dig It' which consisted of variations of the title being sung over a riff.

The version released on *Let It Be* was an excerpt from a much longer jam in which all the Beatles made up lines on the spot, hence the shared composer credit.

There was a lot of time spent hanging around reading newspapers when they record-ed which might account for the references to the FBI and CIA. Transcripts of studio conversations reveal George talking about blues guitarist B B King and distinguishing him from fellow blues man Freddie King. Matt Busby was the heroic manager of Manchester United, one of England's most successful soccer teams.

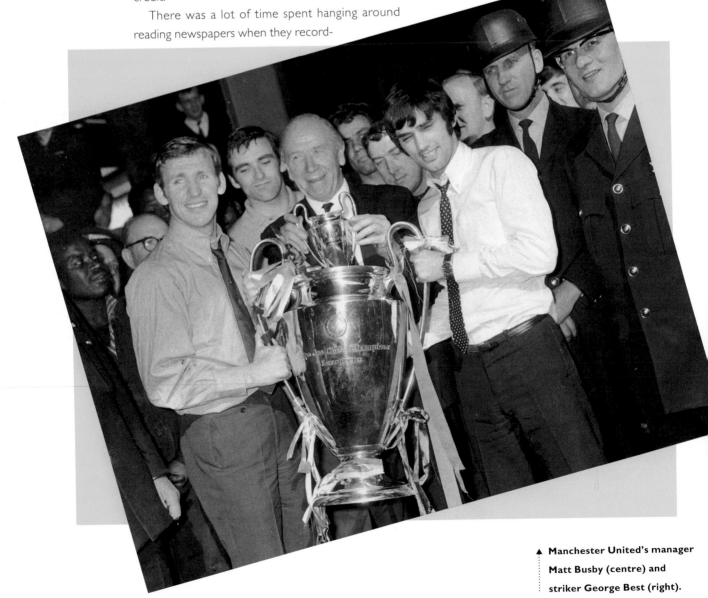

▲ **Manchester United's manager Matt Busby (centre) and striker George Best (right).**

LET IT BE

▲ The arrival of Yoko in
1968 turned John's
affections away from
the Beatles and helped
to end the partnership
between him and Paul.

Released as a single in March 1970, 'Let It Be' sounded as if it had been deliberately recorded as the Beatles' swansong. However, the fact is it was recorded in January 1969. No-one had any idea that it was going to be the last single.

Paul had written 'Let It Be' out of his general feelings of despair, as the Beatles began to fall apart at the seams. The documentary of the same title had started out as a record of a rehearsal followed by a live performance, but it was to become a record of the group's death throes.

By now, John preferred to spend his time with Yoko whose presence around the studio was not welcome with everyone. George had already quit the group once and was discouraged at the way his songs were being instantly rejected. Even Ringo had taken off for a short holiday during the recording of the White Album when the atmosphere got really bad.

Paul was clearly trying to take over the role of leader because he felt that without organization and discipline nothing would be achieved. "I think we've been very negative since Mr Epstein passed away," Paul can be heard saying in the film. "We haven't been positive. That's why all of us in turn have been sick of the group. There's nothing positive in it. It's a bit of a drag. The only way for it not to be a bit of a drag is for the four of us to think – should we make it positive or should we forget it?"

Although Paul's role may have been necessary, it didn't make him popular. The others began to resent his chiding and chivying in the studio. 'Let It Be' was written by Paul as a response to all this pressure: "I wrote it when all those business problems started to get me down," he said. "I really was passing through my 'hour of darkness' and writing the song was my way of exorcizing the ghosts." Written in the style of a modern hymn, the religious feeling was heightened by the invocation of 'mother Mary' which appeared to be a reference to the Virgin Mary but was in fact a reference to Paul's own mother, who he was imagining being there and offering support.

"I used to lie in bed and wonder what was going on and feel quite paranoid," Paul revealed. "I had a dream one night about my mother. She had died when I was 14, so I hadn't heard from her in quite a while and it was very good. It gave me some strength. In my darkest hour, mother Mary had come to me."

▲ On October 18, 1968, John and Yoko appeared at Marylebone Magistrate Court charged with possession of marijuana and obstructing the police. John admitted to possession.

I'VE GOT A FEELING

I've got A Feeling' was again two unfinished songs strung together, this time Paul's 'I've Got A Feeling' and John's 'Everybody's Had A Hard Year'. Paul's song, optimistic as ever, was presumably written for Linda just to tell her that she was the girl he'd always been looking for. John's song was a litany where every line began with the word 'everybody'.

John had indeed been through a hard year. His marriage to Cynthia had ended, he was separated from his son Julian, Yoko had suffered a miscarriage, he had been arrested on a charge of drug possession and he reckoned his personal fortune had dwindled to about £50,000.

During the filming of *Let It Be*, John runs through 'Everybody Had A Hard Year' and states, somewhat tongue in cheek, that it was something he had started writing the night before. If this were true, it would date the song's origin to January 1969, but there is BBC film of him shot in December 1968, where he is singing the song with an acoustic guitar in the garden of his Ascot home.

THE LONG AND WINDING ROAD

Like 'Yesterday', 'The Long And Winding Road' evokes loss without describing any specific situation. The images of wind and rain suggest feelings of being abandoned in the wilderness, while the long and winding road leading to 'her door' is the sign of hope.

The imagery actually comes from Paul's experience of staying at High Park, his farm in Scotland, which is exposed to high winds and frequently lashed with rain. The long and winding road itself is the B842, sixteen miles of twists and turns which runs down the east coast of Kintyre into Campbeltown, the nearest town to the farm.

Paul had the voice of Ray Charles in mind when he wrote it, and this influenced the use of jazzy chords. The road he envisaged as an endless road because the song is about what is eventually unattainable.

It was released as a single in America in May 1970 and reached the Number 1 spot.

ONE AFTER 909

'One After 909' could well be the oldest Lennon and McCartney song ever to be recorded by the Beatles. It was one of 'over a hundred songs' which they often talked about having written before recording 'Love Me Do' and goes back to that time together at Forthlin Road.

The Beatles first recorded 'One After 909' in March 1963 during the same session which produced 'From Me To You' but George Martin was so unimpressed with it that it had never been released. It was an attempt by John, in 1957, to write an American railroad song, after skiffle hits such as 'Last Train To San Fernando' by Johnny Duncan, 'Cumberland Gap' and 'Rock Island Line' by Lonnie Donegan and 'Freight Train' by the Chas McDevitt Skiffle Group.

"We used to sag (play truant) off school, go back to my house and the two of us would write," Paul recalled. "There are a lot of songs from back then that we've never reckoned on because they're all very unsophisticated songs...We hated the words to 'One After 909'."

The landscape of Kintyre in Scotland supplied Paul with the imagery for 'The Long And Winding Road'.

FOR YOU BLUE

GET BACK

Completed in six takes, 'For You Blue' was known as 'George's Blues' and on George's original lyric sheet as 'For You Blues' but became 'For You Blue' on the album.

George was always the Beatle most keen to develop his musical skills and it was through this that he developed close friendships with musicians as diverse as Ravi Shankar and Eric Clapton. It also led him to constantly experiment with different tunings, instruments and styles of playing.

Written for Pattie, 'For You Blue' was an exercise in writing a traditional-sounding blues song. George's only comment on it since has been to say: "It's a simple 12-bar song following all the normal 12-bar principles except that it's happy-go-lucky!"

Paul said that he'd originally written 'Get Back' "as a political song" and surviving demos show that he was planning a satire on the attitudes of those who felt that immigrants to Britain should be repatriated. Sung from the point of view of someone who didn't 'dig no Pakistanis taking all the people's jobs' and so was urging them to 'get back' to where they came from, its satirical intentions could easily have been misconstrued.

Years later, Paul was still having to field questions from journalists who'd heard bootleg editions of this version and who wondered if he'd gone through a racist period. "(The verses) were not racist at all," he said. "They were anti-racist...If there was any group that was not racist, it was the Beatles. All our favourite people were always black."

By the time it was recorded, 'Get Back' had been transformed into a song about Jojo from Tucson, Arizona, (Linda Eastman lived for a while in Tuscon) and Loretta Martin who 'thought she was a woman, But she was another man'. No story was developed

and the orginal 'Get back' chorus was retained. Because it was a rock'n'roll song, 'Get Back' was taken to refer to a return to musical roots and Apple's newspaper advert which bore the slogan 'The Beatles as nature intended' appeared to confirm this notion. "'Get Back' is the Beatles' new single," ran the copy. "It's the first Beatles' record which is as live as can be, in this electronic age. There's no electronic watchamacallit. 'Get Back' is a pure spring-time rock number."

It went on to quote Paul saying, "We were sitting in the studio and we made it up out of thin air...we started to write words there and then...when we finished it, we recorded it at Apple Studios and made it into a song to rollercoast by."

'Get Back' sold over two million copies and was a hit around the world. It reached the Number 1 spot in Britain, America, Australia, Canada, West Germany and France.

John viewed himself and Yoko as a misunderstood and persecuted couple. They married in Gibraltar and increasingly turned their lives together into the main subject of their work.

THE BALLAD OF JOHN AND YOKO

The Ballad Of John And Yoko' – in which John related the details of his marriage to Yoko in Gibraltar and their subsequent 'honeymoon' – was recorded in mid-April and released before the end of May. Paul helped with the final verse. The song portrayed the couple as victims about to be 'crucified': the two are turned back at Southampton docks; can't get a wedding licence in France; then they're misunderstood as they lie in bed 'for peace' and laughed at when they sit in a bag.

Something John failed to mention was the fact that they were turned back at Southampton dock not because of his notoriety but because they were trying to travel to France without passports. The plane they 'finally made' into Paris was not a scheduled airliner but an executive jet which John impatiently asked for when he realized that it was impossible to get married on a cross-Channel ferry.

John's decision to get married appeared to have been made suddenly on March 14, 1969, when he and Yoko were being driven down to Poole in Dorset to visit his Aunt Mimi. This was two days after Paul's registry office wedding to Linda. John asked his chauffeur Les Anthony to go on into Southampton and enquire about the possibility of their being married at sea. When this was found to be impossible, John decided to go to Paris and instructed his office to come up with a way of arranging a quiet wedding there. Peter Brown discovered that this couldn't be organized at short notice but that they could marry in Gibraltar because it was a British protectorate and John was a British citizen.

In the end, the couple flew by private plane to Gibraltar on March 20, and went straight to the British Consulate where the registrar, Cecil Wheeler, conducted a ten-minute marriage ceremony. They were on the ground for less than an hour before taking off for Amsterdam where they had booked the Presidential Suite at the Hilton. Their stay in Amsterdam was to be an extraordinary 'honey-

moon'. Instead of requiring the usual privacy, they invited the world's press to invade their bedroom daily between 10:00 am and 10:00 pm during which time, they said, they would be staying in bed for peace.

Not unnaturally, the world's press hoped that John and Yoko might be intending to consummate their marriage in public. After all, they'd exposed their naked bodies on the cover of their album *Two Virgins* and had recorded the heartbeat of the child that Yoko later miscarried. There seemed to be no area of their lives which they weren't willing to turn into performance art.

To the journalists' frustration, the sight that greeted them in suite 902 was of John and Yoko in neatly pressed pyjamas sitting bolt upright in bed doing nothing more than talking about 'peace'. It was the perfect deal. The media had an insatiable appetite for articles about the Beatles and John would do almost anything to put over his message about peace. The Amsterdam 'Bed In' meant that all parties went away satisfied.

For seven days, they lay there holding court while a stream of media people sat and asked serious questions. The coverage was incredible. They did live interviews with American radio stations, made a sixty-minute documentary for themselves and saw their faces appear on the front pages of newspapers world-wide. "Yoko and I are quite willing to be the world's clowns, if by doing it we do some good," said John. "For reasons known only to themselves people do print what I say. And I'm saying peace. We're not pointing a finger at anybody. There are no good guys and bad guys. The struggle is in the mind. We must bury our own monsters and stop condemning people. We are all Christ and all Hitler. We want Christ to win. We're trying to make Christ's message contemporary. What would he have done if he had advertisements, records, films, TV and newspapers? Christ made miracles to tell his message. Well, the miracle today is communications, so let's use it."

From Amsterdam, they went to Vienna where they stopped overnight at the Hotel Sacher and ate some of it's famous Sacher Torte (a rich chocolate cake) before watching the television premiere of their film *Rape*.

On April 1, they arrived back in London and gave a press conference at the airport. John expected a hostile reception because Yoko (a foreign divorcée, no less) was not considered the ideal partner for a British Beatle. To his surprise, the welcome was warm.

'The Ballad Of John And Yoko' was recorded by Paul and John with Paul playing bass, piano, maracas and drums, while John played lead and acoustic guitars and sang the vocals.

OLD BROWN SHOE

Old Brown Shoe' was one of three songs which George made a demo of at Abbey Road on February 25, 1969. The other two were 'Something', a future Beatles' single, and 'All Things Must Pass', the title track of his first solo album in 1970.

The lyric had its origins in George's religious view that we must free ourselves from the reality of the material world as it is illusory. Once absorbed into the divine consciousness, there would be no right versus wrong, body versus soul, spirit versus matter. Rather like Paul had done with 'Hello Goodbye', George's words were a game based on opposites. It wasn't a song which told much of a story and the intriguing title was pinched from a line about stepping out of 'this old brown shoe'. (George always had a problem coming up with titles.)

The main inspiration was musical. George had been messing around on a piano one day and hit on a chord sequence he liked. Words were added later.

Recorded two months after being demoed, 'Old Brown Shoe' became the B side of 'The Ballad Of John And Yoko'. Much later it was used as a track on the compilation albums *Hey Jude* and *The Beatles 1967-1970*.

▲ John and Yoko used the media's fascination with them to promote the causes they believed in. The Amsterdam 'Bed In' in March 1969 drew journalists from around the world.

YOU KNOW MY NAME

Released as the B side of 'Let It Be', 'You Know My Name' was the strangest single ever released by the Beatles and remains one of their least-known songs.

It had first been recorded shortly after the completion of *Sgt Pepper*, after John arrived at Abbey Road wanting to record a song called 'You Know My Name, Look Up The Number'. When Paul asked to see the lyric, John told him that *was* the lyric. He wanted it repeated in the style of the Four Tops' 'Reach Out, I'll Be There' until it sounded like a mantra. The line was a variation on a slogan John had noticed on the front cover of the Post Office's London telephone directory for 1967 which read; 'You have their NAME? Look up their NUMBER.'

For three days in May and June 1967, the Beatles worked on the song but then abandoned it until April 1969 when the track was taken out for reworking. Although John's original idea of repeating the title phrase was adhered to, the song was transformed from a mantra into what sounded like a karaoke night in Hell, organized by the Goons or the Bonzo Dog Doo Dah Band.

The only departure from the scripted words came when John twice asked for a big hand for 'Denis O'Bell', a reference to the Irish born film producer Denis O'Dell who had been Associate Producer on *A Hard Day's Night* and who had become director of Apple Films and Apple Publicity.

None of the Beatles told O'Dell that they had referred to him in the song and so it came as a shock to him when he started receiving anonymous telephone calls at his home in St George's Square, Pimlico.

"There were so many of them my wife started going out of her mind," says O'Dell. "Neither of us knew why this was suddenly happening. Then I happened to be in one Sunday and picked up the 'phone myself. It was someone on LSD calling from a candle making factory in Philadelphia and they just kept saying 'We know your name and now we've got your number'.

"It was only through talking to the person that I established what it was all about. Then Ringo, who I'd worked with on the film *The Magic Christian*, played me the track and I realized why I'd been getting all these mysterious phone calls. It was because of this experience that I first went ex-directory. We were starting to get people turn up on the doorstep. Once there were 10 or 12 of these people who'd tracked me down and they arrived thinking they could all come and live with us!

"I still don't really know why they put my name in the song. I wasn't in the studio with them at the time as far as I can remember. They've never mentioned it since!"

Seven years on from their first recordings at the Abbey Road Studios, the Beatles returned for what proved to be their final sessions together. Back in June 1962, they were wide-eyed provincial lads keen to make their mark on the music business. By July 1969, they had become world-weary sophisticates, their lives blighted by power and money struggles.

The songs on *Abbey Road* reflected their frustrations. They're about legal negotiations, unpaid debts, being ripped off, bad karma and generally bearing the weight of the world on your shoulders. There was even a mock-jolly song about that silver hammer (namely Maxwell's) that is there waiting to come down hard on you just when things are starting to get better.

Despite this mood – or perhaps because of it – *Abbey Road* was an outstandingly inventive farewell offering. It features two of George's best songs, 'Here Comes The Sun and 'Something'; a stand-out track by John, 'Come Together', and a fascinating medley of half-finished songs skilfully woven together by Paul.

George Martin remembered that after *Let It Be*, Paul came to him and asked him to produce a Beatles' album with the kind of feeling they used to generate together. Martin agreed to help out if the Beatles were prepared to give him their co-operation. "That's how we made *Abbey Road*. It wasn't quite like the old days because they were still working on their old songs and they would bring in the other people to work as kind of musicians for them rather than being a team."

In Britain, *Abbey Road* was released in September 1969 and stayed at Number 1 for 18 weeks. In America, it was released in October and was at Number 1 for 11 weeks.

ABBEY ROAD

COME TOGETHER

Come Together' started life as a campaign song for the Timothy Leary roadshow, when he decided in 1969 that he was going to run as governor of California against America's future president Ronald Reagan.

Leary and his wife Rosemary were invited up to Montreal, where John and Yoko were between the sheets for another major 'bed in' on the 19th floor of the Queen Elizabeth Hotel. They arrived on June 1, 1969, and were promptly roped into singing on the chorus of 'Give Peace A Chance', which was recorded in the hotel bedroom. Leary and his wife were rewarded for their participation by having their names included in the lyric.

The next day, John asked Leary if there was anything that he could do to help him in his campaign and was asked if he could write a song to be used in commercials and performed at rallies. Leary's slogan was 'come together, join the party' – the 'come together' part coming from the *I Ching*, the Chinese book of changes. "There was obviously a double meaning there," said Leary. "It was come together and join the party – not a political party but a celebration of life."

John immediately picked up his guitar and began building on the phrase: 'Come together right now, Don't come tomorrow, Don't come alone, Come together right now over me, All that I can tell you, Is you gotta be free.' After coming up with a few more versions along the same lines, he made a demo tape and handed it to Leary.

Leary had the song played on alternative radio stations throughout California and began to think of it as his own. However, unknown to him, John had returned to England and within seven weeks had recorded a version with the Beatles. In October, it was released on the flip side of 'Something', the first single to be taken from *Abbey Road*.

Leary's campaign to become governor of California came to an abrupt halt in December 1969, when he was charged with possessing marijuana and eventually imprisoned. It was while in prison, that Leary first heard *Abbey Road* on a local rock station and, no doubt, 'Come Together' came as something of a surprise. "Although the new version was certainly a musical and lyrical improvement on my campaign song, I was a bit miffed that Lennon had passed me over this way... When I sent a mild protest to John, he replied with typical Lennon charm and wit that he was a tailor and I was a customer who had ordered a suit and never returned. So he sold it to someone else."

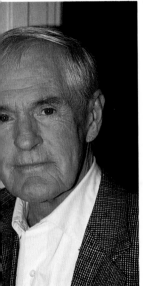

The recorded version, with its semi-nonsense lyric, was largely made up in the studio, the swampy New Orleans bass having been added by Paul. Two of the song lines referring to 'old flat top' were lifted from Chuck Berry's 'You Can't Catch Me' and John was later sued for plagiarism. It was hard to deny where the words had come from, although, in this new context, they were nothing more than an affectionate nod towards the music of his youth. John strenuously denied any musical theft.

The conflict was resolved when John promised to record three songs belonging to the publisher of 'You Can't Catch Me'. He fulfilled this promise when he recorded Berry's 'Sweet Little Sixteen' and 'You Can't Catch Me' for his *Rock'n'Roll* album and Lee Dorsey's 'Ya Ya' on *Walls and Bridges*.

'Come Together' was released as a single in October 1969 and topped the American charts. Teamed up with 'Something' as a double A side in Britain, it only reached Number 4.

SOMETHING

'Something' was the first Beatles' A side to be written by George. Its main source of inspiration was a 1968 album track by James Taylor titled 'Something In The Way She Moves'. Despite what is popularly believed, George has said that it was not written about his wife Pattie.

Taylor, an American, was signed to the Apple label and his eponymous first album was produced by Peter Asher between July and October 1968. Paul played bass on one track. 'Something In The Way She Moves' was the last track on the first side and the opening lines were: 'There's something in the way she moves, Or looks my way or calls my name, That seems to leave this troubled world behind.'

The White Album was being recorded at Abbey Road at exactly the same time as Taylor was recording at Trident Studios in London's Soho. Indeed, on October 3, George was at Trident recording 'Savoy Truffle' with Paul and Ringo and probably heard the track then. "I've always assumed George must have heard it but I never spoke to him about it," says Taylor. "I'd written 'Something In The Way She Moves' about two years before I recorded it and, strangely enough I'd wanted to call it 'I Feel Fine', but of course that was a Beatles' track.

"I often notice traces of other people's work in my own songs," Taylor continues. "If George either consciously or unconsciously took a line from one of my songs then I find it very flattering. It's certainly not an unusual thing to happen. I'd made a tape of 'Something In The Way She Moves' and about seven other songs about a couple of months before I met Peter Asher. I know Paul listened to it at Apple but I'm not sure who else listened to it."

The basic writing of 'Something' must have taken place in October because George has said that he worked it out on piano in Studio 1, while Paul was overdubbing in Studio 2. The only reason it wasn't included on the White Album was because the track selection had already been completed.

When Timothy Leary ran for governor of California, he solicited John's help in composing a campaign song. Leary lost both the song and the chance to be governor when he was arrested and imprisoned on a drugs charge.

John playing with Chuck Berry on the US TV programme *The Mike Douglas Show* in 1972. Berry was one of the Beatles' earliest heroes but when the words from one of his songs found their way into 'Come Together', Berry didn't hesitate to sue.

George first offered 'Something' to Joe Cocker and Jackie Lomax but then, in May 1969, decided to record it with the Beatles for *Abbey Road*. He said that when he wrote it he imagined Ray Charles singing it. 'Something' was an enormously successful song for George, becoming the second most covered Beatles' song after 'Yesterday' (Ray Charles and Smokey Robinson both did versions) and giving him his first American Top 10 hit.

MAXWELL'S SILVER HAMMER

A song, driven by strong rhymes, in which medical student Maxwell Edison uses his silver hammer to kill first his girlfriend, then

▲ George has denied that 'Something' was written for his wife Pattie (pictured here at the premiere of *Yellow Submarine*).

a lecturer and finally a judge. Delivered in a jaunty, vaudevillian style, the only indication of Paul's recent avant-garde leanings was the mention of 'pataphysics', a word invented by Alfred Jarry, the French pioneer of absurd theatre, to describe a branch of metaphysics.

"John told me that 'Maxwell's Silver Hammer' was

OH DARLING

Paul wanted his voice to sound raw on 'Oh Darling', so he sang it through again and again each day for a week before finally recording it. "I wanted it to sound as though I'd been performing it on stage all week," he said.

Inspired by the rock'n'roll ballads of the late Fifties, Jackie Wilson's in particular, it was a simple song pleading for a loved one to stay in exchange for lifelong devotion.

John never rated Paul's job on vocals and reckoned he could have done better. "It was more my style than his," he said.

When Paul went through his phase of being interested in all things avante-garde, he read French playwright Alfred Jarry (1873-1907). A concept of Jarry's found its way into the lyric of 'Maxwell's Silver Hammer'.

◄ ....

about the law of karma," says former Apple employee Tony King. "We were talking one day about 'Instant Karma' (John's 1970 single with Yoko Ono and the Plastic Ono Band) because something had happened where he'd been clobbered and he'd said that this was an example of instant karma. I asked him whether he believed that theory. He said that he did and that 'Maxwell's Silver Hammer' was the first song that they'd made about that. He said that the idea behind the song was that the minute you do something that's not right, Maxwell's silver hammer will come down on your head."

Paul said at the time that the song, "epitomizes the downfalls of life. Just when everything is going smoothly, 'bang bang' down comes Maxwell's silver hammer and ruins everything."

John would remember that the song had taken three whole days of overdubbing, because Paul imagined it could be a future single. "He did everything to make it into a single and it never was and it never could have been."

OCTOPUS'S GARDEN

Ringo's second (and last) Beatles' song was inspired by a family boating holiday in Sardinia which he took in 1968. After Ringo had turned down the offer of an octopus lunch, the vessel's captain started to tell him all he knew about the life of octopuses.

"He told me how they go around the sea bed picking up stones and shiny objects to build gardens with," said Ringo. "I thought this was fabulous because at the time I just wanted to be under the sea too. I wanted to get out of it for a while."

To most listeners, it was a children's seaside song in the vein of 'Yellow Submarine' but, in 1969, George revealed that there were hidden dimensions. Even though Ringo only knew three chords on the piano, George said, the drummer was writing "cosmic songs without really noticing it."

I WANT YOU

Inspired by Yoko's minimalist art, John pared down his lyrics and began contributing his own work to galleries.

Consisting only of the repeated title line and the information that the desire is driving John mad, the lyric of 'I Want You' was once read out on BBC TV's current affairs programme *24 Hours* as an example of the banalities of pop music.

This incensed John who was convinced that its simplicity made it superior to 'Eleanor Rigby' and 'I Am The Walrus'. To him, this was not a reversion to mindless monosyllabic pop but simply economy of language.

'I Want You' was written as a love song to Yoko. John admitted the influence she had on his new style of writing, saying that eventually he wanted to compose a perfect song using only one word. A 1964 poem of Yoko's consisted of the single word 'water'.

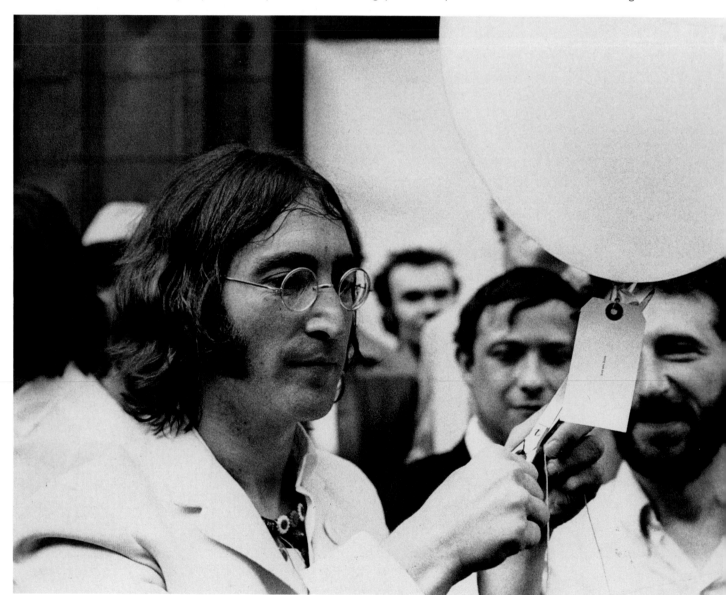

HERE COMES THE SUN

Written by George, 'Here Comes The Sun' was an expression of delight at being able to slip away from the interminable business meetings which were now taking up so much of the Beatles' time.

In January 1969, John and Yoko met with music business manager Allen Klein and shortly afterwards declared that he would be looking after their business affairs, despite the fact that New York laywer John Eastman, brother of Linda, had recently been brought in to represent the Beatles collectively. This was the beginning of a bitter drawn-out conflict over who should manage the Beatles and what should be done about the chaotic state of their finances. Despite the tremendous sales of Beatles' music over the past six years, John claimed, "all of us could be broke in six months."

Klein offered to restructure Apple, organize a takeover bid for the shares the Beatles didn't own in Northern Songs and renegotiate a better royalty deal with EMI. He was able to persuade John, George and Ringo of his ability to do these things but Paul remained loyal to Eastman. As a result the Beatles' existence was now under threat and the frequent meetings at Apple were fraught with tension. One morning in the early spring, George decided it was all getting a bit too much like school, and so he took a day off from the round table routine and went to see his friend Eric Clapton at his country home in Ewhurst, Surrey.

Borrowing one of Eric's acoustic guitars, George took a walk around the gardens and, basking in the first real sunshine of the year, he felt a sudden flush of optimism and started to write 'Here Comes The Sun'. "It was such a great release for me simply being out in the sun," said George at the time. "The song just came to me."

Allen Klein impressed John but worried Paul. This was a major factor in the Beatles' eventual break up.

BECAUSE

John was relaxing on a sofa at home, while Yoko played the first movement of Beethoven's Piano Sonata No 14 in C Sharp Minor ('Moonlight Sonata') on the grand piano. John has said that he asked her if she could play the same chords in reverse order. This she did, and it proved to be the inspiration for 'Because'.

The similarity between the opening of the 'Moonlight Sonata' and 'Because' is striking, although close scrutiny reveals it to be a straightforward lift rather than the reversal of notes John suggested. Musicologist Wilfrid Mellers, author of *Twilight Of The Gods: The Music of the Beatles* puts it this way, "The affinity between the enveloping, arpeggiated C sharp minor triads, with the sudden shift to the flat supertonic, is, in the Lennon and Beethoven examples, unmistakable."

There was a touch of irony in the idea of a Beatle borrowing from Beethoven because there was a common perception at the time that rock'n'roll was antithetical to classical music and that no-one could genuinely appreciate both. It also probably didn't help that the Beatles had recorded Chuck Berry's 'Roll Over Beethoven', an irreverent piece of advice to classical composers asking them to make way for rock'n'roll.

One of the first questions the Beatles were always asked in America was, 'What do you think of Beethoven?' It was Ringo who answered. "I love him," he said. "Especially his poems." But it was John, in particular, who came to regard Beethoven as the supreme composer, and one with whom he felt kinship. By 1969, he was no longer trying to be the artistic equal of Elvis or the Rolling Stones, but of Picasso, Van Gogh, Dylan Thomas and Beethoven.

Music critics, keen to stress the seriousness and significance of the Beatles, often drew not entirely convincing parallels between them and the great composers. In a celebrated *Observer* (London) review of the White Album, critic and film maker Tony Palmer declared the Beatles to be, "the greatest songwriters since Schubert" and promised that the double album would "surely see the last vestiges of cultural snobbery and bourgeois prejudice swept away in a deluge of joyful music making, which only the ignorant will not hear and only the deaf will not acknowledge."

YOU NEVER GIVE ME YOUR MONEY

You Never Give Me Your Money' announced the medley of half-finished songs which dominate the second side of *Abbey Road*. Paul collected the songs and carefully worked out a way of linking them together. 'You Never Give Me Your Money' itself is made up of three distinct fragments. The first, which develops the line in the title, was an allusion to the Beatles' financial problems saying that instead of money all they ever seemed to get was 'funny paper'.

"That's what we get," said George. "We get bits of paper saying how much is earned and what this and that is but we never actually get it in pounds, shillings and pence. We've all got a big house and a car and an office but to actually get the money we've earned seems impossible."

The next fragment, which mentions being penniless after leaving college, may have referred to the same problems but was written in the jolly, nostalgic style of Paul's 'woke up/got out of bed' section of 'A Day In The Life'. The final piece was about the freedom of Paul's new life with Linda, where he could just pack the car and drive out of town leaving his worries behind.

The guitar work of Peter Green of Fleetwood Mac (second from left in line-up) inspired George's playing on 'Sun King'.

SUN KING

As with 'Being For The Benefit Of Mr Kite!', John's opinions on 'Sun King' came to alter over the years but this time, changing from good to bad. In 1971, he referred to it as something that had come to him in a dream, implying that it was an inspired piece of work. By 1980, it had been revalued as just another piece of 'garbage'.

Historically, the Sun King was Louis XIV of France and it could have been he who John dreamt about. Nancy Mitford had recently published a biography of Louis which was titled *The Sun King* and John may have seen it.

The closing lines are composed of those Italian, Spanish and Portuguese words which tourists pick up, strung together in no particular order – 'paparazzi', 'obrigado', 'parasol', 'mi amore'. The original title of the song was 'Los Paranoias'. According to George, the point of musical departure was Fleetwood Mac's 'Albatross', a dreamy instrumental which had been a British Top 10 hit in the early part of 1969.

MEAN MR MUSTARD

John said that 'Mean Mr Mustard' was inspired by a newspaper story about a miser who concealed his cash wherever he could in order to prevent people forcing him to spend it. The line about stuffing a 'ten bob note' (a British ten shilling note) up his nose John admitted was his own invention, claiming that it had absolutely nothing to do with snorting cocaine.

Tony Bramwell believes another colourful London character also provided John with inspiration for this song. "There was an old 'bag lady' who used to hang around the Knightsbridge end of Hyde Park, close to the army barracks," he remembers. "She had all her possessions in plastic bags and slept in the park. I'm sure that she had something to do with the song."

Written in India, 'Mean Mr Mustard' was recorded with 'Sun King' in one continuous piece. In the original version, Mr Mustard had a sister called Shirley but John changed it to Pam when he realized that it could more easily segue into 'Polythene Pam'.

POLYTHENE PAM

Although John initially insisted that 'Polythene Pam' was about "a mythical Liverpool scrubber (promiscuous girl or groupie) dressed up in her jackboots and kilt", the song was actually based on two people who he had known. The name came from Pat Dawson (then Pat Hodgett), a Beatles' fan from the Cavern Club days who, because of her habit of eating polythene, was known to the group as Polythene Pat. "I started going to see the Beatles in 1961 when I was 14 and I got quite friendly with them," she remembers. "If they were playing out of town they'd give me a lift back home in their van. It was about the same time that I started getting called Polythene Pat. It's embarrassing really. I just used to eat polythene all the time. I'd tie it in knots and then eat it. Sometimes I even used to burn it and then eat it when it got cold. Then I had a friend who got a job in a polythene bag factory, which was wonderful because it meant I had a constant supply."

But Polythene Pat never dressed up in polythene bags as the song says. That little quirk was taken from an incident involving a girl called Stephanie, who John met in the Channel Islands while on tour in August 1963.

Although John wouldn't elaborate when he spoke to *Playboy* in 1980, he did supply a few clues. "(Polythene Pam) was me remembering a little event with a woman in Jersey, and a man who was England's answer to Allen Ginsberg, who gave us our first exposure..."

England's answer to American beat poet Ginsberg turned out to be Royston Ellis, a young writer who first met the Beatles in May or June of 1960 when invited to read poetry at Liverpool University.

What John went on reluctantly to tell *Playboy* was that Ellis was the first person to introduce the Beatles to drugs when he showed them how to get high from the strips inside a Benzedrine inhaler.

The "little event with a woman", as John described it, actually took place on the Channel island of Guernsey, not Jersey, when John met up with Ellis who had a summer job there as a ferry boat engineer. After the Beatles' concerts at the Auditorium in Guernsey on August 8, Ellis and his girlfriend Stephanie took John back to the attic flat Ellis was renting and this is where the polythene came into the story.

"(Ellis) said Miss X (a girl he wanted me to meet) dressed up in polythene," John later remembered. "She did. She didn't wear jackboots and kilts. I just sort of elaborated. Perverted sex in a polythene bag. I was just looking for something to write about."

Ellis, who now lives in Sri Lanka and writes travel books, can't recall any 'perverted sex' but he can recall the night spent in a bed with Stephanie and John. "We'd read all these things about leather and we didn't have any leather but I had my oilskins and we had some polythene bags from somewhere," he

Royston Ellis' girlfriend, remembered only as Stephanie, was one of the two major inspirations behind John's song 'Polythene Pam'.

was thinking of bringing a Liverpool group called the 'Beetles' to London to play behind him as he performed his poetry. "I was quite a star for them at that time because I had come up from London and that was a world they didn't really know about," says Ellis. "I stayed with them for about a week in their flat at Gambier Terrace during that 1960 visit. John was fascinated by the fact that I was a poet and that led to deep conversations."

Shortly after introducing John to the delights of polythene, Ellis left England and has spent much of the time since travelling. So far removed has he been from the British pop scene, that he had never even heard 'Polythene Pam' until contacted for this book. He does recall with some pride, though, that in 1973 John wrote to the alternative newspaper *International Times* to correct them about the circumstances of the Beatles' first drug experiences: "The first dope, from a Benzedrine inhaler, was given the Beatles (John, George, Paul and Stuart) by an English cover version of Allen Ginsberg – one Royston Ellis, known as 'beat poet' ... So, give the saint his due."

says. " We all dressed up in them and wore them in bed. John stayed the night with us in the same bed. I don't think anything very exciting happened and we all wondered what the fun was in being 'kinky'. It was probably more my idea than John's. It could have all happened because in a poetry booklet of mine which I had dedicated to the Beatles there was a poem with the lines: 'I long to have sex between black leather sheets, And ride shivering motorcycles between your thighs.'

"I can't really remember everything that happened. At the time, it meant nothing to me. It was just one event during a very eventful time of my life," Ellis adds. Besides being a poet, Ellis was a pundit on teenage life and a chronicler of emergent British rock'n'roll. At the time of their first meeting, he had just completed *The Big Beat Scene*, an excellent survey of late Fifties British beat music.

John was fascinated by Ellis because he stood at the converging point of rock'n'roll and literature. Ellis arranged for the Beatles to back him early on at a beat music and poetry event at the Jacaranda Club. In July 1960, the *Record Mirror* reported that 'the bearded sage'

Stephanie reads while 'beat poet' Royston Ellis takes a nap in the Channel Islands in 1963, the year that Ellis met up again with John.

◄ ·····································

Royston Ellis (with glasses and beard) lands in Guernsey with the Beatles on August 8, 1963. It was that night that some of the events obliquely referred to in 'Polythene Pam' took place.

SHE CAME IN THROUGH THE BATHROOM WINDOW

Fans ranged from those who mobbed the group at airports (right) to the quietly persistent Apple Scruffs, who were on first-name terms with each Beatle. ▸

Paul and George at the time of the recording of *Abbey Road*. ▾

This song was inspired by the activities of an Apple Scruff who climbed into Paul's house in St John's Wood when he was away for the day. "We were bored, he was out and so we decided to pay him a visit," remembers Diane Ashley. "We found a ladder in his garden and stuck it up at the bathroom window which he'd left slightly open. I was the one who climbed up and got in."

Once she was inside the house, she opened the front door and let the rest of the girls in. Fellow Apple Scruff Margo Bird remembers: "They rummaged around and took some

clothes. People didn't usually take anything of real value but I think this time a lot of photographs and negatives were taken. There were really two groups of Apple Scruffs – those who would break in and those who would just wait outside with cameras and autograph books. I used to take Paul's dog for a walk and got to know him quite well. I was eventually offered a job at Apple. I started by making the tea and ended up in the promotions department working with Tony King."

Paul asked Margo if she could retrieve any of his belongings. "I knew who had done it and I discovered that a lot of the stuff had already gone to America," she said. "But I knew that there was one picture he particularly wanted back – a colour-tinted picture of him in a Thirties frame. I knew who had taken this and got it back for him."

Paul wrote 'She Came In Through The Bathroom Window' in June 1968 during a trip to America to do business with Capitol Records. It was here that he resumed his relationship with Linda Eastman, whom he'd been introduced to the previous summer in London and had since met in New York.

The line, 'and so I quit the police department' was inspired by the name of the police officer in New York who was assigned to him. Paul noticed from his licence badge that he was called Eugene Quits and so he worked part of the name into the final verse.

According to Carol Bedford, an Apple Scruff who wrote the book *Waiting For The Beatles*, Paul later said to her: "I've written a song about the girls who broke in. It's called 'She Came In Through The Bathroom Window'." Diane was surprised to have become the subject of a Beatles' song. "I didn't believe it at first because he'd hated it so much when we broke in," she says. "But then I suppose anything can inspire a song, can't it? I know that all his neighbours rang him when they saw we'd got in and I'm sure that gave rise to the lines, 'Sunday's on the 'phone to Monday/Tuesday's on the 'phone to me'."

Now married with four teenage children, Diane keeps a framed photo of herself with Paul on her kitchen shelf and looks back on her days as an Apple Scruff with affection. "I don't regret any of it. I had a great time, a really great time."

GOLDEN SLUMBERS

Paul was at his father's house in Cheshire tinkering around on the piano. Flicking through a songbook belonging to his step-sister Ruth (James McCartney had since remarried), he came across the traditional lullaby 'Golden Slumbers'. Unable to read the music, he went ahead and made up his own melody adding new words as he went along.

'Golden Slumbers' was written by the English writer and dramatist Thomas Dekker, who was a contemporary of Shakespeare. The song was first published in *The Pleasant Comedy of Old Fortunatus* (1600).

A Londoner born around 1570, Dekker was the author of *The Shoemaker's Holiday* (1600), *The Pleasant Comedy of Old Fortunatus* (1600), *The Honest Whore* (1604), *The Gull's Hornbook* (1609), *The Roaring Girl* (1611) and the posthumously published *The Syn's Darling* (1656).

HER MAJESTY

On August 22, 1969, the four Beatles posed together for the last time on John's Tittenhurst estate in Sunningdale, Ascot. Though the Beatles' partnership ended in 1970 amid lawsuits and acrimony, their recordings ensure that they will live forever.

Written by Paul in Scotland, 'Her Majesty' was originally part of the medley, coming between 'Mean Mr Mustard' and 'Polythene Pam' but, on hearing a playback, Paul didn't like it and asked for it to be edited out.

The engineer who cut it out then recycled it to the end of the tape so that it wouldn't be destroyed. Paul must have heard another playback with 'Her Majesty' now tacked on as an apparent afterthought. He liked it enough to keep it there. Because the edit was only meant to be rough, the last chord of 'Mean Mr Mustard' was pressed into service to start 'Her Majesty', which ends abruptly because its own final note was left behind at the beginning of 'Polythene Pam'.

The Beatles met Queen Elizabeth to receive their MBEs on October 26, 1965. Afterwards, asked what they thought of her, Paul answered: "She's lovely. She was very friendly. She was just like a mum to us."

'Her Majesty' has the dubious distinction of being the final track on the last album the Fab Four were ever to record together.

CARRY THAT WEIGHT

Although 'Carry That Weight' appears to be just another song in the medley and is credited as such on the album, it was in fact recorded with 'Golden Slumbers' as a single.

The lyric expressed Paul's fears about the Beatles in their twilight days. He later said that the arguments over finance and management plunged him into the "darkest hours" of his life so far. The atmosphere around the Beatles had changed from light to heavy. "At certain times things get to me so much that I can't be upbeat any more," he told his biographer Barry Miles.

THE END

As the final proper track on the last album recorded by the Beatles, 'The End' was to become the song which would sign off their studio career. Paul saw the couplet 'the love you take is equal to the love you make' as a musical equivalent of the rhyming couplets that Shakespeare ended his plays with, a signal that the events of the drama were now concluded.

It certainly provided a neat symmetry to their recording career – which started with the gawky pleadings of lovesick teenagers in 'Love Me Do', and matured to reveal enigmatic words of wisdom from the group who transformed popular music.

THE **BEATLES**

BRITISH BROADCASTING CORPORATION

'Live at the BBC'

LIVE AT THE BBC

▲ The Beatles outside the BBC's Paris Studio, Lower Regent Street, London, in 1963

In 1982 Kevin Howlett looked through the BBC's archives of radio sessions with the Beatles and produced a programme called *Beatles At The Beeb*. It was the first time that most of this material had been heard since the original broadcasts between 1962 and 1965. Shortly afterwards discussions began between EMI and the BBC to get the material released. However, it wasn't until 1994 that the right climate prevailed between the Beatles, Apple and EMI which enabled the project to be realized.

The BBC tapes were then taken by Kevin Howlett to George Martin at Abbey Road where Martin digitally remastered the 58 tracks which had survived from a total of 88 songs which the Beatles had played live on BBC radio. In fact, only 57 of the tracks had survived in the BBC archives. The 58th was secured from a fan who had contacted Howlett in 1988, during the transmission of another Beatles series, to see if he would be interested in hearing some tapes he had made of the Beatles on air.

"The series was virtually over by then," says Howlett. "It was a bit too late to include anything else but I kept his letter on file and when the question of the album came up we had him come down to London where we took him along to EMI with his tapes. Fortunately he had a copy of 'Keep Your Hands Off My Baby' which didn't exist anywhere else. If you listen to it, you can tell that it's an off-air recording."

These robust live performances, captured by programmes with cute period names like Easy Beat and Top Gear, didn't have the benefit of multitrack recording facilities, overdubs or remixes and so provide an undoctored example of what the Beatles sounded like during the peak of their performing career.

John and Paul learned to write songs by emulating the great singles of their youth. Trying these cover versions out on audiences taught them what worked and helped them to understand why. Gradually they began to drop the cover versions for songs of their own which created the same mood until most of their stage show was made up of Beatles originals.

Live At The BBC illustrates this growth. Of the songs they cover, 76 per cent were from 1954–59, the period when they were serving their apprenticeship in Liverpool. Almost half the cover songs were written by a handful of writers whom they

particularly revered – Chuck Berry, Little Richard, Carl Perkins, Goffin and King and Leiber and Stoller.

When they played their songs they weren't saluting a glorious past but playing music that had thrilled them as it had been released. None of the songs on Live At The BBC was more than a decade old at the time of taping.

The double album *Live At The BBC* was released on 28 November 1994 and went on to sell over 8 million copies.

I'LL BE ON MY WAY

'I'll Be On My Way' was the only unreleased Lennon-McCartney song to be included on *Live At The BBC* and, as such, the first Lennon-McCartney song played by the Beatles to be released since May 1970.

Written by Paul in 1961 in emulation of Buddy Holly it was included in the group's repertoire over the next two years but wasn't played at the Decca audition, an indication that it had already fallen out of favour. It was given to their stablemate Billy J. Kramer who used it as the flip side of 'Do You Want To Know A Secret?' in April 1963.

The lyric serves as a reminder that the Beatles didn't start out as artistic visionaries but as rearrangers of existing cliches. Here 'June light' turns to 'moon light' (naturally) and the lovelorn narrator is forced into exile where 'golden rivers flow' and 'the winds don't blow'. It sounds like the rim of an active volcano, but maybe Paul had something else in mind.

John, typically, poured scorn on the song when asked about it in 1980. It was precisely the sort of pop that had always made him uncomfortable because it stifled the individual point of view with a raft of stock phrases. Paul wasn't quite so harsh when he looked back. It was "a bit too June-moon" he conceded, but it had "worked out quite well" for the group in their early shows.

ANTHOLOGY
1–3

Fielding questions at the launch of Anthology 1 were (l to r) EMI's Rupert Perry, Press Officer Derek Taylor, Jeff Lynne, George Martin and Neil Aspinall.

The three double albums that comprise the *Anthology* set owe their genesis to an exercise in 1984 when engineer John Barrett was given the task of collating all the Beatles material in EMI's archives. Out of hundreds of hours of recordings he identified 13 unreleased tracks. EMI made test pressings and approached the remaining Beatles with the suggestion of an album. At the time, no agreement on a release could be reached.

Five years later, in an unrelated move, Apple's long time manager Neil Aspinall revived a documentary idea he'd abandoned in 1969. He wanted to collect together all the best film footage of the Beatles for a television series that would tell their story in their words. He wanted the remaining Beatles to come together and record some new incidental music. The project would be called *The Long And Winding Road*.

The album of unreleased songs and the documentary series eventually coalesced into *Anthology*. The planned incidental music was dropped in favour of recording two new Beatles tracks. "As the thought of the three of us sitting down in a studio got nearer, I got cold feet about it," said Paul. "I thought, does the world need a three-quarter Beatle record? But what if John was on, the three of us and John, like a real new record? If only we could pull off the impossible, that would be more fun, a bigger challenge."

The apparently impossible was pulled off when Yoko agreed to let them use two demo cassettes of unfinished songs by John as the basis for new Beatles tracks. These eventually became singles which helped to promote not only the six-hour documentary series but the *Anthology* albums.

Anthology was not a soundtrack to the documentary series but an aural counterpart made up of alternative takes, unreleased tracks, live performances, early demos and brief snatches of interview. Out of the 139 songs contained in the collection, 28 were cover versions.

The greatest interest was naturally in the 21 new Beatles compositions, some of which had previously only been heard performed by other artists or on rare bootlegs. These ranged from poor quality home recordings that were purely of historical value to completed studio tracks that had been ousted from albums only for reasons of space.

The general critical response to these rarities was that the Beatles' original judgment to drop them or give them away had been sound. They could probably have had a hit with 'Come And Get It' and it's hard to see why 'Not Guilty' didn't find a place on the *White Album* but otherwise none of these 'new' songs enhanced their reputation. They merely confirmed what we had assumed, which was that the Beatles had already given us their best.

FREE AS A BIRD

'Free As A Bird' was essentially a novelty single designed to attract attention to the *Anthology* project. The novelty was that it would be the first new Beatles single in 25 years and would, in sound at least, reunite the most popular pop group the world has known.

The feverish media excitement surrounding the release of the record was encouraged by EMI's publicity department. An early press release read: "The single, copies of which are currently under armed guard outside the UK, will be released worldwide on Monday December 4."

Nothing could hope to live up to these expectations but, in the event, 'Free As A Bird' was plausibly Beatles-sounding (circa 1969) although obviously hampered by the restraints of having been built around a discarded fragment of a John Lennon song which had a lead vocal recorded on a poorly positioned cassette machine.

The events that led to the recording began on January 1, 1994 when Paul called Yoko to wish her a Happy New Year. This act of reconciliation led to further conversations and then a meeting when Paul attended John's induction into the Rock'n'Roll Hall Of Fame. During this time together they discussed the possibility of the remaining Beatles working on John's home demos. Yoko offered three tracks for consideration – 'Real Love', 'Grow Old With Me' and 'Free As A Bird'.

"I liked 'Free As A Bird' immediately," Paul said. "I

▲ **Sean Lennon, Yoko Ono and Paul McCartney at the Rock and Roll Hall of Fame, January 1994.**

liked the melody. It had strong chords and it really appealed to me...The great thing was that John hadn't finished it. On the middle eight he was just blocking out lyrics that didn't have yet. That meant that we had to come up with something, and that now I was actually working 'with John'."

John probably first worked on the song at home in New York during the latter part of 1977. On October 4 of that year he and Yoko held a press conference in Japan to announce that they were both putting their careers on hold to concentrate on raising their son Sean.

Several of the songs he began during this period dealt with his new life as a house husband. In 'I'm Stepping Out', 'Watching The Wheels', 'Beautiful Boy' and 'Cleanup Time' he wrote of the strange sense of freedom he felt in abandoning the life of a celebrity for domestic duties.

Like many people psychologically wounded in early life, John craved attention and then spurned it when it came. Interviewed by *Rolling Stone* in 1970, his first comment was: "If I had the capabilities of being something other than I am, I would. It's no fun being an artist." His final comment, after being asked how he saw him-

self at 64, was in a similar vein. "I hope we're a nice old couple living off the coast of Ireland or something like that – looking at our scrapbook of madness."

For John, a stable family home had been the one thing that had always eluded him. With Sean and Yoko, he was determined to hang on to what he had got. 'Free As A Bird' was written to express his delight at being set free from the demands of celebrityhood and from the artistic pressure of having to compete with his earlier selves. He was, as he sings, 'home and dry'.

For the middle section of the song John had only the couplet 'Whatever happened to/The life that we once knew?', reminiscent of the belief in a perfect time way back in his past which he had expressed in 'Help!', 'Strawberry Fields Forever' and 'In My Life'. Paul's additional lines subvert this train of thought, turning it into a longing for healed relationships – presumably his own with John.

Recording took place in February and March 1994 at Paul's studio in Sussex with production credits being shared between the Beatles and former Electric Light Orchestra vocalist/guitarist Jeff Lynne. John's original cassette was transferred to tape and the sound digitally remastered. "We then took the liberty of beefing the song up with different chord changes and different arrangements," said George Harrison.

The project was approached as if John was still alive and that he and Paul were still beefing up each other's song ideas. "We came up with this holiday scenario," said Paul. "I rang up Ringo and said let's pretend that John's gone on holiday and he's sent us a cassette and said, 'Finish it up for me'."

George Martin, who had produced every other Beatles single, gave it a cautious blessing but felt that it lacked dynamics because they hadn't been able to successfully separate the piano and vocals on the original cassette and thus had put it in a rigid time beat to make overdubbing easier.

"They stretched it and compressed it and put it around until it got to a regular waltz control click and then they were done," he said. "The result was that in order to conceal the bad bits they had to plaster it fairly heavily so that what you ended up with was quite a thick homogeneous sound that hardly stops."

'Free As A Bird' reached Number 2 in the British charts.

REAL LOVE

'Real Love' was a song that John had worked on for at least two years and, although a large proportion of the public weren't aware of it, a version was used in the 1988 soundtrack to Andrew Solt's documentary *Imagine*.

It began as a song called 'Real Life', the verses of which later became 'I'm Stepping Out', posthumously released on *Milk And Honey*. The remaining chorus — 'It's real life/Yes, it's real life' — he obviously thought too good to throw away. The theme of the tune — I'm back to what really counts in life — was the essential theme of all his post-Beatle work. He was stripping away myths, dispensing with the unnecessary and in this case, getting down to the reality of kitchens, cigarettes, babies, newspapers and early morning blues.

The revamped song, still called 'Real Life', was coming closer to the version that the Beatles would work on. The references to 'little girls and boys' and 'little plans and schemes' were there but the verses were not yet in the final order.

When John finally changed the chorus from 'real life' to 'real love' the theme became the transforming love of Yoko Ono. He said many times in interview that he felt that she was the woman that all his longings for love and acceptance had been directed towards even before he met her. She was the 'girl with kaleidoscope eyes'. She was, as he wrote in his essay *The Ballad Of John And Yoko*, "Someone who I had already known, but somehow had lost."

During February 1995 producer Jeff Lynne worked at deleting any extraneous noises on John's cassette copy of 'Real Love' and then transferred the mono recording to two 24-track analogue tapes at Paul's Sussex studio. Paul, George and Ringo then added guitars, drums, bass, percussion and backing vocals. At one point Paul even used the upright bass he owns which once belonged to Bill Black and was used on Elvis Presley's 'Heartbreak Hotel'.

'Real Love' made it to Number 4 in the British charts.

John and Yoko at the Watergate hearings, June 1973.

CHRISTMAS TIME (IS HERE AGAIN)

Dressed up for a sketch in 1964's 'Another Beatles' Christmas Show' at the Hammersmith Odeon, London.

Particularly for the British, The Beatles became inextricably tied up with the Christmases of the Sixties. Six of their albums were released to capitalise on the Christmas market and four of their singles were Christmas Number 1s. In 1963 and 1964 they presented special Christmas shows in London theatres which were a mixture of music and pantomime and had support acts ranging from the Yardbirds to Rolf Harris.

Between 1963-1969 they produced a flexi-disc exclusively for members of their official fan club which offered spoken greetings from each Beatle and some light-hearted studio banter. The earliest messages were clearly scripted but as their music developed so did the discs. In 1965 they fooled around with a version of 'Auld Lang Syne' and the next year Paul wrote a mini-pantomime for the group.

'Christmas Time (Is Here Again)', the only original song written for fan club members, came out in 1967, the year that *Magical Mystery Tour* was being screened on Boxing Day. The unedited version, recorded on November 28, was more than six minutes long and parts of it were used to punctuate a satirical sketch written by all four Beatles.

Although it consists largely of a single line repeated like a musical mantra, 'Christmas Time (Is Here Again)' is illustrative of their fascination with children's songs and rhymes which began with 'Yellow Submarine' in 1966. This in part reflected nostalgia for the Liverpool of the Forties but was also part of the psychedelic tendency to regress to simpler states of mind where it wasn't out of place for an adult to wear ripped jeans, blow bubbles and think buttercups were 'far out'.

IN SPITE OF ALL THE DANGER

A rough recording transferred from a slightly worn 78 rpm shellac disc cut in the spring or summer of 1958, this has historical value in that it is the earliest taping of the soon-to-be Beatles as well as being the group's first songwriting effort to make it into the archives.

It was recorded on a £400 portable tape recorder at a small studio in the terraced home of a 63-year-old electrical goods shop-owner in the Kensington district of Liverpool. The Quarry Men, which then consisted of John, Paul, George, pianist John 'Duff' Lowe and drummer Colin Hanton, paid 17 shillings and six pence (87p) to cut two songs.

The first song they chose was 'That'll Be The Day', a September 1957 hit in Britain for the Crickets (with Buddy Holly), and the second was the McCartney-Harrison number 'In Spite Of All The Danger'. "It says on the label that it was me and George but I think it was written by me and George played the guitar solo," said Paul in 1995. "It was my song. It was very similar to an Elvis song."

It was in fact very similar to one particular Elvis song – 'Trying To Get To You' – which was written by Rose Marie McCoy and Margie Singleton and recorded by Elvis on July 11, 1955. It was the only Sun recording by Elvis to use a piano and was released as a single in September 1956.

John Lowe remembers 'In Spite Of All The Danger'

as being the only original song the Quarry Men played at the time. "I can well remember even at the rehearsal at his house in Forthlin Road, Paul was quite specific about how he wanted it played and what he wanted the piano to do," he says. "There was no question of improvising. We were told what we had to play. There was a lot of arranging going on even back then."

It was recorded on a single microphone and Lowe thinks that it must have gone straight to disc because he can't recall waiting around for it to be transferred from tape and there are mistakes in John's vocal which would otherwise have been corrected. The disc was then passed on from member to member and eventually came down to Lowe who kept it in a sock drawer until 1981 when a colleague suggested to him that it might have some commercial value. He had it valued by Sotheby's which led to the discovery of the disc being reported by *Sunday Times* columnist Stephen Pile in July 1981.

"Before midday an that Sunday Paul McCartney had called my mum in Liverpool," says Lowe. "I eventually spoke to him on the phone and we had long conversations over the next few days because he wanted to buy it from me. I was living in Worcester at the time and he sent his solicitor and his business manager up. I deposited the disc in a small briefcase at the local Barclay's Bank and we met up in a small room the bank kindly let me use. The deal was done, I handed the record over and we all went home."

Although Paul didn't have a specific project in mind at the time, part of the deal was that Lowe had to assign over all rights to the track and promise not to perform the song for the next 15 years. "That took us up to August 1996," says Lowe. "Isn't it strange that two months later the final album in the *Anthology* set came out?"

YOU'LL BE MINE

Recorded during April 1960 on a borrowed tape machine at Paul's family home at Forthlin Road, this is the first recording of a Lennon and McCartney song, although that's the extent of its interest. It sounds like nothing more than a couple of minutes of musical hilarity put together by teenagers in awe of the sound of their own voices.

Without a drummer but with the addition of fourth guitarist Stuart Sutcliffe, the group experimented with the echo facilities of the McCartney bathroom during an Inkspots parody with John delivering a melodramatic spoken section that owed a lot to his fascination with the Goons. Appropriately the whole track is signed off with a wild squeal of laughter. You can almost see them wetting themselves as they played it back again and again.

The restored living room of the McCartney family home in ▼ Liverpool.

CAYENNE

P aul has said that the instrumental 'Cayenne', or 'Cayenne Pepper' as it was originally titled, was written before he met John, probably at the age of 14 when he got his first, £15 guitar. Another instrumental he wrote around the same time, 'Cat's Walk', was recorded by the Chris Barber Band in 1967 as 'Cat Call'.

When Paul committed 'Cayenne' to tape in the summer of 1960 rock'n'roll instrumentals were a regular chart phenomenon. Since January there had been hit singles by Johnny and the Hurricanes, the Ventures, Duane Eddy, Bert Weedon, Sandy Nelson, Jerry Lordan, the John Barry Seven and the Shadows.

"It's not brilliant," Paul said recently of 'Cayenne', "but when you listen to it you can hear a lot of stuff I'm *going* to write. So, it's interesting from that point of view."

Paul at the Cavern in 1961, six months after recording 'Cry For A Shadow'.

CRY FOR A SHADOW

W hen this track was recorded in June 1961, Cliff Richard and The Shadows were Britain's premier rock 'n' roll act. Since his first hit with 'Move It' in October 1958 Cliff had been in the Top 10 ten times and the Shadows were now making their own instrumental hits.

Although the Beatles found Cliff a bit too tame for their liking, they were early admirers of the Shadows. Paul learned the opening chords of 'Move It' from watching lead guitarist Hank Marvin's finger movements on the *Oh Boy!* TV show and when Cliff first played the Liverpool Empire on October 12, 1958, Paul was in the audience.

'Cry For A Shadow', an instrumental intended to sound like mock Shadows, was credited to Harrison-Lennon. It was the Beatles' first composition to make it onto record when it appeared on Tony Sheridan's 1962 German album *My Bonnie* where the 'backing group' were listed as the Beat Brothers.

The story is that the composition came about by accident. Rory Storm was in Germany and had asked George to play him a recent British hit by the Shadows – either 'Apache' or 'Frightened City' – and George came up with something new, either because he couldn't remember the Shadows' tunes or as a joke on Storm. At first he was going to title it 'Beatle Bop' but then, out of homage to his original inspiration, he called it 'Cry For A Shadow'.

"It doesn't sound like 'Frightened City' or 'Apache'," says Shadows guitarist Bruce Welch. "It has the same instrumentation that we used but melodically it's nowhere near either of them. I had heard that it was a piss-take because we had a stranglehold on the British group scene and we'd never been to Germany as almost every other group did."

It was recorded in Germany when the orchestra leader and record company producer Bert Kaempfert hired the Beatles for 300 marks to back Sheridan on a Polydor record. Norwich-born Sheridan, a veteran of London's 2 I's coffee bar, had spent a lot of time in Germany and Kaempfert wanted him to do rocked-up versions of such standards as 'My Bonnie' and 'When The Saints Go Marching In'. The Beatles were allowed their own spot on 'Ain't She Sweet' and 'Cry For A Shadow'.

Brian Epstein, who was responsible for getting the Beatles out of leather jackets and into tailored suits, encouraged them to emulate the Shadows in their attire and on-stage courtesies. The two groups first met in 1963 at a party in London and in June of that year Hank, Bruce and Brian Locking came to Paul's 21st in Liverpool.

LIKE DREAMERS DO

Merseybeat consisted largely of covers of recent American hits and selections from Buddy Holly, Chuck Berry, Ray Charles and Jerry Lee Lewis. The Beatles stood out initially by discovering unknown acts and obscure B sides but even these were soon copied and became standard fare on Merseyside. This was what pushed them into serious songwriting. It was the only guarantee of uniqueness. If you had your own material then you were set apart from the copyists. Their goal was to come up with material that not only went down well with their audiences but which remained unique to their act.

Paul has said that 'Like Dreamers Do' was one of the first of his own compositions that he tried at the Cavern. This implies that he wrote it for the Cavern audience but the Quarry Men were performing it as far back as 1958. What he probably meant was that it was one of the first songs from his back catalogue that he felt confident enough to slip into the Beatles regular set.

The early arrangement of the song, he thought was weak although "certain of the kids" at the Cavern liked it. When the Beatles came to audition for Decca on January 1, 1962, it was one of three Lennon-McCartney songs that they included in a 15-song set (the others were 'Hello Little Girl' and 'Love Of The Loved').

By the time of their EMI audition nine months later, none of these songs were offered, all of them having been replaced by better material. Shortly afterwards they were offered to other artists, 'Like Dreamers Do' to The Applejacks, a Birmingham six-piece group with a female bassist, who reached Number 20 with it in July 1964.

'Like Dreamers Do' is a typically optimistic McCartney song. He dreams about a girl, meets someone who resembles this dream girl and knows that he will love her. There is no mention of whether the girl will love him. It was his foregone conclusion that his emotions would be reciprocated.

HELLO LITTLE GIRL

John frequently referred to 'Hello Little Girl' as his earliest composition. Written in 1958, it became the first of his songs to be performed by the Quarry Men.

He credited its origin to the Cole Porter song 'It's De-Lovely', with its chorus of 'It's delightful, it's delicious, it's de-lovely', which was first sung by Bob

Brian Epstein in June 1963 with the cream of merseybeat – the Beatles, Gerry and the Pacemakers and Billy J. Kramer and the ▼ Dakotas.

Hope in the 1936 stage musical *Red, Hot And Blue* and was recorded in Britain by Carroll Gibbons and The Savoy Hotel Orpheans in 1938.

"That song always fascinated me for some reason or another," John said. "It was possibly connected to my mother. She used to sing that one. It's all very Freudian. So I made 'Hello Little Girl' out of it. It was supposed to be a Buddy Holly style song."

There is no similarity between the two songs other than the device of repeating the title as a chorus. It may have been more the playful spirit of the song and, as with 'Please Please Me', the association with his mother's musical interests. The imprint of Buddy Holly is more easily detectable. In its earliest incarnation the middle eight was apparently swiped wholesale from 'Maybe Baby'.

Just as Paul's early songs always bore the hallmark of optimism, John's bore the hallmark of pessimism. Paul assumed acceptance and love where John braced himself for rejection. In 'Hello Little Girl' he attempts to attract a girl's attention but she remains unaware of him. He sends her flowers but she is unmoved. He ends up lonely about to 'lose my mind'.

Recorded for the Decca audition in January 1962, 'Hello Little Girl' was out of the running by the time they signed for EMI later in the year. "It was then offered to Gerry and the Pacemakers," remembers Tony Bramwell. "It was considered as the follow up to 'How Do You Do It?'. They recorded a demo of it (included on *Gerry and the Pacemakers; The Best of the EMI Years*, 1992) but by that time Mitch Murray had come up with 'I Like It'."

The song was then offered to The Fourmost, another Liverpool group managed by Brian Epstein. After a Sunday concert in Blackpool where the two groups had appeared John invited The Fourmost to his house to see the lyrics. The following morning they were sent a demo tape. "We had to record on the Wednesday and so we only had two days to record it," said bass guitarist Billy Hatton. "As a matter of fact, when we were recording, we were just learning the song as we went along."

The record was a hit after its release on August 23 and reached Number 7 in the British charts. It was released in America on September 16.

YOU KNOW WHAT TO DO

A languid country-flavoured song written by George and recorded on June 3, 1964. Ringo had been taken ill that morning, on the verge of a tour, and so the studio time booked to record a fourteenth and final song for the *A Hard Day's Night* album had to be used to rehearse substitute drummer Jimmy Nicol. As a result only three new demos were recorded that day – Paul's 'It's For You' (later given to Cilla Black), John's 'No Reply' and this new song from George.

Being the youngest Beatle, George always had a hard time getting his ideas to be taken seriously. This was only the second song of his to be taped by the group (the first being 'Don't Bother Me') but it was never developed and, due to misfiling, it was lost for the next three decades. It it had been worked on by the group, it would surely have been a contender for *Beatles For Sale*.

Although it is undoubtedly a formula song with no deep revelation at the core, it's interesting to note that George was just 12 weeks into his courtship of Pattie Boyd. Could he have written a song at the time about wanting to be with his girl 'every hour of the day' without having her in mind?

IF YOU'VE GOT TROUBLE

J ohn and Paul never gave Ringo their best songs but neither did they only give him their worst. However, 'If You've Got Trouble' must rate as the worst one they ever expected him to sing. Melodically, it's uninspiring. Lyrically, it's embarrassing. It's hard to believe that the team that had just written 'Ticket To Ride' and 'You've Got To Hide Your Love Away' could come up with this. Recorded in one take, the song sounds as though it was also composed in one take.

The theme of the song could be roughly summarised as 'If you think you've got problems, you should see mine!' The vitriol in the song sounds like John. Did it start out as a barbed attack on Cynthia, telling her to quit complaining about his abilities as a husband and a father and to be grateful for the luxuries afforded by the Beatles' new stardom?

An interview that year in the *Saturday Evening Post* conducted by Al Aronowitz suggests such a context for the song: "Their friends say that she (Cynthia) was in awe of John when they first met and she still is; a feeling, in fact, which has grown as his stardom rockets him further into the entertainment heavens, troubling her with the occasional thought that she might be left behind. When the Beatles are on tour, she often is left behind. 'Well, she certainly doesn't seem to mind spending the money I'm making,' John says."

Intended for the *Help!* album, it was left to die after this session.

THAT MEANS A LOT

Written primarily by Paul, this was another song intended for *Help!* but the Beatles were never able to record what they considered to be a definitive version. During sessions on February 20 and March 30 1965 they attempted the song 24 times before finally abandoning it.

The song takes the point of view of a third party looking in on a relationship, a device first used by the Beatles in 'She Loves You'. The shift in viewpoint opened up the possibility of writing in voices other than their own and expressing attitudes that were not necessarily their own.

"We found that we just couldn't sing it,' summarised John some time later. "In fact, we made such a hash of it that we thought we'd better give it to someone who could do it well." That someone was P. J. Proby, an American singer who'd been invited to Britain by Jack

Good in April 1964 to take part in a Beatles TV special, and who had become friendly with the group. Proby recorded 'That Means A Lot' and it made Number 30 in the British charts in October 1965.

12-BAR ORIGINAL

Recorded between 'What Goes On' and 'I'm Looking Through You' in November 1965, was this the soul intended for *Rubber Soul?* Two takes were recorded and one of them was mixed but neither was ever released.

It is one of the most untypical of Beatle tracks and appears to be an attempt to mimic the Memphis soul sound. The obvious template is Booker T. & The MGs – keyboard player Booker T. Jones, drummer Al Jackson, bass player 'Duck' Dunn and guitarist Steve Cropper – the Stax Records session musicians who played behind such soul greats as Otis Redding, Sam and Dave, and Eddie Floyd and who had a string of instrumental hits under their own name beginning with 'Green Onions' in 1962.

'12-Bar Original', which is credited to all four Beatles, sounds like a pastiche of 'Green Onions' and its follow-up 'Jellybread' minus the distinctive keyboard playing.

The track was recorded at a point when the Beatles were striving for recognition as musicians. It was also at a juncture in British pop when the heavier sounds of the Animals, Yardbirds, Kinks and Pretty Things were taking over from Tin Pan Alley.

JUNK

Paul wrote 'Junk' while in India and first recorded it in May 1968 when all four Beatles met up at George's home on Claremont Drive, Esher, Surrey. It's this version, an acoustic demo with unfinished lyrics, that appears on

Anthology. Paul hoped to complete it for inclusion on *Abbey Road* but instead recorded it for his first solo album, *McCartney*, which was released in April 1970.

The demo is nothing more than a rough sketch. An unfinished verse is repeated twice, and the gaps are filled with humming and giggling. It's impossible to determine the story because Paul is obviously only interested in the sounds of the words. In this case the words had to do with a scrap yard and a junk shop. In the press release that went out with his solo album his only comment was; "Originally written in India, at Maharishi's camp, and completed bit by bit in London."

NOT GUILTY

This was recorded during the White Album sessions in August 1968. George had already spent two months in the studio with only one of his songs – 'While My Guitar Gently Weeps' – having been picked up by the group. Over 100 takes and rehearsals of this song were produced between August 7 and August 12 but for some reason it wasn't included in the final line-up.

The song didn't surface until 1979 when a re-recorded version was used on the album *George Harrison*. Structurally the song remained the same, with the exception of the addition of the lines 'Not guilty for being on your street/ Getting underneath your feet'.

Around this time George explained the song as being about the problems that were beginning to affect him as a part of the Beatles in 1968: "Paul – John – Apple – Rishikesh – Indian friends etc." Written at a time when he was starting to be regarded as the freaky, mystical Beatle, he seems to be saying: "Don't blame me for getting you involved with freak culture. Hey, I'm not asking for too much. I just want to do my job and get a bit of respect.'

It's hard not to see such lines as, 'I'm not trying to be smart/ I only want what I can get' as a bitter comment on his inability to increase his presence within the group and become regarded as a songwriting equal to John and Paul. Maybe that's why it didn't get on the album.

WHAT'S THE NEW MARY JANE

This was a thing I wrote half with our electronic genius Alex," said John in 1969. "It was called 'What A Shame Mary Jane Had A Pain At The Party' and it was meant for *The Beatles* album."

Written in India when the Greek-born John Alexis Mardas paid a visit, it was demoed at George's Esher home in May 1968. At this stage it was a little over two and a half minutes long and as the Beatles improvised towards the end of the track, one of them shouted, "Ooh. What's the news?…What are you saying? What a shame Mary Jane had a pain at the party. What's the new Mary Jane…Oh, my God! Mary! Mary!" This gave rise to the unusual title.

The studio version, recorded by John and George with help from Yoko and Mal Evans, went on for over six minutes with a two-minute 'freak out' before the final verse. The lyric remained the same as demoed in May except for the line 'He cooking such groovy spaghetti' which came out, whether by accident or creative play, as ' He groovy such cooking spaghetti'.

The syntax of the lyric is unorthodox. There is a deliberate use of wrong tenses and wrong words which suggest that John may have been imitating the way that Indians sometimes speak English as a second language. The story told is either surreal or a coded putdown of someone in the Maharishi's circle. Perhaps significantly, John had been recording 'Sexy Sadie' the day before, which was originally a scathing attack on the guru who he felt let down by.

At the end of the recording John can be heard saying, "Let's hear it before we get taken away." A year later he planned to have it released as a B side to 'You Know My Name (Look Up The Number)' as a Plastic Ono Band single but it was pulled at the last minute. "It was real madness," said John describing the track in 1969. "I'd like to do it again."

STEP INSIDE LOVE

Cilla Black, real name Priscilla White, was a Liverpool typist signed by Brian Epstein and given a contract with Parlophone. Her first single, released in February 1963, was 'Love Of The Loved', an old Quarry Men song written by Paul and used by the Beatles at their Decca audition. Paul turned up for the recording.

In 1964 he wrote 'It's For You' for her and then in 1968, after hearing that she was to front her own BBC TV series, he offered to write the theme song for her. Entertainment shows of the time were traditionally book-ended by big band numbers but Cilla wanted to change that.

"Paul understood what I felt," she said. "He said to me: 'I know what they're doing. They're sending you these Billy Cotton Band type of numbers and that's not you. You're the kind of person that should invite people into your house. You should have a song that that starts of very quietly and then builds up.' "

Paul did a demo of 'Step Inside Love' at his home in Cavendish Avenue and double tracked it with his own voice.

"All he had given us was one verse and a chorus with him playing on guitar," remembers director and producer Michael Hurll. "We played it that way for the first couple of weeks and then decided that we needed a second verse. Paul came over to the BBC Theatre in Shepherd's Bush and sat with me and Cilla and worked on a second verse. It started off with the line 'You look tired, love' because Cilla was tired after a lot of rehearsing and most of what he wrote related to what was going on that day."

The version of the song included on *Anthology* was captured in September 1968 while the Beatles were waiting to record 'I Will'. Paul begins with the chorus and slips straight into the second verse which he misremembers, singing 'kiss me goodnight' instead of 'love me tonight', leaving a line out and concluding with the last line of what should have been the third verse.

'Step Inside Love' became a Top 10 hit for Cilla in Britain, was released in America in May and earned her a ban in South Africa where it was considered to be a play on a prostitute's invitation. It could have

been worse. Tony Bramwell remembers that Paul's initial idea was 'Come Inside Love'.

"I quite like the song," said Paul. " It was just a welcoming song for Cilla. It was very cabaret. It suited her voice."

John, Paul and Cilla Black during the filming of *The Music of Lennon and McCartney*, ▼ in 1965.

LOS PARANOIAS

This was nothing more than an extended studio joke initiated by Paul when, at the end of his bossa nova version of 'Step Inside Love' he announced in the voice of an MC, 'Joe Prairie and the Prairie Wall Flyers'. John responded with 'Los Paranoias' which was enough to get Paul improvising a South American spoof about Los Paranoias.

The likely inspiration was the Paraguayan group Trio Los Paraguayas led by Luis Alberto Del Parana who appeared in variety shows on British TV during the Fifties with their 'Latin American rhythms' and released a *Best Of* album in 1957.

TEDDY BOY

"Another song started in India," announced Paul in 1970 when 'Teddy Boy' was included on his first solo album. "It was recorded for the *Get Back* album but later not used." It was started during one of the Maharishi's lectures at Rishikesh when Paul turned to John and sung the first line in his ear; it was then finished in Scotland and London.

Strictly speaking, it was never 'recorded' by the Beatles because there was no final take, no mixing and in January 1969 Paul had still not completed the lyric. What is presented on *Anthology* is a rough sketch of a song offered by Paul in the hopes that John, George and Ringo would like it. The atmosphere is so informal that Paul laughs in parts, whistles over the unwritten patches and John can be clearly heard talking to others in the studio as he played along.

This inconsequential tale of a boy called Ted who is told to be good by his mother is not one that would have warmed John's heart. He once referred to Paul's story songs as being about "boring people doing boring things". This is probably why as the song ended during this session John picked up the rhythm on his gui-

tar and turned it into a clunky square dance song;: 'Take your partners do-si-do/ Hold them tight and don't let go'. That was his none-too-subtle comment about where 'Teddy Boy' fitted into Sixties rock culture.

ALL THINGS MUST PASS

In November 1968, after finishing up his work on the White Album, George had gone to Woodstock to stay with Bob Dylan. Here he also spent time with the Band, Dylan's former backing group, who had just recorded *Music From Big Pink*.

This album was seen at the time as a reaction against the excesses of psychedelia and as a return to the mainstream of American music. The bluntness of the group's name and the rustic simplicity of their publicity photos suggested a swing away from surrealism and a return to the roots of American culture.

Their music was particularly appealing to seasoned musicians weary of the demands of fan hysteria. It was instrumental in the break-up of Cream, for example. "I got the tapes of *Music From Big Pink* and I thought this is what I want to play," Eric Clapton explained in 1974. "Not extended solos and maestro bullshit but just good, funky songs."

George's song 'All Things Must Pass', which he played during Beatles recording sessions in January 1969 and then recorded alone on February 25, was an attempt to evoke the feeling that the Band had captured on their single 'The Weight'. In fact, when George first played it through to John and Paul he openly enthused about the Band and their music.

The lyric was based on a poem from Timothy Leary's book *Psychedelic Prayers After The Tao Te Ching* (Poets Press, New York, 1966). The poem was a 'translation from English to psychedelese' of part of the 23rd chapter of the Tao which Leary had titled 'All Things Pass'; '*All things pass/ A sunrise does not last all morning/ All things pass/ A cloudburst does not last all day...*' As George was to admit: "I remembered one of these prayers and it gave me the idea for this thing."

Bob Dylan and the
Beatles were the great
rock innovators of the
1960s. George became
particularly close to
Dylan and stayed at his
Woodstock home in
1968.

Despite George's frequent references to the song while the others were recording, it wasn't considered for either *Let It Be* or *Abbey Road*. Instead it became the title track of his debut solo album in December 1970.

COME AND GET IT

Apple Films, which was being run by Denis O'Dell, were planning a film of Terry Southern's 1958 novel *The Magic Christian* and O'Dell asked Paul to do the music. Paul agreed, reluctantly it now seems, and with a shooting script in hand began to write.

He started with a song to be used over a scene where Sir Guy Grand, the world's richest man (played by Peter Sellers) throws banknotes into a vat of filth and gets pleasure from seeing respectable people wallowing in slime in the hopes of grabbing some free cash. The idea came to him late at night while at Cavendish Avenue and he came downstairs and taped it in a whisper so as not to wake Linda. When he played it back the next day he believed that he had come up with "a very catchy song".

On July 5, 1969 one of the Apple label signings, a

group called The Iveys, gave an interview to *Disc & Music Echo* in which they complained of being neglected by the Beatles. Three weeks later Paul contacted the group and on July 29 he met them at their home and offered them 'Come And Get It' which he'd recorded alone with engineer Phil MacDonald five days previously at Abbey Road. He also suggested that they might make other contributions to the film soundtrack as he was trying to put his energies into recording the *Abbey Road* album.

Paul produced the group on August 2, choosing Tom Evans to do the lead vocal and encouraging them to stick to the simplicity of his demo on which he'd played only piano, drums, bass and maracas. He told them that if they did it right he could guarantee them a hit and if they didn't do it right then he'd keep it for a Beatles' single. "That challenge really made us work hard," said Evans.

By the time 'Come And Get It ' came out The Iveys were Badfinger (after John's 'Badfinger Boogie'). The single reached the Top 5 and the group could no longer say they were neglected. The soundtrack to *The Magic Christian* contained three Badfinger songs and in a move to capitalise on this they titled their next album *Magic Christian Music*.

Asked whether 'Come And Get It' was a veiled message to those squabbling over the Beatles fortune in 1968, Paul said: "It was just a straightforward pop song with all the old innuendoes. Come and get what?"

CHRONOLOGY
TO 1970

1940

July 7 — Ringo Starr born in Liverpool as Richard Starkey

Oct 9 — John Lennon born in Liverpool as John Winston Lennon

1942

June 18 — Paul McCartney born in Liverpool as James Paul McCartney

1943

Feb 25 — George Harrison born in Liverpool

1956

Oct 31 — Paul's mother, Mary, dies of breast cancer

1957

March — John Lennon forms the Quarry Men skiffle group with school friend Pete Shotton

July 6 — The Quarry Men play at the garden fete of St Peter's Church, Woolton, after which John is introduced to Paul by Ivan Vaughan

Oct 18 — After weeks of rehearsals Paul McCartney makes his debut with the Quarry Men

1958

Feb — George Harrison meets John and Paul and shortly afterwards is invited to join the Quarry Men

July 15 — John's mother, Julia, is killed in a hit-and-run accident

1959

Aug 29 — The Quarry Men play the newly opened Casbah Club which is run by Mona Best, mother of drummer Pete Best

1960

Jan — John's art school friend Stuart Sutcliffe joins the group on bass guitar. They start to be known variously as the Beatals, the Silver Beetles and the Silver Beats

May — London poet Royston Ellis uses the group to back him at a Liverpool reading. While staying with John and Stuart at their flat in Gambier Terrace, Ellis introduces them to the high produced by sniffing a broken-down benzedrine inhaler

May 10 — The Silver Beetles audition before Britain's top rock 'n' roll manager, Larry Parnes, and Liverpool's best known pop star, Billy Fury. They aren't offered the job of backing Fury but instead get a tour of Scotland playing for Johnny Gentle

May 20 — Silver Beetles begin seven-date tour with Johnny Gentle

July 9 — Record Mirror reveals that Royston Ellis is considering bringing a Liverpool group called the Beetles to London

Aug 12 — Pete Best auditions for the group and later joins on drums

Aug 17 — Now known as the Beatles, the group begins its first season in Hamburg, Germany – 48 nights at the Indra Club

Oct 4 — They then appear at the Kaiserkeller for a further 58 nights

1961

Feb 9 — The Beatles play the Cavern Club in Mathew Street, Liverpool, for the first time

April 1 — The Beatles return to Hamburg for a 13-week engagement at the Top Ten Club

June — The Beatles return to Hamburg and back English guitarist-vocalist Tony Sheridan Polydor in Germany release 'My Bonnie' which is credited to Tony Sheridan and 'The Beat Brothers'

Sept — During a holiday trip to Paris, Paul and John change their hairstyles into what would later become known as the 'Beatle haircut' or 'mop top'

Nov 9 — Brian Epstein visits the Cavern Club and sees the Beatles for the first time

1962

Jan 1 — Fifteen audition track recorded for Decca Records in London

Jan 24 — The Beatles sign a management contract with Brian Epstein

April 10 — Stuart Sutcliffe dies of a brain haemorrhage while in Germany with his girlfriend Astrid Kirchherr

April 13 — Start of a seven-week residency at the Star-Club in Hamburg

June 4 — The Beatles sign a contract with EMI in England

June 6 — First session at EMI Studios in Abbey Road with producer George Martin

Aug 16 — Pete Best is dismissed as drummer

Aug 18 — Ringo Starr joins the Beatles. The first John, Paul, George and Ringo concert is held at Hulme Hall in Birkenhead

Aug 23 — John marries Cynthia Powell at Mount Pleasant Register Office, London

Sept 3 — Second session at Abbey Road

Sept 11 — Third Abbey Road session at which 'Love Me Do' is re-recorded with session drummer Andy White

Oct 5 — British release of 'Love Me Do', the Beatles' first single

Nov 1 — Return to the Star-Club, Hamburg, for 14 nights

Nov 26 — Second single, 'Please Please Me', recorded at Abbey Road

Dec 18 — Final return to club dates in Hamburg – 13 nights at the Star-Club

1963

Feb 2 — Start of Beatles' first British tour. They support 16-year-old Helen Shapiro

Feb 4 — Last lunchtime session at the Cavern

Feb 11 — Debut album Please Please Me recorded in just over nine hours

Mar 9 — Nationwide tour with American stars Tommy Roe and Chris Montez

April 8 — Julian Lennon born as John Charles Julian Lennon in Liverpool

April 18 — After an appearance at London's Royal Albert Hall, Paul meets teenage actress Jane Asher for the first time

Aug 3 — The Beatles' final performance at the Cavern Club where they had played almost 300 times

Sept 11 — Work starts on With The Beatles LP

Oct 13 — An appearance on the top-rated British TV show Sunday Night At The London Palladium helps create the phenomenon the press later dub 'Beatlemania'

Oct 25 — Start of a short tour of Sweden

Nov 1 — The Beatles' Autumn Tour opens in Cheltenham, Gloucestershire

Nov 4 — Royal Command Performance at Prince of Wales Theatre, London, before the Queen Mother and Princess Margaret

Dec 24 — 'The Beatles' Christmas Show' opens at the Astoria Cinema, Finsbury Park, London for a 16-night run

1964

Jan 16 — An 18-day run at the Olympia Theatre, Paris, France

Feb 7 — The Beatles fly to New York where they are greeted by 3,000 screaming fans

Feb 9 — First appearance on the Ed Sullivan Show to an estimated audience of 73 million

Feb 11 — First American concert takes place at the Washington Coliseum

Mar 2 — Shooting begins on A Hard Day's Night

Mar 23 — John's first book, In His Own Write, is published

June 4 — Beatles leave for a tour of Denmark, Holland, Hong Kong, Australia and New

Zealand with Jimmy Nicol substituting for Ringo who is hospitalized with tonsillitis and pharyngitis

June 14 Ringo re-joins the Beatles in Melbourne

July 6 World premiere of *A Hard Day's Night* at the London Pavilion

July John buys a home in Weybridge, Surrey

Aug 19 The Beatles' second visit to America but their first American tour. The first concert is at the Cow Palace in San Francisco

Aug 28 In New York City they are introduced to Bob Dylan and smoke marijuana for the first time

Oct 9 British tour begins in Bradford, Yorkshire

Dec 24 Another Beatles' Christmas Show opens for 20 nights at the Odeon Cinema, Hammersmith, London

1965

Feb 11 Ringo Starr marries Maureen Cox

Feb 23 – May 11 Filming *Help!*, the Beatles' second feature film

March – April John and George experience LSD for the first time when a dentist friend spikes their after-dinner coffees

June 12 Each Beatle is awarded an MBE in the Queen's Birthday Honours list

June 24 John's second book, *A Spaniard In The Works*, is published

July 29 World premiere of *Help!*

Aug 14 Beatles arrive in New York for their second American concert tour

Aug 15 First appearance at Shea Stadium in Queens, New York. The attendance of almost 56,000 makes it the biggest pop concert ever

Aug 27 The Beatles meet Elvis Presley at his home in Bel Air

Aug John and George take their second LSD trip in the company of actor Peter Fonda

Aug 31 Final concert of 1965 North American tour takes place at Cow Palace, San Francisco

Dec 3 The first date of what would

turn out to be their final British tour

Dec 25 George gets engaged to Pattie Boyd

1966

Jan 21 George marries Pattie Boyd

Mar 4 John's interview with Maureen Cleave in which he claims that the Beatles are now "more popular than Jesus" is published in London's *Evening Standard*

April 6 – June 22 Recording *Revolver* at Abbey Road

June 24 Beginning of Far Eastern tour which goes from Germany to Japan and on to the Philippines

July John's comments about the Beatles being bigger than Jesus are appear in the American magazine *Datebook* and trigger a Beatles backlash in the Bible Belt states

Aug 12 Final tour of America begins in Chicago

Aug 29 The last-ever concert performance by John, Paul, George and Ringo takes place at Candlestick Park, San Francisco

Sept 6 – Nov 6 John films *How I Won The War* in Germany and Spain

Nov 9 John meets Japanese artist Yoko Ono for the first time, in London

Nov 24 Beatles enter Abbey Road to begin recording *Sgt. Pepper's Lonely Hearts Club Band*

1967

Jan 1 – April 2 Recording continues on *Sgt Pepper's Lonely Hearts Club Band*

April 3 Paul flies to San Francisco

June 1 *Sgt Pepper's Lonely Hearts Club Band* is released in America

June 16 Paul becomes the first Beatle to confess to having taken LSD, in a *Life* cover story

June 25 *Our World* television programme in which the Beatles sing the specially composed 'All You Need Is Love'.

July 24 Beatles sign petition for the legalization of cannabis which is published in the London *Times*

Aug 1 George and Pattie fly to Los Angeles and later on to San Francisco where they visit the

Haight Ashbury district

Aug 24 All four Beatles attend a lecture given by the Maharishi Mahesh Yogi at the Hilton Hotel in London's Park Lane

Aug 25 At the personal invitation of the Maharishi the Beatles travel to Bangor, North Wales, for a summer school in Transcendental Meditation

Aug 27 Brian Epstein dies

Sept 11 – 24 *Magical Mystery Tour* is filmed

Sept 22 Beatles make the cover of *Time* magazine

Oct 18 World premiere of *How I Won The War*, starring John Lennon

Dec 5 Apple Boutique opens at 94 Baker Street, London W1

Dec 25 Paul announces his engagement to Jane Asher

Dec 26 *Magical Mystery Tour* premiered on British television (BBC)

1968

Feb 15 John, Cynthia, George and Pattie fly out to India to join the Maharishi at his ashram in Rishikesh where they will study meditation

Feb 19 Paul, Jane, Ringo and Maureen join the rest of the Beatles in India

May 15 John and Paul travel to New York to announce the formation of Apple. Paul is reunited with Linda Eastman

May John begins his affair with Yoko Ono

May 30 Beatles demo the songs written during their stay in India

May 31 – Oct 14 Recording *The Beatles*, better known as The White Album

June 20 – 24 Paul is in Los Angeles on business and again meets up with Linda Eastman

July 20 Jane Asher announces that her engagement to Paul is off

July 31 The Apple Boutique is closed down

Oct 16 George goes to California to produce Apple artist Jackie Lomax

Oct 18 John and Yoko arrested on a charge of drug possession

Nov 8 Divorce granted to John and Cynthia

Nov 10 John puts his Weybridge home on the market

1969

Jan 2 Filming begins in Twickenham for what will eventually become the documentary *Let It Be*

Feb 2 Yoko Ono and Tony Cox divorce

Feb 10 George temporarily leaves the group after disagreements with John and Paul

Mar 12 Paul marries Linda Eastman at Marylebone Registry Office in London

Mar 20 John marries Yoko Ono in Gibraltar

Mar 25 – 31 John and Yoko organize their first 'bed-in' at the Amsterdam Hilton

Mar 28 It is announced that ATV are poised to buy Northern Songs

May 26 – June 2 John and Yoko arrange a bed-in at the Queen Elizabeth Hotel in Montreal

July 1 Work begins in earnest on the *Abbey Road* album

Aug 8 Iain MacMillan shoots the celebrated cover photo of the four Beatles walking across Abbey Road

Aug 11 John and Yoko move to Tittenhurst Park, Sunningdale, Ascot

Aug 20 The last day on which all four Beatles would be together in a recording studio

Aug 31 John, George and Ringo see Bob Dylan perform at the Isle of Wight festival

Sept 13 The Plastic Ono band (John, Yoko, Eric Clapton, Klaus Voorman and Alan White) makes its live debut in Toronto

Nov 25 John returns his MBE to Buckingham Palace

1970

Jan 4 The final taping of *Let It Be*

Apr 10 Paul announces that he has left the Beatles due to "personal, business and musical differences"

May – Aug Battles over the ownership of Northern Songs and involvement of Allen Klein continue

Aug 4 Apple's press office closes down

Dec 31 Paul files a suit against The Beatles and Co to dissolve the partnership

DISCOGRAPHY, 1962 – 1996

UK RELEASES

SINGLES

'Love Me Do'/'PS I Love You', October 5, 1962, Parlophone 45-R 4949.

'Please Please Me'/'Ask me Why', January 11, 1963, Parlophone 45-R 4983.

'From Me To You'/'Thank You Girl', April 11, 1963, Parlophone R 5015.

'She Loves You'/'I'll Get You', August 23, 1963, Parlophone R 5055.

'I Want To Hold Your Hand'/'This Boy', November 29, 1963, Parlophone R 5084.

'Can't Buy Me Love'/'You Can't Do That', March 20, 1964. Parlophone R 5114.

'A Hard Day's Night'/'Things We Said Today', July 10, 1964, Parlophone R 5160.

'I Feel Fine'/'She's A Woman', November 27, 1964, Parlophone R 5200.

'Ticket To Ride'/'Yes It Is', April 9, 1965, Parlophone R 5265.

'Help!'/'I'm Down', July 23, 1965, Parlophone R 5305.

'We Can Work It Out'/'Day Tripper', December 3, 1965, Parlophone R 5389.

'Paperback Writer'/'Rain', June 10, 1966, Parlophone R 5452.

'Eleanor Rigby'/'Yellow Submarine', August 5, 1966, Parlophone R 5493.

'Strawberry Fields Forever'/'Penny Lane', February 17, 1967, Parlophone R 5570.

'All You Need Is Love'/'Baby, You're A Rich Man', July 7, 1967, Parlophone R 5620

'Hello, Goodbye'/'I Am The Walrus', November 24, 1967, Parlophone R 5655.

'Lady Madonna'/'The Inner Light', March 15, 1968, Parlophone R 5675.

'Hey Jude'/'Revolution', August 30, 1968, Apple [Parlophone] R 5722.

'Get Back'/'Don't Let Me Down', April 11, 1969, Apple [Parlophone] R 5777.

'The Ballad Of John And Yoko'/'Old Brown Shoe', May 30, 1969, Apple [Parlophone] R 5786.

'Something'/'Come Together', October 31, 1969, Apple [Parlophone] R 5814.

'Let It Be'/'You Know My Name (Look Up The Number)', March 6, 1970, Apple [Parlophone] R 5833.

'Free As A Bird'/'I Saw Her Standing There'/'This Boy'/ 'Christmas Time (Is Here Again)', December 4 1995, Apple [Parlophone] CDR 6422

'Real Love'/'Baby's In Black'/'Yellow Submarine'/'Here, There And Everywhere', March 4, 1996, Apple [Parlophone] CDR 6425

EPS

Twist And Shout, July 12, 1963, Parlophone GEP 8882 (mono)– 'Twist And Shout'; 'A Taste Of Honey'/ 'Do You Want To Know A Secret'; 'There's A Place'.

The Beatles' Hits, September 6, 1963, Parlophone GEP 8880 (mono) – 'From Me To You'; 'Thank You Girl'/'Please Please Me'; 'Love Me Do'.

The Beatles (No 1), November 1, 1963, Parlophone GEP 8883 (mono) – 'I Saw Her Standing There'; 'Misery'/'Anna (Go To Him)'; 'Chains'.

All My Loving, February 7, 1964, Parlophone GEP 8891 (mono) –
'All My Loving'; 'Ask Me Why'/'Money (That's What I Want)'/'PS I Love You'.

Long Tall Sally, June 19, 1964, Parlophone GEP 8913 (mono) –
'Long Tall Sally'; 'I Call Your Name'/'Slow Down'; 'Matchbox'.

Extracts From The Film A Hard Day's Night, November 6, 1964, Parlophone GEP 8920 (mono) – 'I Should Have Known Better'; 'If I Fell'/'Tell Me Why'; 'And I Love Her'.

Extracts From The Album A Hard Day's Night, November 6, 1964, Parlophone GEP 8924 (mono) – 'Any Time At All'; 'I'll Cry Instead'/'Things We Said Today'; 'When I Get Home'.

Beatles For Sale, April 6, 1965, Parlophone GEP 8931 (mono) – 'No Reply'; 'I'm A Loser'/'Rock And Roll Music'; 'Eight Days A Week'.

Beatles For Sale (No 2), June 4, 1965, Parlophone GEP 8938 (mono) –
'I'll Follow The Sun'; 'Baby's In Black'/'Words Of Love'; 'I Don't Want To Spoil The Party'

The Beatles' Million Sellers, December 6, 1965, Parlophone GEP 8946 (mono) –
'She Loves You'; 'I Want To Hold Your Hand'/'Can't Buy Me Love'; 'I Feel Fine'.

Yesterday, March 4, 1966, Parlophone GEP 8948 (mono only)– 'Yesterday'; 'Act Naturally'/'You Like Me Too Much'; 'It's Only Love'.

Nowhere Man, July 8, 1966, Parlophone GEP 8948 – 'Nowhere Man'; 'Drive My Car'/'Michelle'; 'You Won't See Me'.

Magical Mystery Tour, December 8, 1967, Parlophone MMT-1 (mono), SMMT-1 (stereo) – 'Magical Mystery Tour'; 'Your Mother Should Know'/'I Am The Walrus'; 'The Fool On The Hill'; 'Flying'/'Blue Jay Way'.

ALBUMS

Please Please Me, March 22, 1963, Parlophone PMC 1202 (mono), PCS 3042 (stereo) –
'I Saw Her Standing There'; 'Misery'; 'Anna (Go To Him)'; 'Chains'; 'Boys'; 'Ask Me Why'; 'Please Please Me'/'Love Me Do'; 'PS I Love You'; 'Baby It's You'; 'Do You Want To Know A Secret'; 'A Taste Of Honey'; 'There's A Place'; 'Twist And Shout'.

With The Beatles, November 22, 1963, Parlophone PMC 1206 (mono), PCS 3045 (stereo) –
'It Won't Be Long'; 'All I've Got To Do'; 'All My Loving'; 'Don't Bother Me'; 'Little Child'; 'Till There Was You'; 'Please Mister Postman'/ 'Roll Over Beethoven'; 'Hold Me Tight'; 'You Really Got A Hold On Me'; 'I Wanna Be Your Man'; '(There's A) Devil In Her Heart'; 'Not A Second Time'; 'Money (That's What I Want)'.

A Hard Day's Night, July 10, 1964, Parlophone PMC 1230 (mono), PCS 3058 (stereo) – 'A Hard Day's Night'; 'I Should Have Known Better'; 'If I Fell'; 'I'm Happy Just To Dance With Me'; 'And I Love Her'; 'Tell Me Why'; 'Can't Buy Me Love'/'Any Time At All'; 'I'll Cry Instead'; 'Things We Said Today'; 'When I Get Home'; 'You Can't Do That'; 'I'll Be Back'.

Beatles For Sale, December 4, 1964, Parlophone PMC 1240 (mono), PCS 3062 (stereo) – 'No Reply'; 'I'm A Loser'; 'Baby's In Black'; 'Rock And Roll Music'; 'I'll Follow The Sun'; 'Mr Moonlight'; 'Kansas City'/'Hey-Hey-Hey!'/'Eight Days A Week'; 'Words Of Love'; 'Honey Don't'; 'Every Little Thing'; 'I Don't Want To Spoil The Party'; 'What You're Doing'; 'Everybody's Trying To Be My Baby'.

Help!, August 6, 1965, Parlophone PMC 1255 (mono), PCS 3071 (stereo) –
'Help!'; 'The Night Before'; 'You've Got To Hide Your Love Away'; 'I Need You'; 'Another Girl'; 'You're Going To Lose That Girl'; 'Ticket To Ride'/'Act Naturally'; 'It's Only Love'; 'You Like Me Too Much'; 'Tell Me What You See'; 'I've Just Seen A Face'; 'Yesterday'; 'Dizzy Miss Lizzy'.

Rubber Soul, December 3, 1965, Parlophone PMC 1267 (mono), PCS 3075(stereo) –
'Drive My Car'; 'Norwegian Wood (This Bird Has Flown)'; 'You Won't See Me'; 'Nowhere Man'; 'Think For Yourself'; 'The Word'; 'Michelle'/'What Goes On'; 'Girl'; 'I'm Looking Through You'; 'In My Life'; 'Wait'; 'If I Needed Someone'; 'Run For Your Life'.

Revolver, August 5, 1966, Parlophone PMC 7009 (mono), PCS 7009 (stereo) – 'Taxman'; 'Eleanor Rigby'; 'I'm Only Sleeping'; 'Love You To'; 'Here, There And Everywhere'; 'Yellow Submarine'; 'She Said She Said'/'Good Day Sunshine'; 'And Your

Bird Can Sing'; 'For No One'; 'Doctor Robert'; 'I Want To Tell You'; 'Got To Get You Into My Life'; 'Tomorrow Never Knows'.

A Collection Of Beatles Oldies, December 9, 1966, Parlophone PMC 7016 (mono), PCS 7016 (stereo) – 'She Loves You'; 'From Me To You'; 'We Can Work It Out'; 'Help!'; 'Michelle'; 'Yesterday'; 'I Feel Fine'; 'Yellow Submarine'/'Can't Buy Me Love'; 'Bad Boy'; 'Day Tripper'; 'A Hard Day's Night'; 'Ticket To Ride'; ' Paperback Writer'; 'Eleanor Rigby'; 'I Want To Hold Your Hand'.

Sgt Pepper's Lonely Hearts Club Band, June 1, 1967, Parlophone PMC 7017 (mono), PCS 7027 (stereo) – 'Sgt Pepper's Lonely Hearts Club Band'; 'With A Little Help From My Friends'; 'Lucy In The Sky With Diamonds'; 'Getting Better'; 'Fixing A Hole'; 'She's Leaving Home'; 'Being For The Benefit Of Mr Kite!'/ 'Within You Without You'; 'When I'm Sixty Four'; 'Lovely Rita'; 'Good Morning Good Morning'; 'Sgt Pepper's Lonely Hearts Club Band (Reprise)'; 'A Day In The Life'.

The Beatles, November 22, 1968, Apple [Parlophone] PMC 7067-7068 (mono), PCS 7067-7068 (stereo) – 'Back In The USSR'; 'Dear Prudence'; 'Glass Onion'; 'Ob-La-Di, Ob-La-Da'; 'Wild Honey Pie'; 'The Continuing Story Of Bungalow Bill'; 'While My Guitar Gently Weeps'; 'Happiness Is A Warm Gun'/'Martha My Dear'; 'I'm So Tired'; 'Blackbird'; 'Piggies'; 'Rocky Raccoon'; 'Don't Pass Me By'; 'Why Don't We Do It In The Road'; 'I Will'; 'Julia'/'Birthday'; 'Yer Blues'; 'Mother Nature's Son'; 'Everybody's Got Something To Hide Except Me And My Monkey'; 'Sexy Sadie'; 'Helter Skelter'; 'Long Long Long'/'Revolution 1'; 'Honey Pie'; 'Savoy Truffle'; 'Cry Baby Cry'; 'Revolution 9'; 'Good Night'.

Yellow Submarine, January 17, 1969, Apple [Parlophone] PMC 7070 (mono), PCS 7070 (stereo) – 'Yellow Submarine'; 'Only A Northern Song'; 'All Together Now'; 'Hey Bulldog'; 'It's All Too Much'; 'All You Need Is Love' / [Seven soundtrack instrumental cuts by the George Martin Orchestra].

Abbey Road, September 26, 1969, Apple [Parlophone] PCS 7088 (stereo only) – 'Come Together'; 'Something'; 'Maxwell's Silver Hammer'; 'Oh! Darling'; 'Octopus's Garden'; 'I Want You (She's So Heavy)'/'Here Comes The Sun'; 'Because'; 'You Never Give Me Your Money'; 'Sun King'/'Mean Mr Mustard'; 'Polythene Pam'/'She Came In Through The Bathroom Window'; 'Golden Slumbers'/'Carry That Weight'; 'The End'; 'Her Majesty'.

Let It Be, May 8, 1970, Apple [Parlophone] PCS 7096 (stereo only) – 'Two Of Us'; 'Dig A Pony'; 'Across The Universe'; 'I Me Mine'; 'Dig It'; 'Let It Be'; 'Maggie Mae'/'I've Got A Feeling'; 'The One After 909'; 'The Long And Winding Road'; 'For You Blue'; 'Get Back'.

Live At The BBC, November 30, 1994, Apple [Parlophone] CDPCSP 726 TC (mono) – 'From Us To You'; 'I Got A Woman'; 'Too Much Monkey Business'; 'Keep Your Hands Off My Baby'; 'I'll Be On My Way'; 'Young Blood'; 'A Shot Of Rhythm And Blues'; 'Sure To Fall (In Love With You)'; 'Some Other Guy'; 'Thank You Girl'; 'Baby It's You'; 'That's All Right (Mama)'; 'Carol'; 'Soldier Of Love'; 'Clarabella'; 'I'm Gonna Sit Right Down And Cry (Over You)'; 'Crying, Waiting, Hoping'; 'You Really Got A Hold On Me'; 'To Know Her Is To Love Her'; 'A Taste Of Honey'; 'Long Tall Sally'; 'I Saw Her Standing There'; 'The Honeymoon Song'; 'Johnny B Goode'; 'Memphis, Tennessee'; 'Lucille'; 'Can't Buy Me Love'; 'Till There Was You'; 'A Hard Day's Night'; 'I Wanna Be Your Man'; 'Roll Over Beethoven'; 'Things We Said Today'; 'She's A Woman'; 'Sweet Little Sixteen'; 'Lonesome Tears In My Eyes'; 'Nothin' Shakin''; 'The Hippy Hippy Shake'; 'Glad All Over'; 'I Just Don't Understand'; 'So How Come (No One Loves Me)'; 'I Feel Fine'; 'I'm A Loser'; 'Everybody's Trying To Be My Baby'; 'Rock And Roll Music'; 'Ticket To Ride'; 'Dizzy Miss Lizzy'; 'Kansas City/'Hey! Hey! Hey!'; 'Matchbox'; 'I Forgot To Remember To Forget'; 'I Got To Find My Baby'; 'Ooh! My Soul'; 'Don't Ever Change'; 'Slow Down'; 'Honey Don't'; 'Love Me Do'.

Anthology 1, November 21, 1995, Apple [Parlophone] CDPCSP 727 – 'Free As A Bird'; 'That'll Be The Day'; 'In Spite Of All The Danger'; 'Hallelujah, I Love Her So'; 'You'll Be Mine'; 'Cayenne'; 'My Bonnie'; 'Ain't She Sweet'; 'Cry For A Shadow'; 'Searchin''; 'Three Cool Cats'; 'The Sheik Of Araby'; 'Like Dreamers Do'; 'Hello Little Girl'; 'Besame Mucho'; 'Love Me Do'; 'How Do You Do It'; 'Please Please Me'; 'One After 909'; 'Lend Me Your Comb'; 'I'll Get You'; 'I Saw Her Standing There'; 'From Me To You'; 'Money (That's What I Want)'; 'You Really Got A Hold On Me'; 'Roll Over Beethoven'; 'She Loves You'; 'Till There Was You'; 'Twist And Shout'; 'This Boy'; 'I Want To Hold Your Hand'; 'Moonlight Bay'; 'Can't Buy Me Love'; 'All My Loving'; 'You Can't Do That'; 'And I Love Her'; 'A Hard Day's Night'; 'I Wanna Be Your Man'; 'Long Tall Sally'; 'Boys'; 'Shout'; 'I'll Be Back'; 'You Know What To Do'; 'No Reply' (Demo); 'Mr Moonlight'; 'Leave My Kitten Alone'; 'No Reply'; 'Eight Days A Week'; 'Kansas City'/'Hey! Hey! Hey!'.

Anthology 2, March 18, 1996, Apple [Parlophone] CDPCSP 728 – 'Real Love'; 'Yes It Is'; 'I'm Down'; 'You've Got To Hide Your Love Away'; 'If You've Got Trouble'; 'That Means A Lot'; 'Yesterday'; 'It's Only Love'; 'I Feel Fine'; 'Ticket To Ride'; 'Yesterday'; 'Help!'; 'Everybody's Trying To Be My Baby'; 'Norwegian Wood (This Bird Has Flown)'; 'I'm Looking Through You'; '12-Bar Original'; 'Tomorrow Never Knows'; 'Got To Get You Into My Life'; 'And Your Bird Can Sing'; 'Taxman'; 'Eleanor Rigby' (Strings Only); 'I'm Only Sleeping' (rehearsal); 'I'm Only Sleeping' (take 1); 'Rock And Roll Music'; 'She's A Woman'; 'Strawberry Fields Forever' (Demo); 'Strawberry Fields Forever' (Take 1); 'Strawberry Fields Forever' (Take 7); 'Penny Lane'; 'A Day In The Life'; 'Good Morning Good Morning'; 'Only A Northern Song'; ' Being For The Benefit Of Mr Kite! (Takes 1 and 2); 'Being For The Benefit Of Mr Kite!' (Take 7); 'Lucy In The Sky With Diamonds', 'Within You Without You' (Instrumental); 'Sgt Pepper's Lonely Hearts Club Band' (Reprise); 'You Know My Name (Look Up The Number); 'I Am The Walrus'; 'The Fool On The Hill' (Demo); 'Your Mother Should Know'; 'The Fool On The Hill' (Take 4); 'Hello, Goodbye'; 'Lady Madonna'; 'Across The Universe'.

Anthology 3, October 28, 1996, Apple [Parlophone] CDPCSP 729 – 'A Beginning'; 'Happiness Is A Warm Gun'; 'Helter Skelter'; 'Mean Mr Mustard'; 'Polythene Pam'; 'Glass Onion'; 'Junk'; 'Piggies'; 'Honey Pie'; 'Don't Pass Me By'; 'Ob-La-Di, Ob-La-Da'; 'Good Night'; 'Cry Baby Cry'; 'Blackbird'; 'Sexy Sadie'; 'While My Guitar Gently Weeps'; 'Hey Jude'; 'Not Guilty'; 'Mother Nature's Son'; 'Glass Onion'; 'Rocky Raccoon'; 'What's The New Mary Jane'; 'Step Inside Love'/'Los Paranoias'; 'I'm So Tired'; 'I Will'; 'Why Don't We Do It In The Road'; 'Julia'; 'I've Got A Feeling'; 'She Came In Through The Bathroom Window'; 'Dig A Pony'; 'Two Of Us'; 'For You Blue'; 'Teddy Boy'; 'Rip It Up'/'Shake, Rattle and Roll'/ 'Blue Suede Shoes'; 'The Long And Winding Road'; 'Oh! Darling'; 'All Things Must Pass'; 'Mailman, Bring Me No More Blues'; 'Get Back'; 'Old Brown Shoe'; 'Octopus's Garden'; 'Maxwell's Silver Hammer'; 'Something'; 'Come Together'; 'Come And Get It'; 'Ain't She Sweet'; 'Because'; 'Let It Be'; 'I Me Mine'; 'The End'.

US RELEASES

SINGLES

"Please Please Me'/'Ask Me Why', February 25, 1963, Vee Jay VJ 498.

'From Me To You'/'Thank You Girl', May 27, 1963, Vee Jay VJ 522.

'She Loves You'/'I'll Get You', September 16, 1963, Swan 4152.

'I Want To Hold Your Hand'/'I Saw Her Standing There', December 26, 1963, Capitol 5112.

'Please Please Me'/'From Me To You', January 30, 1964, Vee Jay VJ 581.

'Twist And Shout'/'There's A Place', March 2, 1964, Tollie 9001.

'Can't Buy Me Love'/'You Can't Do That', March 16, 1964, Capitol 5150.

'Do You Want To Know A Secret'/'Thank You Girl', March 23, 1964, Vee Jay VJ 587.

'Love Me Do'/'PS I Love You', April 27, 1964, Tollie 9008.

'Sie Liebt Dich'/'I'll Get You', May 21, 1964, Swan 4182.

'A Hard Day's Night'/'I Should Have Known Better', July 13, 1964, Capitol 5222.

'I'll Cry Instead'/'I'm Happy Just To Dance With You', July 20, 1964, Capitol 5234.

'And I Love Her'/'If I Fell', July 20, 1964, Capitol 5235.

'Matchbox'/'Slow Down', August 24, 1964, Capitol 5255.

'I Feel Fine'/'She's A Woman', November 23, 1964, Capitol 5327.

'Eight Days A Week'/'I Don't Want To Spoil The Party', February 15, 1965, Capitol 5371.

'Ticket To Ride'/'Yes It Is', April 19, 1965, Capitol 5407.

'Help!'/'I'm Down', July 19, 1965, Capitol 5476.

'Yesterday'/'Act Naturally', September 13, 1965, Capitol 5498.

'We Can Work It Out'/'Day Tripper', December 6, 1965, Capitol 5555.

'Nowhere Man'/'What Goes On', February 21, 1966, Capitol 5587.

'Paperback Writer'/'Rain', May 30, 1966, Capitol 5651.

'Eleanor Rigby'/'Yellow Submarine', August 8, 1966, Capitol 5715

'Strawberry Fields Forever'/'Penny Lane', February 13, 1967, Capitol 5810.

'All You Need Is Love'/'Baby, You're A Rich Man', 17 July 1967, Capitol 5964.

'Lady Madonna'/'The Inner Light', March 18, 1968, Apple [Capitol] 2138.

'Hey Jude'/'Revolution', August 26, 1968, Apple [Capitol] 2276.

'Get Back'/'Don't Let Me Down', May 5, 1969, Apple [Capitol] 2490.

'The Ballad Of John And Yoko'/'Old Brown Shoe', June 4, 1969. Apple [Capitol] 2531.

'Something'/'Come Together', October 6, 1969, Apple [Capitol] 2654.

'Let It Be'/'You Know My Name (Look Up The Number)', March 11, 1970, Apple [Capitol] 2764.

'The Long And Winding Road'/'For You Blue', May 11, 1970, Apple [Capitol] 2832.

'Free As A Bird'/'I Saw Her Standing There'/'This Boy'/'Christmas Time (Is Here Again)', December 4, 1995, Apple [Capitol] C2 7243 8 584 972

'Real Love'/'Baby's In Black'/'Yellow Submarine'/'Here, There And Everywhere', March 4, 1996, Apple [Capitol] C2 7243 8 585 442

ALBUMS

Introducing The Beatles, July 22, 1963, Vee Jay VJLP 1062 (mono), SR 1062 (stereo) –
'I Saw Her Standing There'; 'Misery'; 'Anna (Go To Him)'; 'Chains'; 'Boys'; 'Love Me Do'/'PS I Love You'; 'Baby It's You'; 'Do You Want To Know A Secret'; 'A Taste Of Honey'; 'There's A Place '; 'Twist And Shout'.

Meet The Beatles!, January 20, 1964, Capitol T-2047 (mono), ST-2047 (stereo) – 'I Want To Hold Your Hand'; 'I Saw Her Standing There'; 'This Boy'; 'It Won't Be Long'; 'All I've Got To Do'; 'All My Loving'/'Don't Bother Me'; 'Little Child'; 'Till There Was You'; 'Hold Me Tight'; 'I Wanna Be Your Man'; 'Not A Second Time'.

Introducing The Beatles, January 27, 1964, Vee Jay VJLP 1062 (mono; no stereo release) –
'I Saw Her Standing There'; Misery'; 'Anna (Go To Him)'; 'Chains'; 'Boys'; 'Ask Me Why'/'Please Please Me'; 'Baby It's You'; 'Do You Want To Know A Secret'; 'A Taste Of Honey'; 'There's A Place'; 'Twist And Shout'.

The Beatles' Second Album, April 10, 1964, Capitol T-2080 (mono), ST-2080 (stereo) –
'Roll Over Beethoven'; 'Thank You Girl'; 'You Really Got A Hold On Me'; '(There's A) Devil In Her Heart'; 'Money (That's What I Want)'; 'You Can't Do That'/ 'Long Tall Sally'; 'I Call Your Name'; 'Please Mister Postman'; 'I'll Get You'; 'She Loves You'.

A Hard Day's Night, June 26, 1964, United Artists UA 6366 (mono), UAS 6366 (stereo) – 'A Hard Day's Night'; 'Tell Me Why'; 'I'll Cry Instead'; 'I'm Happy Just To Dance With You'; plus two soundtrack instrumental cuts by George Martin & Orchestra/ I Should Have Known Better'; 'If I Fell'; 'And I Love Her'; 'Can't Buy Me Love'; plus two soundtrack instrumental cuts by George Martin & Orchestra.

Something New, July 20, 1964, Capitol T-2108 (mono), ST-2108 (stereo) – 'I'll Cry Instead'; 'Things We Said Today'; 'Any Time At All'; 'When I Get Home'; 'Slow Down'; 'Matchbox'/'Tell Me Why'; 'And I Love Her'; 'I'm Happy Just To Dance With You'; 'If I Fell'; 'Komm, Gib Mir Deine Hand'.

The Beatles' Story, November 23, 1964, Capitol TBO-2222 (mono), STBO-2222 (stereo) – 'Interviews plus extracts from 'I Want To Hold Your Hand'; 'Slow Down'; 'This Boy'/Interviews plus extracts from 'You Can't Do That'; 'If I Fell'; 'And I Love Her'/Interviews plus extracts from 'A Hard Day's Night'; 'And I Love Her'/Interviews plus extracts from 'Twist And Shout' (live); 'Things We Said Today'; 'I'm Happy Just To Dance With You'; 'Little Child'; 'Long Tall Sally'; 'She Loves You'; 'Boys'.

Beatles '65, December 15, 1964, Capitol T-2228 (mono), ST-2228 (stereo) –
'No Reply'; 'I'm A Loser'; 'Baby's In Black'; 'Rock And Roll Music'; 'I'll Follow The Sun'; 'Mr Moonlight'/ 'Honey Don't'; 'I'll Be Back'; 'She's A Woman'; 'I Feel Fine'; 'Everybody's Trying To Be My Baby'.

The Early Beatles, March 22, 1965, Capitol T-2309 (mono), ST-2309 (stereo) – 'Love Me Do'; 'Twist And Shout'; 'Anna (Go To Him)'; 'Chains'; 'Boys'; 'Ask Me Why'/'Please Please Me'; 'PS I Love You'; 'Baby It's You'; 'A Taste Of Honey'; ' Do You Want To Know A Secret'.

Beatles VI, June 14, 1965, Capitol T-2358 (mono), ST-2358 (stereo) – 'Kansas City'/'Hey-Hey-Hey-Hey!'; 'Eight Days A Week'; 'You Like Me Too Much'; 'Bad Boy'; 'I Don't Want To Spoil The Party'; 'Words Of Love'/ 'What You're Doing'; 'Yes It Is'; 'Dizzy Miss Lizzy'; 'Tell Me What You See'; 'Every little Thing'.

Help! August 13, 1965, Capitol MAS-2386 (mono), SMAS-2386 (stereo) – 'Help!'; 'The Night Before'; 'You've Got To Hide Your Love Away'; 'I Need You'; plus three soundtrack instrumental cuts by George Martin & Orchestra/'Another Girl'; 'Ticket To Ride'; 'You're Going To Lose That Girl'; plus three soundtrack instrumental cuts by George Martin & Orchestra.

Rubber Soul, December 6, 1965, Capitol T-2442 (mono), ST-2442 (stereo) – 'I've Just Seen A Face'; Norwegian Wood (This Bird Has Flown)'; 'You Won't See Me'; 'Think For Yourself'; 'The Word'; 'Michelle'/ 'It's Only Love'; 'Girl'; 'I'm Looking Through You'; 'In My Life'; 'Wait'; 'Run For Your Life'.

"Yesterday"…And Today, June 20, 1966, Capitol T-2553 (mono), ST-2553 (stereo) –
'Drive My Car'; 'I'm Only Sleeping'; 'Nowhere Man'; 'Doctor Robert'; 'Yesterday'; 'Act Naturally'/'And Your Bird Can Sing'; 'If I Needed Someone'; 'We Can Work It Out'; 'What Goes On'; 'Day Tripper'.

Revolver, August 8, 1966, Capitol T-2576 (mono), ST-2576 (stereo) – 'Taxman'; 'Eleanor Rigby'; 'Love You To'; 'Here, There And Everywhere'; 'Yellow Submarine'; 'She Said She Said'/'Good Day Sunshine'; 'For No One'; 'I Want To Tell You'; 'Got to Get You Into My Life'; 'Tomorrow Never Knows'.

Sgt Pepper's Lonely Hearts Club Band, June 2, 1967, Capitol MAS-2653 (mono), SMAS-2653 (stereo) – tracks as UK release

Magical Mystery Tour, November 27, 1967, Capitol MAL-2835 (mono), SMAL-2835 (stereo) – 'Magical Mystery Tour'; 'The Fool On The Hill'; 'Flying'; 'Blue Jay Way'; 'Your Mother Should Know'; 'I Am The Walrus'/'Hello, Goodbye'; 'Strawberry Fields Forever'; 'Penny Lane'; 'Baby, You're A Rich Man'; 'All You Need Is Love'.

The Beatles, November 25, 1968, Apple [Capitol] SWBO-101 (stereo) – tracks as UK release

Yellow Submarine, January 13, 1969, Apple [Capitol] SW-153 (stereo) – tracks as UK release

Abbey Road, October 1, 1969, Apple [Capitol] SO-383 (stereo) – tracks as UK release

Hey Jude, February 26, 1970, Apple [Capitol] SW-385 (stereo) – 'Can't Buy Me Love'; 'I Should Have Known Better'; 'Paperback Writer'; 'Rain'; 'Lady Madonna'; 'Revolution'/ 'Hey Jude'; 'Old Brown Shoe'; 'Don't Let Me Down'; 'The Ballad Of John And Yoko'.

Let It Be, May 18, 1970, Apple [Capitol] AR-34001 (stereo) – tracks as UK release

Live At The BBC, November 30, 1994, Apple [Capitol] (mono) – tracks as UK release

Anthology 1, November 21, 1995, Apple [Capitol] – tracks as UK release

Anthology 2, March 18, 1996, Apple [Capitol] – tracks as UK release

Anthology 3, October 28, 1996, Apple [Capitol] – tracks as UK release

BIBLIOGRAPHY

BOOKS ABOUT THE BEATLES

Bacon, David and Maslov, Norman. *The Beatles' England*. Columbus Books, London ,1982; 910 Books, San Francisco, 1982.

Baird, Julia. *John Lennon My Brother*. Grafton, London, 1988.

The Beatles Lyrics. MacDonald, London, 1969.

Bedford, Carol. *Waiting For The Beatles*, Blandford Press, Newron Abbot, 1984.

Braun, Michael. *Love Me Do*. Penguin, London, 1964.

Brown, Peter. *The Love You Make*. MacMillan, London,1983.

Coleman, Ray. *Lennon*. McGraw Hill, New York, 1984.

Dalton, David and Cott, Jonathan. *The Beatles Get Back*. Apple, London, 1969.

Davies, Hunter. *The Beatles*. Heinemann, London 1968.

Elson, Howard. *McCartney: Songwriter*. W.H.Allen, London, 1986.

Freeman, Robert. *The Beatles: A Private View*. Pyramid, London, 1992.

Fulpen, H.V. *The Beatles: An Illustrated Diary*. Plexus, London, 1982.

Giuliano, Geoffrey. *Blackbird*. Smith Gryphon, London, 1991.

Goldman, Albert. *The Lives Of John Lennon*. Bantam Press, London, New York.

Gottfridsson, Hans. *The Beatles from Cavern to Star Club*. Premium Publishing, Stockholm, 1997.

Harrison, George. *I Me Mine*. W.H.Allen, London, 1980.

Harry, Bill (Editor). *Mersey Beat; The Beginnings Of The Beatles*. Columbus Books, London, 1977.
The Ultimate Beatles Encyclopedia. Virgin, London, 1992.

Lennon, Cynthia. *A Twist Of Lennon*. W.H. Allen, London 1978.

Lennon, John. *In His Own Write*. Jonathan Cape, London,1964.

Lewisohn, Mark. *The Complete Beatles Recording Sessions*. Hamlyn, London, 1988.

The Complete Beatles Chronicle. Pyramid, London, 1992.

McCabe, Peter and Schonfeld, Robert. *Apple To The Core*. Sphere Books, London, 1972.

McCartney, Mike. *Thank U Very Much*.Weidenfeld & Nicolson, London, 1982.

Mellers, Wilfrid. *Twilight Of The Gods*. Schirmer Books, New York, 1973.

Miles, Barry. *Paul McCartney: Many Years from Now*. Secker & Warburg, London, 1997.

Norman, Philip. *Shout*, Elm Tree, London, 1981.

Rolling Stone magazine. *The Ballad Of John and Yoko*. Michael Joseph, London, 1982.

Salewicz, Chris. *McCartney: The Biography*. MacDonald, London, 1986.

Schafiner, Nicholas. *The Beatles Forever*. MSF Books, New York, 1978.

Schultheiss,Tom. *A Day In The Life*. Pierian Press, Ann Arbor, 1980.

Sheff, David. *The Playboy Interviews with John Lennon and Yoko Ono*. New English Library, London, 1981; Playboy Press, Chicago, 1981.

Shepherd, Billy. *The True Story of the Beatles*. Beat Publications, London, 1964.

Shotton, Pete. *John Lennon In My Life*. Stein & Day, New York, 1983.

Stuart Ryan. David, *John Lennon's Secret*, Kozmik Press Center, New York, 1982.

Taylor, Alistair. *Yesterday*. Sidgwick and Jackson, London; Pioneer Books, Las Vegas, 1989.

Wenner, Jann. *Lennon Remembers*. Straight Arrow Books, San Francisco, 1971.

Wiener, Jon. *Come Together: John Lennon In His Time*. Faber & Faber, London, 1984; Random House, New York, 1984

GENERAL BOOKS

Anthony, Gene. *Summer Of Love*. Celestial Arts, Berkeley, 1980.

Buglioso, Vincent. *Helter Skelter*. Bantam, New York, 1974.

Fein, Art. *The LA Musical History Tour*. Faber and Faber, Boston, 1990.

Gaines, Steven. *Heroes and Villains*. MacMillian, London,1986; New American Library, New York, 1986.

Gibran, Kahlil. *Sand and Foam*, 1927.

Gillett, Charlie. *The Sound Of The City*. Sphere Books, London, 1970.

Goodman, Pete. *The Rolling Stones: Our Own Story*. Bantam, New York, 1965.

Guinness Book of Rock Stars. Guinness, London, 1989.

Hotchner, A.E. *Blown Away*. Simon and Schuster, London, 1990.

Leary, Timothy. *Flashbacks*. Heinemann, London, 1983.

Maharishi Mahesh Yogi,. *The Science of Being and the Art of Living*. International SRM Publications, London, 1963.

Mascaró, Juan. *Lamps of Fire*, Methuen, London 1958.

Marsh, Dave. *The Heart of Rock and Roll*. Penguin, London, 1989; New American Library, New York, 1989

Smith, Joe. *Off The Record*. Sidgwick and Jackson, London, 1989.

Stein, Jean. *Edie*. Jonathan Cape, London, 1982.

Turner, John M. *A Dictionary of Circus Biography* (unpublished).

White, Charles. *Little Richard*. Pan, London, 1984.

Wolfe, Tom. *The Electric Kool-Aid Acid Test*. Bantam, New York, 1968.

Worth, Fred and Tamerius, Steve. *Elvis: His Life from A-Z*. Contemporary Books, New York, 1988.

Wyman, Bill. *Stone Alone*. Viking, London, 1990

INDEX